Craig Hall's
BOOK OF
REAL ESTATE
INVESTING

Also by Craig Hall
THE REAL ESTATE TURNAROUND

Craig Hall's
BOOK OF
REAL ESTATE
INVESTING

Craig Hall

 HOLT, RINEHART and WINSTON/New York

Published by Holt, Rinehart and Winston,
383 Madison Avenue, New York, New York 10017.

Published simultaneously in Canada by Holt, Rinehart and
Winston of Canada, Limited.

Library of Congress Cataloging in Publication Data
Hall, Craig, 1950–
    Craig Hall's book of real estate investing.
    Includes index.
    1. Real estate investment. I. Title. II. Title:
Book of real estate investing.
HD1382.5.H34   332.63'24   81-47468
                                 AACR2

ISBN: 0-03-059516-9

First Edition

Designer: Nancy Dale Muldoon
Printed in the United States of America
10 9 8 7 6 5 4 3 2 1

This book is dedicated to the memory of
LAWRENCE W. "PETER" HEACOCK,
whose spirit and strength will always serve as a humbling example
to those of us who knew him;
and to the women in my life:
My MOTHER, my four daughters—MARCIA, MELISSA, BRIJETTA,
and my newest, KRISTINA—
and last, but far from least, my loving wife,
MARYANNA.

Acknowledgments

FIRST and foremost, I would like to thank my father, Herbert Hall, both for his extensive assistance and involvement in rewriting various drafts of the book and for his sage wisdom and counsel.

I would also like to extend my deep appreciation to Barbara Diedrich and Kimaron J. Gardner, who assisted me in the research as well as in pulling together all the pieces of this book. For their many long hard hours of typing, copying, proofreading, and organizing of materials, I owe great thanks to Denise Polasky, Margaret Roberts, Davina Hom, Tanya Kirkland, Martie Tanner, Natalie Tupilow, Kathy Cumiskey, Cathy Corbett and Kit Noruk. I owe a special debt of gratitude to my friend and agent-lawyer, Robert L. Fenton, and agent, Phillip Spitzer, for their fine advice in picking Holt, Rinehart and Winston as a publisher. Special thanks also go to Donald Hutter, Editor-in-Chief of Holt, Rinehart and Winston, whose fine editing and counsel greatly improved the book. Thanks also go to my friend Robert Cohen, who is the Hall Real Estate Group's General Counsel. Bob's tax expertise was most helpful in making the chapters on taxes understandable and interesting.

I would also like to thank my friends and business associates, who really made the Hall Real Estate Group what it is today and have given me the knowledge and background to write this book. To name just a few who deserve credit, they are Peter Nunez, Robert

Flynn, Robert Hobbs, Ronald Berlin, Larry Levey, Robert Cohen, William Poore, Mark Douglas, and Thomas Jahncke. I would also like to thank my friends and business associates who read and critiqued various drafts of the book: Martin Rom, Lloyd Semple, Hugh Makens, Allan Nachman, James Karpen, Saul Shiefman, and Subrata Ghosh.

Last, but never least, I would like to thank the ladies in my life. First my mother, for the source of my inherited drive and single-minded dedication to tackle every project with great vigor. Finally my wife and four daughters, for putting up with my single-minded dedication to projects like this book, which occupied all of my spare waking hours for over a year.

Contents

Preface   1

*A Book for Successful People *Who Should Read This Book?
*The Challenge of the Eighties *What This Book Offers You

Part One

WHY REAL ESTATE IS RIGHT FOR YOU   7

Chapter 1: The Age of Economic Turbulence   9

*The Save-and-Prosper Period *Inflation Takes Its Toll *Tax-
es: The Second Half of the Problem *What Happened to Savings? *Why Has the Stock Market Changed? *Will Inflation
Go Away? *New Rules for Economic Preservation

**Chapter 2: The Magic of Real Estate Investment in
Fighting Inflation and Taxes**   25

*Where the Action Is *Maximum Return with Minimum Risk
*Real Estate Is Basic *The Government Is Your Partner
*Taming Inflation with Real Estate *Basic Vehicles for Pas-
sive Real Estate Investment

**Chapter 3: How Limited Partnerships Work for
the Investor**   37

*The Power of Pooling Dollars *Limited Partnerships Aid
Diversification *The Right Opportunity at the Right Time

*The Fine Art of Negotiation *Due Diligence *Day-to-Day
Management *Timing the Turnover *Selecting the Right
General Partner *Understanding the Differences between
Public and Private Limited Partnerships

**Chapter 4: Is Limited-Partnership Real Estate
Investing for You?**   47
*What Can You Expect as a Return on Real Estate Invest-
ment? *Public Limited Partnerships *Do You Have the Fi-
nancial and Emotional Staying Power for Success? *Are You
in a High Enough Tax Bracket to Benefit? *What Kind of
People Invest in Real Estate Limited Partnership? *A Very
Personal Decision

Part Two
**TAX AND LEGAL ASPECTS OF REAL ESTATE
INVESTMENT**   61
**Chapter 5: Why Tax Shelter Can Be the Cornerstone
of Your Economic Survival**   63
*Tax-Dollar Power *Tax Shelters Are Investment Incentives
and Are Your Legal Right *How Tax Shelters Work *Tax Ba-
sis *Special Tax Risks Inherent in Tax-Shelter Investment
*Reducing Withholding Tax

Chapter 6: Why Real Estate Is the Super Tax Shelter   79
*Economic Investment Strength *Legislative Advantages
Provided for Real Estate Investment *The Value of Lever-
age *Tax Loss Provides Current Return *The Importance of
Property Maintenance Instead of Cash-Flow Maintenance
*River View Associates—A Case History *The Special Tax
Benefit of an Installment Sale *The Importance of Capital-
Gains Taxation *Stepped-up Basis for Estate Tax *The Eco-
nomic Recovery Act of 1981 and Congressional Plans for
Future Real Estate Investment Taxation

Chapter 7: IRS Practices and Pitfalls   92
*The IRS Position on Tax Shelters *The Relationship Be-
tween Partnership and Individual Audits *The Nature of
Tax-Law Risks *How to Report Limited Partnerships on
Your Personal Income-Tax Return

Chapter 8: How to Use Financial Advisors Effectively   107
*The Importance of Using Advisors Only in Their Qualified
Areas *You Owe It to Yourself to Become a "Professional"

Client *The Role of the Financial Counselor or Financial-Investment Advisor *The Role of the Attorney *The Role of Your Accountant *The Potential Role of Your Securities Broker

Part Three
SELECTING YOUR GENERAL PARTNER   115
   Chapter 9: Why the General Partner Is the Key to
   Your Success   117
   *Personal Control *The Legal Position of Your General Partner *The Operational Position of Your General Partner *Essential Qualities of a Successful General Partner *General Partners Come in Different Shapes and Sizes *Don't Short-Change Your Selection Effort

   Chapter 10: How to Find and Evaluate Potential
   General Partners   129
   *Locating Public Limited Partnerships *Why Private Limited Partnerships Are a Well-kept "Secret" *Locating Private Limited Partnership Sources in Your Community *A Proven Plan to Evaluate Private-Placement General Partners *The Desirability Rating for Prospective General Partners *Continuing Your Vigilance after You Enter a Limited Partnership *What to Do If You Feel the General Partner Is Not Serving You Properly

Part Four
SELECTING SPECIFIC INVESTMENTS   151
   Chapter 11: Evaluating the Deal   153
   *Consideration of Risks *Types of Real Estate *How Important Is It to Select the Right Kind of Property? *What Return on Investment Is Reasonable to Expect from a Real Estate Limited Partnership? *Factors to Consider in Comparing Returns on Investment *The Importance of Understanding Return-on-Investment Calculation Methods *Specific Returns to Anticipate from Real Estate Limited Partnerships *Timing and Return of Money *How to Review Assumptions *Don't Let Overoptimism Rub Off *Evaluating the Fees Involved in Limited-Partnership Investing *Evaluating Fees as Part of a Total Business Relationship *Timing Real Estate Investments

Chapter 12: Evaluating the Documentation   187

*The Offering Memorandum *The Partnership Agreement
*Subscription Documents *Securities-Bureau Involvement
*How to Decrease Your Liability During the Life of Your In-
vestment

Part Five

**FINANCIAL PLANNING FOR REAL ESTATE
INVESTMENT**   203

Chapter 13: The Happy Road to Long-Range Security   205

*Planning Is Essential for Success *How to Decide on the
Size of Your First Tax-Sheltered Real Estate Investment *A
Planning Concept for Higher-Income People That Can Turn
Them into Millionaires *Cash-Flow Planning *Borrowing to
Invest *How Planning Can Eliminate the Tax-Preference
Shock Syndrome *The Tax-Preference Set-Aside Concept
*Diversification for Safety and Profit *The Value of Overall
Planning

**Chapter 14: Evaluating the Total Investment
Opportunity for You**   229

*Ten Critical Areas of Evaluation *Three Basic Principles
That Make or Break a Deal

Part Six

THE OUTLOOK FOR THE EIGHTIES   237

**Chapter 15: Real Estate Investment Enters the
"Growth Stock" Era**   239

*The "Too-Late" Trap *Real Estate Comes of Age as a
"Growth Stock" Investment *Rent-Lag Theory *The Rent
Revolution—The Approaching Period of Major Increases in
Apartment Rent *How Do Current Apartment Investment
Costs Compare to Replacement Construction Costs? *The
Changing Nature of Housing in the United States *The Sig-
nificance of Single-Family Affordability *What Demograph-
ics Tell Us about Apartment Demand in the Eighties *While
Demand Is Growing, Apartment Supply Is Slipping *The
Pressure for Condominium Conversion *Fundamental
Changes in the Mortgage Market *The Possibility of Political
Interference in Anticipated Free-Market Action *The Bot-
tom Line in Terms of Real Estate Investment Timing *What
Does It Mean to You Today and Tomorrow?

Epilogue: A Better Tomorrow   258

Appendix 1: Sources of Additional Information   267

Appendix 2: Public Limited-Partnership Sponsors and Their
Offerings   270

Appendix 3: National and Regional Brokerage Houses and
the Sponsors They Carry   284

Appendix 4: Largest Public-Partnership Sponsors Ranked by
Total Dollars Raised   287

Appendix 5: Guide to Property Inspection   288

Appendix 6: Glossary   291

Index   303

Craig Hall's
BOOK OF
REAL ESTATE
INVESTING

Preface

FOURTEEN years ago, when I was eighteen years old, I made my first real estate investment. Since then I have purchased or built properties worth more than $350 million, but only that first investment was made without the participation of investor-partners.

Initially my reason for seeking investors was simply that my first purchase tied up every penny of my capital—all $4,000 of it. After some early problems were resolved, it was obvious this investment would prove to be successful. I was anxious to move ahead. I had an abundance of good ideas, opportunities, enthusiasm, and energy. The only thing I lacked was money.

Following the long tradition of American entrepreneurs, I formed one partnership after another in which I was the active or working partner, and friends became the investors.

As the years went by, my small business became Standard Realty Corporation, and finally Hall Real Estate Group—a sizable, sophisticated organization specializing in the formation and operation of real estate limited partnerships. The properties involved became larger, the partnerships and the investment sums grew in size, but the essence of our work remained that of investing money on behalf of other people.

I found that creating and operating worthwhile real estate investment opportunities for others was a service in great demand, and frequently in short supply. The reason was that *knowledgeable* investment in real estate offers a unique opportunity not only to profit, but also to ease the ravages of taxation and inflation.

I emphasize the word "knowledgeable" because as I grew into a substantial syndicator of real estate investments, I realized there is a serious void in the information available to help people use real estate investments intelligently. That realization is the reason for this book.

A BOOK FOR SUCCESSFUL PEOPLE

In our culture we tend to make the mistake of equating intelligence in any field with intelligence in all fields. The person who can make enough money to have some left over for investment is assumed automatically to have the knowledge to make wise investments.

The truth is, the more brilliant and dedicated an individual is in his or her special field, the more difficult it is to focus the energy and effort required to become personally involved in a unique investment area such as real estate.

This dictates the job of this book: to offer financially successful people a complete but concise base of knowledge that will allow them to intelligently use passive real estate investment to beat inflation and taxes.

The word "passive" does not mean without effort, care, and a great deal of wise selection. It merely means without active day-to-day management, since those who most need the benefits of real estate investment usually cannot handle the active management role.

With all the growing interest in real estate as an investment vehicle, a substantial number of books on the subject have been published in recent years. Most of them have concentrated on individual do-it-yourself investments, which require personal work along with some degree of financial involvement. Essentially these books have catered to the dreams of individuals who have not yet experienced financial success through their regular jobs. Some of the authors have been knowledgeable and realistic, but many have chosen to tout real estate as a get-rich-quick opportunity. They grossly understate the dollars and the time involved, and overplay the profit potential. Real estate can provide opportunities for individuals with more time than money, but the rewards never come without knowledge and real work.

At best, most of the current real estate how-to books are of little value to people who are working hard at a productive career. The achievers of our society have no time to buy and operate real estate personally, and they are not seeking ways to get rich quick. They do want to make intelligent investments geared to protecting and multiplying the money they make from their main efforts. This book is for them.

For anyone interested in real estate as a profession, I have written a book called *The Real Estate Turnaround*. It describes the techniques I have developed for profitably investing in underperforming real estate as an active participant in the investment.

WHO SHOULD READ THIS BOOK?

This book is written for those who are on the road to financial success or who are already there and are interested in expanding their horizons. It is a guide for achievers in any career who are concerned with how to protect, conserve, and multiply their investment capital.

Some years ago I became a close friend of a now-retired senior executive of one of the major automobile manufacturers in Detroit. As I got to know this gentleman, I started to realize the difficulties that achievers face in our chaotic economy.

This individual paid higher and higher income taxes as he rose through the ranks and finally achieved the high earning level of a vice-president. His problem was that he possessed good general business sense and outstanding skill in his area of specialty, but he had neither the time nor the background knowledge to understand how to defend, let alone exploit, his financial situation through skillful investment.

He completely misunderstood the reason the government allows, and even encourages, tax-shelter investments. As a result he consistently paid annual income tax in excess of $50,000, and as high as $100,000 in some years. As he approached retirement, this man could look back on a career of many accomplishments, but a very modest accumulation of wealth. Excessive taxation and the inflationary erosion of buying power had stolen the rewards this man should have earned from a lifetime of successful work. I'm proud to say our friendship and our business relationship have helped this gentleman improve his economic well-being.

THE CHALLENGE OF THE EIGHTIES

There was a time in this country when the right thing to do was save money, invest in bonds, pay off your home, and trust the banks. At least for now, those days are gone.

We live in a very volatile economy. Until some basic changes take place—changes not yet in sight—those who continue to follow the old truths will end up with depleted buying power and little to show for their efforts to accumulate and save.

Both the history of the 1970s and the outlook for the 1980s indicate an economy largely governed by inflation and growing financial chaos. This does not mean ruin and doom for everyone. As always, there will be winners and losers. Great amounts of wealth will change hands. The winners will be those who recognize current reality rather than those relying on rules learned twenty or thirty years ago.

No achiever in any field can afford to be an uninformed investor in the 1980s. You may have to rely on others for the active management of your investments, but it is economic suicide not at least to understand the basic advantages and disadvantages of major investment arenas, and not to understand how to evaluate and select the professionals you are going to trust with your financial future.

The 1980s will be a time of change and a time of frustration, except for those who are willing to gain the fundamental knowledge necessary to guide their own destinies.

WHAT THIS BOOK OFFERS YOU

- It will help you decide whether or not real estate limited partnership investing is right for you.
- It will explain the basic tax and legal aspects of real estate investment, and it will dispel some widely held myths.

- It will help you decide which types of real estate investment will best meet your needs.
- It will show you how to evaluate and select General Partners who will contribute to your success.
- It will show you how to analyze specific real estate investment opportunities.
- It will give you basic tips on how to avoid investing with promoters who will lose your money.
- It will help you use the advice and counsel of your own experts effectively.
- It will show you a foolproof method to avoid the financial problem of income-tax recapture.
- It will provide a flexible approach to overall long-term financial planning.

Above all else, this book will help you realize your desire to be a winner in the economy of the eighties.

Part One

WHY REAL ESTATE IS RIGHT FOR YOU

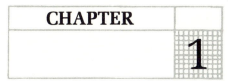

CHAPTER 1

The Age of Economic Turbulence

To GET some perspective on the economic situation today, let's think back to the early 1960s, just twenty years ago. As time goes, that's not very long, but the difference in financial atmosphere makes the sixties seem like ancient history.

The keynote of the sixties was economic dependability. The financial world was dependable, logical, and predictable. It was entirely reasonable to concentrate on advancement in your chosen profession and be assured that financial progress would come along automatically.

THE SAVE-AND-PROSPER PERIOD

Safe investment simply meant saving your money. First and foremost you put your excess in a bank and earned a modest, but worthwhile, interest rate. Paying off your home mortgage was a desirable goal since debt was viewed as a costly inconvenience to be borne only as long as absolutely necessary.

People were aware of inflation, and when it got up as high as 5 or 6 percent annually, there were those who forecast trouble ahead. However, there was a simple answer. Just invest some of your savings in blue-chip stocks, and they would act as a virtually automatic hedge against inflation. As the cost of living went up, so would the value of the stocks, and so would their dividends.

While taxes were not low by any means, they were generally acceptable when weighed against the purchasing power of the after-tax dollars left to average middle- and upper-middle-class families. In other words, most achievers felt they were making strides forward, even after they had paid their annual tax obligations.

Now you are in the early 1980s, twenty years later. From a practical point of view it should be easy to make your own comparison. If you can compare your purchasing power from after-tax earnings with what it was in the early sixties, it's a safe bet you don't feel you've made much real progress. Even if your age doesn't allow a direct comparison, you know intuitively that you are living in a turbulent time, and you realize that without some defensive measures your financial situation is going to erode. The old-fashioned work ethic alone is no longer enough, because conditions have changed and the rules of the financial game have changed.

I believe it is this realization that was largely responsible for the overwhelming election of Ronald Reagan, which took place as my work on this book was being completed. I sincerely hope President Reagan will be able to accomplish his goals of reducing our present economic turmoil. However, I believe that under the best of circumstances it will take many years to achieve the substantial changes required, and I am not at all convinced the people of our country are ready to make the necessary sacrifices.

Unfortunately, when you are caught in the middle of a storm, it's not easy to see the signs that point to safety. It will be worth a few minutes to try to understand the nature of our present problem.

INFLATION TAKES ITS TOLL

Everyone knows that a big part of the problem is inflation. Unfortunately, we don't have a really long-term view of inflation.

The basic causes of inflation are loss of productivity, waste, deficit spending by the government, and attempts to artificially stimulate the economy. Essentially, inflation is a by-product of political policies.

One reason this downward spiral has been accepted is that the government's attention has been focused on short-term changes. We tend to talk about "the inflation rate last month" or "how much inflation we had last year." With this kind of focus, we're bound to think we see improvement from time to time. In fact, we are just seeing the ratchet effect of alternate cooling and heating, constantly working from a higher level of inflation. Thus, we are lulled into acceptance of policies that may ultimately lead to the destruction of our economy. In fact, so many of us in one way or another have a vested interest in inflation that, despite opinion polls to the contrary, most people want inflation; they just want it their way—increase their house value and wages and hold the line otherwise.

What has really been happening is much more clearly illustrated in Chart 1: a comparison of the last two fifteen-year periods of our economy—1950 to 1964 and 1965 to 1980—in terms of inflation (Consumer Price Index), total government spending, per capita productivity, and annual government deficits. The cause-and-effect relationships speak for themselves.

The purpose of this book is not to try to solve the problem of inflation but rather to help productive Americans protect themselves against the ravages of inflation and taxes. The first step is to clearly recognize the size and shape of the enemy, and then decide if the recent past is in fact the prologue to the future. In this regard, what can we learn from these comparisons?

First, let's accept the fact that inflation is not a new phenomenon in our country. It is instead a condition that is steadily growing in degree.

From 1950 to 1964 the dollar lost almost 24 percent of its buying power, but during the last five years of that period the rate of decline eased dramatically. Hope for a secure future was indicated, for during that period there was general stability in the economy, and individuals were able to handle their financial investment with a minimum of effort.

During the 1965 to 1980 period, the value of the dollar fell by nearly 60 percent—two and a half times the inflationary loss of the preceding fifteen-year period. And the rate of inflation steadily increased throughout the period. There does not seem to be any rational expectation for a lasting change in direction, although there certainly will be ups and downs.

CHART 1

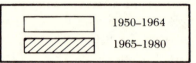

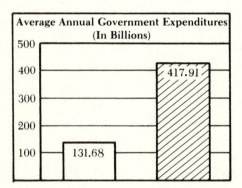

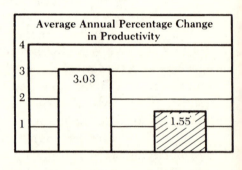

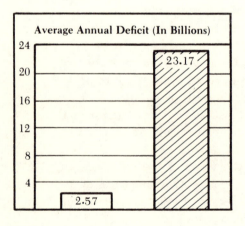

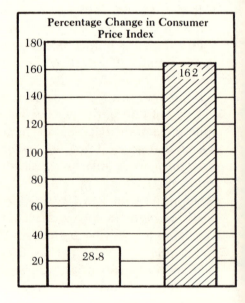

If we can learn anything from the past, it is the strong suggestion that the financial turbulence of the 1970s can be expected to continue and intensify in the 1980s. The real question is not whether inflation will come down for a year or two but rather whether it can be stopped over the long run. Personally, I doubt that the people of our country are going to be willing to pay the necessary price in social and human terms to end inflation. I hope President Reagan will be able to bring it down, but meanwhile defense against inflation should be the most important goal of intelligent investors.

TAXES: THE SECOND HALF OF THE PROBLEM

Even if you have managed to increase your earnings, and have invested your savings to keep up with inflation, you are still a loser! The reason is the extra tax bite taken by Uncle Sam from your added earnings.

You may or may not have realized what is happening, but as your earnings have increased (in dollars, not in buying power) you have been getting into higher and higher tax brackets. Thus, an ever-increasing percentage of your inflated earnings has been going to pay your income tax.

To put this insidious situation into real terms, let's assume your earnings have just kept pace with inflation over the last fifteen years. If you were making $30,000 in 1965, you would have to be making about $75,000 per year in 1980 to have the same buying power in pretax dollars. Remember, every dollar you make today will buy only what 40¢ bought in 1965.

Of course, a comparison of pretax earnings adjusted for inflation is only a part of the story. The fact that you must earn much more money today just to stay even with 1965 makes a big difference in your income-tax situation.

For the sake of realistic tax comparisons, we'll assume typical deductions for a family of four in each year, including appropriate interest and taxes on a home, and we'll even assume you are now in a much more expensive house complete with a larger mortgage, due to inflation.

In 1965 you were in the 36 percent tax bracket and paid $6,020 in income tax, leaving you with $23,980 in after-tax expendable income. In 1980, your comparable inflated $75,000 income put you into the 54 percent tax bracket, and you paid $21,568. This left $53,432 in after-tax dollars.

To compare the buying power of 1965 dollars with that of 1980 dollars, just multiply your 1965 after-tax income of $23,980 by 2.5 to reflect the 60 percent loss to inflation. That's right, you need $59,950 after taxes to maintain the same buying power. The point is, because of your promotion to a much higher tax bracket, you aren't staying abreast, even if your pretax income has increased as rapidly as inflation!

We won't take the time to go through the arithmetic, but the fact is that for a family of four to have the same after-tax buying power in 1980 that they had from pretax earnings of $30,000 in 1965, the pretax earnings in 1980 would have had to be $98,908. That is what has happened to us in just fifteen years as a result of inflation coupled with taxation in higher and higher brackets.

We all hope for improvement, but can we seriously expect a return to little or no inflation? Suppose the Reagan administration is indeed able to bring inflation down from the 1980 level of 12.4 percent to perhaps 7 percent in a short time. That will be an enormous achievement, and psychologically we may all think we are out of trouble. But even the effect of that 7 percent level would cause your *pretax* purchasing power to be cut in half from today's level in just over ten years. Being taxed at higher brackets would reduce your earnings even more. You can see how serious our future situation may be.

Despite any improvement that may be achieved, you cannot just drift along without taking every possible defensive measure to protect your economic achievement.

WHAT HAPPENED TO SAVINGS?

To continue with our example, let's suppose you work harder and make even more than enough to stay even with inflation. You pay your higher taxes, and you actually have $1,000 left over to invest in your future. Remember, back in the early sixties, the smart money went into the bank. How will that work out in the eighties?

If you put that $1,000 into a good old dependable savings account with instant availability, you'll earn $55 interest over a year. You must consider what will happen to the buying power of your money while it is in the bank. We'll assume 12.4 percent inflation, the rate for 1980. (There are several approaches to measuring inflation. I use the federal Consumer Price Index because it's the measure used for cost-of-living adjustments in wages, social security, etc.) Here's how it works out:

Placed in savings account	$1,000.00
Interest earned (5.5 percent)	55.00
Total in savings account	1,055.00
Loss of buying power through 12.4 percent inflation	−130.82
Buying power of $1,000 after one year in savings	$ 924.18

That's disheartening, but let's see how it works out if you are really fortunate and can save a much larger sum of money—say $10,000—and you decide to put it in the bank's money-market fund at much higher interest. Of course now the money is tied up, and as the banks tell you, "There is a substantial penalty for early withdrawal."

Invested in money-market fund	$10,000.00
Interest earned (13 percent average)	1,300.00
Total available	11,300.00
Income tax on interest over $200 (54 percent bracket)	−650.00
Total available after taxes	10,650.00
Buying power loss through 12.4 percent inflation	−1,320.60
Buying power of $10,000 after one year money-market investment	$ 9,329.40

It is sad but true—the more you save, the worse off you are! Is it any wonder our country is finding that people are turning away from savings? The fact is, the rules of the game have changed for those who want to protect and conserve the fruits of their labor.

WHY HAS THE STOCK MARKET CHANGED?

Investments in stocks still go up and down, and from a speculative point of view, I suppose the stock market is still as good a place as any to risk your money. However, even the most avid stock investor is not touting the market as an automatic hedge against inflation.

American business is suffering from a special aspect of the inflation and tax disease we have been considering from a personal point of view. As a business produces its product, it generally uses up its tools of production. Machinery, buildings, and everything else involved must eventually be replaced. In the days of economic stability, these costs were more or less anticipated by a depreciation allowance, which gave tax relief and allowed the accumulation of reserves for replacement.

Today, antiquated depreciation methods do not allow for the higher replacement costs being created by inflation. This means that in many cases profits are being grossly overstated. Taxes and dividends are, in effect, being paid out of the real equity capital of our corporations, and the companies are being partially liquidated. This is one reason the Reagan tax cut program has shortened depreciation lives.

As long as the companies represented on the stock market are themselves victims of inflation, we can hardly expect their growth and dividends to protect our investments from the same enemy. While it is not my purpose to speculate on such matters, the effects of inflation on corporate America are certainly a good explanation for the current seemingly bargain-basement stock market. This is not to say that the market, which appears grossly undervalued, couldn't have a nice sustained rise in price.

WILL INFLATION GO AWAY?

As a nation we are always hopeful, and we usually think very positively. This is one of our strengths, but it can also work against us when our positive thinking leads us into false hope.

Frankly, I do not believe there will be any sharp and lasting improvement in our inflationary situation soon. If we do a lot of things right, we can look forward to a better future, but it will take many years to institute the necessary fundamental changes. As a result, my own financial plans assume continued relatively high inflation. My advice to others is to make that assumption, act accordingly, but keep a contingency plan; the economy of the 1980s could produce unexpected sharp changes that would be ruinous to people with all of their eggs in one basket. Keep reviewing conditions so you can adjust your thinking when there is definite reason to do so.

NEW RULES FOR ECONOMIC PRESERVATION

If you agree we are in an age of economic turbulence, and the rules of the financial game have indeed changed, then it makes good sense to update your personal guidelines. Adjusting to change can be difficult. The only thing I know that is worse is to watch the world around you change while you refuse to budge.

For your consideration, I offer ten economic rules I have established for myself. These may or may not be acceptable to you. A lot depends on your financial position, and even more on your fiscal temperament. The important thing is that you seriously review present-day conditions, and then weigh their effect on your investment approach. Establish your own firm rules. Put them in writing, and review them often so you have a rational sense of direction guiding all of your investment decisions. You owe this to yourself and those who depend on you for security.

1. Preserve your income through tax-shelter investments. If you are single and have a pretax gross income of $35,000 or more, or if you are married and your income is $40,000, it is essential that you improve your net after-tax position by investing in tax-incentive situations that will shelter some of your ordinary income. My reference is to solid, relatively conservative investments that are made first because they offer good potential profit, and only secondarily because of their tax advantages.

It is important that you understand that real estate tax-shelter investments are both legal and moral. They are not "loopholes" but are in fact created by law to meet needs found desirable by Congress. Depending on your particular ability to invest, and your objectives, tax-advantaged real estate investments may be made for as little as a few thousand dollars. They are realistically within the reach of many modest investors.

This book will discuss tax shelters in much more detail in later chapters. I will focus particularly on real estate investments, which I believe are the most favorable tax-shelter opportunities for most people. For broader information and specific application to your needs, you should get professional tax counseling from the most knowledgeable practitioner you can locate. Your accountant or attorney may be able to counsel you, or at least recommend a specialist to you.

2. Borrow the maximum dollars possible on your home. Your home is one of your few possessions that can collateralize a fixed-rate loan for an extended period of years, and long-term debt is extremely favorable during inflationary times. The fundamental reason is that as inflation continues to erode purchasing power, you are able to pay back your long-term obligation with cheaper dollars than those you borrowed.

To illustrate this, let's draw again on Chart 1. If you had borrowed heavily on your home in 1965, you would still be paying off the mortgage today. However, the current payments would be made with dollars worth only 40¢ compared to the dollars you borrowed fifteen years ago.

True, you would have paid interest on the borrowed money ever since 1965, but that interest would have been at the fixed rate of 5.25 percent, a lot cheaper than what you pay to borrow money today. Further, the interest cost is reduced because it is a legitimate tax-deductible expense.

The real value of borrowing the excess equity that inflation has probably created on your home depends on what you do with the money. If you were to put the mortgage proceeds into money-market instruments, you might break even at first, then realize some profit as interest rates cycled to still higher levels, as they have been doing over the last fifteen years. On the other hand, using the money in a tax-sheltered investment with capital-gains appreciation potential should far outweigh the value of leaving the cash as equity in your home.

The question at the moment is less whether you should borrow more money on your home at a fixed interest rate, than whether you can do so on reasonably favorable terms. At the time this book is being written, long-term mortgage rates are at record high levels, and heavy front-end fees are also demanded by lenders. Further, many financial institutions are experimenting with floating-rate mortgages of various types, which will allow them to increase the rate of interest as inflation moves up. Floating-rate loans, otherwise known as adjustable-rate loans or adjustable mortgage loans, should be avoided if at all possible. They transfer a great deal of the benefits from inflation from you the borrower to the lender.

My suggestion is patience. Interest rates, loan terms, and loan availability fluctuate with economic conditions. In this turbulent period, the aggressive borrower will eventually be offered opportunities. Be ready to move when conditions are favorable, but resist the temptation to turn your inflated home equity into cash unless you can get a reasonable interest rate and good terms. This may be difficult in the future as long-term lenders see the error of lending at fixed rates, but toward the end of recessions there is often an excess of lendable capital over demand, and you may indeed find the opportunity. Most mortgages on homes provide that you can prepay the loan at any time with little or no penalty. Therefore, if rates go down after you borrow, you can prepay the existing loan with the proceeds from a more favorable loan.

3. Avoid keeping excess investment money in financial institutions. Look at banks and savings-and-loans as temporary parking places for cash, not as viable elements in your financial investment plan.

The first reason for this rule is simply that the rates of interest offered are just not up to the returns you can achieve elsewhere. As I have pointed out earlier, most money deposited in an interest-bearing account in a financial institution is losing purchasing power every day it is there. If you consider that loss as a short-term "parking fee," that makes sense. If you believe money in the bank is a safe, sane way to build your fortune, you are simply deluding yourself.

The second reason to generally avoid financial institutions is risk.

We have been carefully conditioned since the huge bank failures of the early 1930s to accept banks once again as an absolute safe haven for dollars. This simply is not true.

Many of our financial institutions are highly leveraged businesses, and in this time of turbulence they are vulnerable to bankruptcy. I am not suggesting that banks or savings-and-loans cannot be used for short-term deposit of modest amounts of money, but I do not think they are the best place for your important funds.

The Federal Deposit Insurance Corporation, a government agency, supposedly provides insurance on accounts up to $100,000. In fact, this insurance is only backed by reserves sufficient to pay a very small percentage of the potential claims from depositors. In 1980, when they raised the insured amounts from $40,000 per account to $100,000, no additional reserves were provided. The intent was to have people "keep the faith." In a time of serious economic chaos, I would hate to count on that kind of insurance to protect my investment capital.

It should be noted that in 1980 Congress passed the Depository Institutions Deregulation and Monetary Control Act, which will deregulate the limits on the interest banks can pay over the following six years. This may make banks a more lucrative parking place for your money. And I would be remiss if I did not state that while I believe many banks are highly leveraged and are riskier than many people believe, there are many very conservative and safe banks. In my business dealings I choose a bank not only on its interest in making loans to my company but on its stability and financial strength too.

4. Diversify your investment portfolio. In these times, you owe it to yourself to study your investment needs and opportunities, and to maintain a specific purpose and direction in your decisions. But this does not mean that all of your dollars should go into the same type of investment, no matter how ideal it seems.

First, define as investment funds only those dollars not required for other higher priorities. There should certainly be a reasonable amount of liquid cash for unforeseen emergencies, and there should be a secure cash flow for your normal living expenses. Only after these priorities are covered can you consider investment.

Some percentage of your investment fund should be kept liquid to allow you to take advantage of good opportunities as they occur. This might fluctuate from 5 to 20 percent. Such liquid assets are best kept in U.S. Treasury bills, or in very conservative money-market funds.

Primary investments should be in inflation-oriented vehicles that also offer substantial tax-shelter benefits. There are a number of investments that may be inflation-oriented but have no tax advantages. Other than possibly a minor position in gold, I do not believe these opportunities are for most investors, since they tend to be highly speculative.

The two vehicles that meet the combined need for inflationary growth and tax shelter are real estate and oil and gas exploration. There are ample diversification opportunities within either or both of these fields to safeguard most investors. This book will deal only with real estate opportunities, because that is my area of expertise and because I feel it offers the best opportunities to most investors. If you also want to consider oil and gas investments, I urge you to secure at least as much in-depth knowledge in that field as this book offers about real estate.

5. Select investments that have a high amount of fixed-rate debt. As I have already explained, fixed-rate debt is advantageous during inflationary times. This is even more true when the debt is tied to an investment property. As the debt becomes worth less due to inflation, the equity portion of the asset is automatically enhanced due to inflation.

When properly structured, the debt can be transferred along with the property when it is sold. Assuming that inflation will increase interest rates, there will be a definite economic value to the existing fixed-rate debt when the investment is sold in the future.

This will be discussed in much more detail in later chapters. For now, suffice it to say that the nature and type of debt underlying any investment should be a key consideration.

6. Avoid variable-rate debt. Tied to the desire to obtain as much fixed-rate debt as possible is the equally important desire to shun variable-rate debt. Variable-rate debt is simply borrowing under an agreement that allows the interest rate to be adjusted in line with the "prime rate" or with other economic factors.

High interest rates *per se* do not necessarily make an investment bad. That depends on what interest was anticipated when the deal was structured; in other words, what the investment can afford in interest costs. The danger is in rate fluctuation, which can create interest costs far higher than those anticipated when the investment was planned.

We have seen interest rates skyrocket in very short periods. This has been disastrous to investors who made decisions on estimates or pro formas that assumed interest rates far lower than those their investments ultimately had to pay.

When you are unable to predict important costs with reasonable assurance, you are adding serious risk. I would generally avoid investments structured with variable-rate loans or short-term balloon-payment loans for which no long-term replacement is assured. The only time to borrow variable-rate money is when it is for a short-term purpose and you're able to pay the loan off without severe prepayment penalties.

7. Avoid personal liability for investment debt. In all likelihood, you will have to accept personal liability for the debt on your home. However, it is not necessary, and it is definitely not desirable, to accept personal liability for debt involved in investments.

Protection against personal liability is one of the important advantages of "limited-partnership" investment, and this will be examined in greater detail later in this book.

In each separate investment, you should risk only the amount of money that you agree to put into the investment. This may be immediate cash, or it may also include deferred additional contributions. However, money borrowed by the investment entity should not be your personal liability if you are a passive investor.

The risk of your actual investment should be minimized by the tax savings you achieve immediately upon making the investment. Thus, you should never be able to lose more than you invest, and generally your maximum exposure should be substantially less than the actual investment.

8. Do not confuse high risk with high reward. The key to intelligent investment in today's troubled times is selectivity to gain desired objectives with an absolute minimum of risk. Beware of the promoter who overrides your questions concerning risk by pointing out the tremendous potential rewards. The two do not necessarily go together.

There is always some degree of risk in every decision and in every investment. The risk of unforeseen economic change is always there. The risk of unexpected natural disasters or violent change must be accepted. But those are quite different from built-in risks that can best be described as "crap-shooting."

As you evaluate opportunities, keep in mind the times in which we live and the realities of the financial world. The safe investments of fifteen or twenty years ago may well spell doom through financial erosion. The speculation of the past may well be the most conservative approach of today because of tax considerations.

Select investments with an antirisk bias. Look for projections that are conservatively structured, and for active partners who have a track record of success. Your money is too valuable to waste.

9. Avoid gambling and don't get greedy. As times become even more turbulent, you are bound to hear stories of big financial gains made on a quick flier. True, a great deal of money does change hands in these times, and some money can be made by luck, but much more is lost on the same kind of gambling. Most people who are gamblers and have some luck usually give it all back by pressing that luck out of sheer greed.

It is exciting and infectious to play high-finance in fast-moving areas such as gold, silver, commodities, and stock options. As inflation seems to be getting the best of us, it is very alluring to try to make a killing. These are games for the pros who have spent a lifetime learning how to participate in a very specialized area.

When you start to feel a little greedy, just remember the gambling odds are always with the house. But for the achiever who truly wants to conserve and multiply his investment funds, today's economy offers endless opportunity to make money consistently and without great risk.

10. Set goals—establish your "financial living plan." In your investments, as in most any practical aspect of life, the shortest distance between two points is a straight line. Take the direct, straight-line approach by establishing written goals and knowing where you want to be in the future. Today more than ever, it is essential to have a financial plan that deals with the growth of your net worth and the taxes on your current income in order to have a fighting chance to maintain your purchasing power. Chapter 13 discusses goal-setting and your financial living plan in more detail.

The Magic of Real Estate Investment in Fighting Inflation and Taxes

"Ninety percent of all millionaires become so through owning real estate. More money has been made in real estate than in all industrial investments combined. The wise young man or wage earner should invest his money in real estate."
—Andrew Carnegie, 1835–1919

MANY people think of Andrew Carnegie as a philanthropist who gave millions of dollars to establish free public libraries throughout the United States. Of course, before he could be a philanthropist he had to earn the millions of dollars he eventually gave away. So Carnegie is also remembered as the tough Scotsman who was largely responsible for the development of our steel industry.

What most people do not realize is that many of the millions of dollars accumulated by Carnegie came not from steel, but from real estate investment!

I use Carnegie as an example because I particularly admire his rags-to-riches life story. I could just as effectively have cited John Ringling of the famous circus family, or Marshall Field, who developed the largest department store in Chicago. These men, like so many of the financial giants in the early history of our country, made vast fortunes in real estate as they sought intelligent ways to invest the profit of their basic business success.

Today, the same holds true. Real estate investment tends to attract people who have earned outstanding financial success in other careers. If you check around your own community, you are sure to find its leaders in industry, banking, retailing, and the professions almost all involved to some degree in real estate investment.

WHERE THE ACTION IS

This attraction to real estate is based on the simple fact that it offers outstanding opportunity. Averaged over many decades, income from real estate has been higher and resale profit consistently larger than from almost any other kind of investment.

To top it off, as income tax became a major deterrent to the accumulation of wealth, real estate investment was given a very favored status by the government in terms of tax shelter and tax deferment. And more recently, as inflation became our dominant concern, real estate proved itself to be among the most reliable inflation hedges available.

In Chapter 4, I will present details of several typical passive real estate investments. To fully appreciate the opportunities offered, just compare the actual after-tax profits of these investments with the profits of any other investments you may have made in recent years. As you will see throughout this book, you too can use real estate to accumulate wealth even on a passive-investment basis.

MAXIMUM RETURN WITH MINIMUM RISK

Most investors base their ideas of risk and reward on the stock market. As a result they have the idea that an investment offering a particularly high potential yield must automatically be particularly risky. That is generally true of investments in stocks or bonds, where the marketplace adjusts prices to reflect inordinate risk.

Certainly there is risk involved in real estate, as there is in any investment, along with a broad range of rewards. The difference in real estate is that high potential yield need not be tied to high risk. The two factors do not necessarily go together as they do in the stock market.

Real estate investment can be extremely conservative and relatively risk-free for the knowledgeable investor. The key to limiting risk lies in professional property judgment, acquisition skills, management capability, and thorough knowledge of income-tax regulations. Since few individuals outside the real estate business have this know-how, conservative real estate investment usually requires some form of investment with and through a professional. Most frequently this is carried out through a limited partnership, the form of investment that is the main focus of this book.

As to the profitability of real estate investment, it varies of course, but it tends to be high because of a number of unique conditions. Among these are the following:

- Real estate investment is given highly favorable income-tax treatment that legitimately reduces the investment cost and increases after-tax earnings.
- Real estate has shown a remarkable ability to reflect inflationary increases, thus adding value.
- Real estate investments usually benefit from more favorable leverage than is available in most other forms of investment.

As a result, the after-tax profit of real estate investment is extremely favorable. Of course, there are no absolutes, but an average return on investment per year of 15 to 20 percent or even higher is not considered at all unusual. Remember, those percentages are in *after-tax* dollars, so an investor in the 50 percent tax bracket would have to achieve 30 to 40 percent pretax return to do as well.

If I have made real estate investment sound easy or glamorous, let me state that it is not, nor is it guaranteed. There are losers as well as winners. In my observation, the losers are characterized by being in over their heads. They lack the staying power and the resources necessary to make it through market lows when property should not be sold. Sales that are made because owners are emotionally tired or lack the capital to hang on are what create the big losers.

The key to avoiding losses for most investors is to select carefully the right professional partner: one with both knowledge and staying power. A major purpose of this book is to show you how to do this.

REAL ESTATE IS BASIC

All of the foregoing really doesn't deal with the "magic" of real estate investment in terms of tax shelter and inflation. Before we examine those timely considerations, it is important to put real estate investing into a longer-term perspective. Too many Americans are starting to think of real estate as another of the "financial survival" gimmicks, and I think that is dangerously misleading.

The need today is for investing that is sound and secure in a general sense, while offering special advantages in terms of inflation and taxation. There is danger in investments that address only the needs of taxation and inflation without offering intrinsic investment value as well.

As we have seen, the opportunities offered by real estate were recognized long ago. Other investment opportunities appear and disappear like Hula Hoop fads; real estate continues because it is tangible and essential.

The real estate product serves a fundamental need for all society. Every individual, every business, every service requires the use of some form of real estate. As a result, while economic ups and downs may affect price, the underlying demand for real estate is directly tied to our constantly increasing population and the changing needs of our various lifestyles. These factors tend to maintain a significant upward bias in real estate values.

THE GOVERNMENT IS YOUR PARTNER

Every businessman, every investor, every factory worker realizes the government is his partner in everything he does to earn money.

Unfortunately, this is not generally a desirable partnership. You contribute the labor, or investment risk, and through taxation the government takes a disproportionate share of the proceeds. In 1980, it was estimated the average American taxpayer worked from January 1 to May 11 to earn the share taken by the government. Only after that "Liberation Day" did the rewards of labor belong to the worker.

As a matter of perspective, it's interesting to note that in 1930, the average American taxpayer worked only until February 13 for the government. In other words, our average total tax payment now takes almost three times as much of our total productive effort as it did fifty years ago. The partnership seems to be getting more and more lopsided.

A Truly Constructive Partnership. For real estate investors, the government partnership is quite a different story. Tax laws are actually designed to support and encourage this one type of investor above all others! These laws provide for certain "paper" write-offs from real estate investments, which include depreciation and other items that can be deducted from other taxable income. The net effect is that your real estate investment creates a "paper" loss that can be deducted from taxes that would otherwise have to be paid on other taxable income. In fact, your real estate may concurrently be increasing in value, and may be producing an actual cash flow instead of a cash loss.

Some people refer to these favorable laws as "loopholes," suggesting government error or oversight. Actually, Congress, with the help of the Internal Revenue Service, regularly reconsiders the entire matter of tax shelters and all the other complex machinery of taxation. Over the years, many shelters in other fields have been reduced or eliminated. Today, in all investments except real estate, the maximum paper loss you can deduct from income is equal to the amount of money you have at risk. Real estate tax shelter is essentially unlimited as long as the investment has sound business purposes. So real estate continues to be the most favored investment in terms of the government partnership. The 1981 tax law clearly demonstrates the intent of the President and Congress to give special tax incentives to real estate.

There is a reason for this position on the part of the government: it encourages steady flow of investment into real estate. The special tax benefits offered to real estate investors are simply an incentive.

In a sense, they are subsidies that assure the continuing expansion of real estate, and a relatively low level of rent for the users. Perhaps even more to the point, if the tax benefits were taken away from real estate there would be total chaos in real estate markets, with badly needed new construction brought to a virtual standstill. The tax benefits are an ingrained part of the economics of this vital industry.

For the real estate investor, tax shelter offers not only great opportunity for superior financial return, but also a degree of safety not offered in other kinds of investment. In most realty investment situations, the greatest returns from tax shelter come in the first year or two. Thus, if something goes sour later and the total investment is lost, the investor is almost always better off than if he had a total loss in any other form of investment. Obviously, no such loss is ever desirable, and losses are relatively infrequent in real estate ventures. The point is that tax-shelter benefits in real estate do soften losses as well as sweeten profits.

The whole area of tax shelter and how tax loss works in real estate is discussed much more fully in Chapter 5. Of necessity, this is a somewhat technical area, but it is one you should understand broadly if you are to be successful in real estate investment.

I believe in free enterprise, and I would prefer the government did not use tax incentives to encourage real estate investment. On the other hand, I am also pragmatic. I believe that every player in any game owes it to himself to take full advantage of the rules as they exist. Since tax shelter is available, the only way to win in real estate today is to know how to make the most of tax-shelter opportunities.

The Government's Role in Inflation. In terms of concern about your personal finances, the ravages of inflation are even more important than the bite of taxation. Here, too, the government is a contributing partner when you invest properly in real estate.

The government contributes in that it is the primary creator of inflation, and its continuing economic needs strongly suggest that inflation will stay with us in the foreseeable future. Thus, you can quite safely plan to put inflation to work for you instead of allowing it to work against you.

At the end of fiscal year 1980, the total U.S. national debt was approximately $909 billion. The government depreciates this debt and pays it off with cheaper dollars by lowering the value of the currency. It must do this in order to remain solvent as various portions of the debt become due and must be refinanced. In a real sense our government is now in a no-win situation: inflate or collapse.

Because inflation brings difficult times to most people, and misery to many, the administration in power will constantly give lip service to stopping inflation. But the record of our economy since the end of World War II speaks for itself.

The fact is, politicians in power are far more fearful of recession or depression than they are of inflation. After all, they know their chances for reelection go down as unemployment goes up. Thus, we have seen the development of the inflation roller coaster: growing inflation, cooled off by recession, followed quickly by more government spending to create a quick job solution, followed by even higher inflation.

Just as the government counts on inflation to help pay its debts, so do many of our fellow citizens. Our economy today is built on an overextension of consumer credit, encouraged by the government. Most home purchases, and many other consumer purchases, are planned on the assumption of inflation. Thus, if the government ever took the steps necessary to really stop inflation, hundreds of thousands of individual families would face bankruptcy, and a severe depression would be inevitable.

I am not saying this situation will never occur, but I am betting most of my money on the premise that politicians will do everything possible to avoid it. President Reagan's administration will put up a valiant fight against inflation, but I don't believe it will accept the deflationary depression that would result if it were truly to end inflation. Moreover, through the tremendous powers of the Federal Reserve System, except for an economic accident, it can avoid a deflationary depression. That means continued inflation. Despite all of the double-talk, and all of the promised action, in the end inflation will win out over the risk of a severe recession leading to a shattering depression.

If the Reagan "supply side" economics were to work, your real estate investment would benefit from the real prosperity in the system. In any event, Reagan's economists are predicting inflation will be over 7 percent for at least the next five years. While this is not high compared to the 12.4 percent of 1980, by historic standards this "optimistic" view itself represents very high inflation. Based on these broad assumptions of government economic action, you, the financial achiever, have only one intelligent choice. Put inflation to work as part of your investment program. Become a beneficiary instead of a victim.

TAMING INFLATION WITH REAL ESTATE

Real estate is a particularly effective inflation hedge because it offers steady user demand coupled with the availability of favorable financing. Normally, real estate is the most easily financed of all investment vehicles. Because it is tangible, immovable, insurable, in constant demand, and will probably increase in value, bankers prefer to make loans secured by real estate over most other forms of collateral. Interest and terms are usually among the most favorable offered for any kind of investment, and the portion of the investment that can be financed is among the highest.

With a large proportion of fixed debt, inflation enhances your profitability. In most cases, as all prices inflate you will be able to sell a property for more than you paid for it. You will pay off the fixed debt, and the profit as a percentage of your cash down payment will far outstrip the rate of inflation. As 60 to 80 percent or more of most real estate purchases can be financed, good leverage is assured, and this has a positive effect in staying ahead of inflation.

If you were to invest in real estate as an active, personal owner, you would have to reckon with the fact that leverage is a two-edged sword. In the event of a serious loss, you would be responsible for the borrowed money as well as your cash investment, and this could increase your loss substantially. However, in this book we are dealing only with passive investment, and one of the extra advantages of that position is that you are protected against any loss beyond your actual investment. More about this "magic" in the next chapter.

BASIC VEHICLES FOR PASSIVE
REAL ESTATE INVESTMENT

Now that you have some idea as to why real estate is a very favorable investment for the eighties, you are probably wondering just how such investments are made.

There are three principal forms of real estate investment other than direct ownership, which is not the province of this book. These widely available types of passive real estate investment are stock corporations, real estate investment trusts, and limited partnerships. They vary considerably in their nature, so we will consider each one individually.

Real-Estate-Oriented Corporations. These are stock corporations listed on the major exchanges just like any other corporation in which you invest through the purchase of stock. They may or may not pay dividends to their shareholders, and your investment profits come through appreciation of the stock price. Shares in real-estate-oriented corporations may be bought and sold through local stock brokerages just as any other stocks may.

While corporate investment is a method of participating in the advantages of real estate, and it certainly can prove profitable, I do not believe it is the most effective method. Its essential problem is that the unique elements of real estate do not fit especially well into the stock-corporation mold.

One negative factor is that the stock market does not generally understand tax-loss operations, oriented as it is to cash profit. Since earning statements of a corporation holding a great deal of real estate must reflect the paper losses created by that real estate, they are not impressive unless you consider the tax benefits. Furthermore, generally accepted accounting principles for stock corporations show real estate at depreciated cost values on the corporate statement, rather than at current market value. This tends grossly to understate the achievement of these corporations and to hold down the price of the stock. One of the greatest values of real estate investment is the opportunity to create paper losses, which can be applied to reduce or defer taxes due on other income. This will be explored in more detail in Chapter 5. The important point here is that real-estate-oriented corporations cannot pass these tax losses on to their investors and thereby enable the investors to apply the losses to their own personal income. Instead, the corporation realizes their value only by applying them to income from properties and other corporate business activities. And it is frequently difficult for the corporation to use up all of the real estate tax losses in a timely fashion.

Then too, real estate stock corporations suffer the same problem of double taxation faced by all corporations. They must pay a heavy corporate income tax on earnings, especially if they do not have enough tax shelter prior to the payment of dividends to their shareholders. Then, the shareholder must in turn declare the dividends as taxable income. As you will soon see, other forms of real estate investment provide for single taxation of real estate earnings.

My final hesitation about the corporate vehicle for real estate investment stems from my strong belief that real estate generally reacts best to an entrepreneurial form of management. Decision-making is required on the firing line of the projects involved, and this implies a decentralization rare in big corporations. An indication of this can be seen in the unsuccessful real estate programs attempted by subsidiaries created by Chrysler and a number of other Fortune 500 corporations.

On the positive side, real estate investment through stock in large corporations does offer the liquidity of any stock investment, and there are many cases of excellent returns and opportunities for more in the future. I will not explore the real estate corporation further, but if you are interested, I suggest you discuss the subject with a qualified stockbroker.

Real Estate Investment Trusts (REITs). A real estate investment trust is a special form of investment in real estate that avoids the corporate double-taxation problem. Dividends are distributed to shareholders without corporate taxation. However, tax losses cannot be passed through to the shareholders and must be used against profits of the trust within a specified period of years.

As in the case of corporations, REIT stocks are traded widely, and many are on the major exchanges. Investment in REITs is handled through stockbrokers and in all respects is similar to the standard buying and selling of stock.

REITs are frequently involved in the financing of major real estate developments, and they are also allowed to own, buy, sell, and operate real estate projects. They are heavily leveraged with borrowed money, and in times of stability they can show excellent profits. During the financial crunch of 1973 and 1974, however, many REITs found themselves overextended, and many suffered severe losses from which they never recovered. Today, many of the surviving REITs appear to be back in good shape and, in fact, may be undervalued in the marketplace.

While REITs do indeed offer a method of participating in the advantages of real estate, they will not be our focus either, primarily because of the lack of opportunity for an investor to gain full advantage of the tax-shelter opportunities.

The Best of Both Worlds: Real Estate Limited Partnership. Most passive real estate investment is done through a special legal entity known as a "limited partnership." This investment vehicle offers a unique combination of corporate and individual ownership benefits.

A limited partnership has many of the benefits of a corporation, but it is not taxed like a corporation. Rather, the depreciation and tax benefits pass through to the individual partners in proportions specified by the partnership agreement. This arrangement allows the special tax-shelter benefits of real estate investment to be passed on to investors just as though those investors were individual property owners.

A limited partnership consists of two classes of partners: general and limited. The general partners are the active members of the business, the entrepreneurs and managers. They also have unlimited and exclusive liability for partnership debts. Limited partners are the passive members. They invest in the business, but are not active in its operation.

While the entity is treated as a partnership for tax purposes, the limited partners have a legal position similar to corporate shareholders in that they have no liability for financial loss beyond their original investment. Thus when a limited partnership finances the

purchase of property largely through a mortgage, the limited partners are not personally liable in the event of default, nor are they
even liable for debts of the operation.

Structurally, the limited partnership provides the best of both
worlds for the individual who wants the benefits of real estate investment without the operating responsibility. Assuming proper
knowledge and caution in selecting a specific limited partnership, I
believe this is without question the most favorable vehicle for real
estate investment. And so, limited partnerships will be the central
focus of this book. My purpose will be to prepare you for the most
effective utilization of the opportunities they offer to fight back
against inflation and taxation.

3

How Limited Partnerships Work for the Investor

OPERATIONALLY, limited partnerships vary tremendously, so the investor's selection becomes a matter of critical importance. This selection process is considered in great detail in Part Three of this book. For now, let's examine the potential values of investment through a limited partnership, assuming you will be dealing with an experienced and ethical organization.

THE POWER OF POOLING DOLLARS

The successful operation of a real estate investment is dependent on a thousand and one small details. Whether a property is large or small, the basic requirements are usually the same: mechanical maintenance, lawn care, snow removal, painting, advertising, rental showings, deposits, rent collection, security, and so on. As these factors are accounted for, it quickly becomes obvious that economies of scale make larger properties far more desirable than smaller ones.

An apartment property with 350 or more rental units can easily support an experienced professional resident manager. In addition, there will be a small clerical, bookkeeping, and maintenance staff. On the other hand, a typical individual investment in a building with perhaps 20 to 30 apartments will be hard put to afford more than a Mom-and-Pop management team working in exchange for an apartment. The difference in capability is apt to show up quickly in greater turnover, higher vacancy rate, and far lower return on investment.

Furthermore, the small property is constantly in jeopardy from relatively small problems, which become overwhelming in terms of operational percentages. Suppose the boiler goes bad in a small building—replacement can wipe out the owner's total cash flow for an entire year. In a larger project, the economies of scale allow such unforeseen economic bumps to be absorbed with relatively little discomfort.

We could go on and on with this comparison, but that really isn't necessary. The bottom line is that large properties are more efficient and effective to manage. Their operational profitability and value appreciation are generally superior.

Limited partnerships usually invest in large properties through the pooling of funds from a number of investors. An individual who might buy a $250,000 building with a cash investment of $50,000 can instead become one of forty investors in a limited partnership that will put $2 million down to purchase an $8 to $10 million property. There is, of course, a cost for the services of the General Partner, but in most cases the individual investor more than balances that cost with peace of mind, as well as an equal or superior return.

LIMITED PARTNERSHIPS AID DIVERSIFICATION

Diversification is a basic element of sound investing. Because of the large sums required, it is extremely difficult for the individual real estate investor to buy really attractive properties. Thus, most individual investors end up with all of their eggs in one or two baskets.

Through limited-partnership investment, there is no reason not to spread your total funds over any number of different properties. You simply buy a smaller portion of each partnership. For greatest avoidance of risk, your portfolio should also be diversified in terms of location and type of property.

In addition, you can diversify over a certain period of time to tailor your portfolio to meet your projected needs for tax shelter, cash flow, and cash return. While you cannot absolutely count on what phase each investment will be in, year after year, you can get estimates from a professional General Partner that will be valid for planning purposes. Then, by making various investments over a period of years, you can have some properties coming up for sale while others are providing cash flow and still others are at the stage of maximum tax shelter. In Chapter 13, I describe a particular portfolio approach we call the Step Investing Plan. It is designed to minimize taxes during highest earning years, and to add liquidity through a planned sequence of cash returns from old investments and reinvestment in new partnerships. Obviously, this kind of flexibility can be achieved only by taking relatively small segments of numerous investment partnerships.

THE RIGHT OPPORTUNITY AT THE RIGHT TIME

Real estate is not a business in which you can decide on any given day that you're ready to buy, then act on that urge and expect outstanding results. Locating and buying property is an ongoing process requiring virtually full-time involvement if the results are to be effective.

Much more than price is involved. A buying decision depends on current local market conditions and future economic forecasts for the area. It depends on location, age, design, appearance, earnings, physical condition, neighbors, competitive rental rates, competitive vacancies, opportunities to upgrade, utilization, existing financing, and the owner's terms and desires, to mention just a few factors.

To give you an idea of the complexity of this task, my own company, Hall Real Estate, Inc., is currently considering fifty property offerings for each one we buy for our limited partners. In our operation, each partnership is usually organized around a specific property, and this selection process actually goes on before a partnership is formed. It is really an advance contribution from the General Partner.

Of course, our deciding that we want a property is not the end of the acquisition process; it is really just another beginning.

THE FINE ART OF NEGOTIATION

Here is where it all comes together: knowledge, skill, experience, and creativity.

Certainly real estate investment is a business, but it is far from a rigid, routine kind of business. I consider it more an art than a science, because creativity plays an important role in putting together the best opportunities. There is no one right way to buy, operate, or sell real estate. There are many right ways, and even more wrong ways. Thus, the ability to structure each investment using its unique characteristics is a major contribution of the General Partner.

Real estate purchases and sales are among the few that can be "non-zero-sum" transactions. That is, in order for one party to win a point in negotiation, the other party need not necessarily lose on that point. A recent negotiation in which I was involved illustrates this fact.

We were interested in purchasing a very desirable property, but the seller was asking what we felt was too high a price, and he appeared to be adamant. After we dug out more background information about the seller's situation, it became apparent the high price was necessary for him to show a good return because he had not yet held the property long enough to get the savings of a capital-gains tax on the profit. All the income from the sale profit would be treated as ordinary income, subject to high taxation.

I could understand the seller's point of view, so I took it as my job to give him what he needed while still structuring a deal we could afford. The solution was to induce the seller to give us long-term financing that would make the high price reasonable from the cash flow potential of the project.

In return for a long-term note at a substantial interest rate, and with a stiff penalty for prepayment, the seller agreed to lower the price a bit as well as spread the down payment over many years. We each reached our objective. Even with the somewhat lower price, the seller got the profit he sought through the combination of the sale and high interest protected by a prepayment penalty. Since his profit would all be ordinary income anyway, it didn't matter in what form he received it. We got a payment schedule we could handle, and in addition we expected to gain from the tax deductibility of the interest. Everyone won, no one lost, thanks to creative negotiation.

The acquisition stage is absolutely critical in real estate investment because it usually affects everything that happens thereafter. If you don't buy well, you can spend your entire period of ownership just trying to dig your way out of the hole. That is no pleasure.

DUE DILIGENCE

One of the duties a General Partner owes to the limited partners is "due diligence" in the investment and expenditure of their money. A very important part of the acquisition of a property thus becomes the detailed verification of all of the assumptions and physical conditions on which the purchase is calculated. Therefore, as part of the purchase process as general partners we tie a property up but insist on fourteen to twenty-one days to fully inspect both the physical assets and all records before our purchase decision is final. At this point at Hall Real Estate, we send in a team of specialists in the various functions of real estate operation. The books are checked, and verification is made of rent rolls, vacancy rate, delinquency rate, personnel payrolls, accounts payable, operating costs, and all the other details that will affect the investment. Physical inspections are made of such things as boilers, roofs, wiring, and other elements to assure that their condition is as we assumed it to be in our purchase planning.

These activities are extremely important to the partnership if it is to avoid the traps that await unwary real estate investors. It is very easy to buy a pig in a poke. Due diligence on the part of the General Partner is an essential service.

DAY-TO-DAY MANAGEMENT

One of the major differences between real estate investment and most other investments is that the property cannot be put in a safe-deposit box and forgotten. Not even for a single day. With the exception of vacant land, real estate requires a fairly high degree of management attention. Even net-lease properties cannot be completely ignored.

The usual approach for the individual investor is to put the property in the hands of a management company. In theory this is workable, but in practice it is very difficult to find management companies that have the depth and motivation to do the proper job for the relatively small fee the property can support. What you, as an investor, really need is a management that approaches its responsibility from the owner's point of view. The question shouldn't be "How little must be done?" but rather "How much can be done to make the property worth more?"

I can be very sympathetic with independent management companies, because theirs is a thankless task, and one at which it is very difficult to make money without cutting corners. Early in my real estate career, I operated a management company that took care of investments in which I was not involved as General Partner. I soon learned that trying to do a proper job was close to a nonprofit proposition. I then got out of the management business except for those properties owned by our own limited partnerships. My experience over many years indicates the best management is that provided by the General Partner, and it is most efective if the same General Partner organization provides management for a substantial number of limited partnerships.

TIMING THE TURNOVER

Every aspect of a real estate investment is important, if the gains to be made all along the way through tax shelter and cash flow are to be meaningful. But nothing can touch the financial or psychological value of selling a property well, and receiving the ultimate reward of the investment.

Timing is usually the key to maximizing the profit on a sale. Unfortunately for many individual investors, the right time is usually that point at which they become emotionally attached to the property. This is the time when all the problems have been solved, when cash flow is at its best and not a problem is in sight. It seems like the time to hang on forever, but in fact is the best time to sell if you have the discipline to cash in.

The greatest money in real estate is made by those who go against the cycles. "Buy low, sell high" is an easy slogan to understand. It is not so easy to do if it means buying when everyone else is selling, or selling when everyone else is buying. Nevertheless, swimming against the stream and taking the opposite action from that of the crowd is how fortunes are made. For those with courage and foresight, the greatest buying opportunities are found in the midst of recession. The maximum profit on sale is available during the rosy days of prosperity, when the future looks limitless and no one wants to sell.

Beyond timing, each sale raises structural questions. There are opportunities to sell for cash, or to participate in financing. The total price must be weighed against risks and tax consequences. Once again, experience and objectivity are required.

One of the most serious responsibilities of a General Partner is to decide when and how to sell. He may ask for an advisory vote from his partners, but in the long run this difficult decision must be made on the basis of professional judgment, and must be free of emotion. This is one of the high points and special requisites of the service rendered to investors by the General Partner.

SELECTING THE RIGHT GENERAL PARTNER

The theory of limited-partnership investment in real estate is simple and sound. The investor joins with others in an inactive financial role, entrusting the complex management decisions and actions to a General Partner. That General Partner may be an individual, several individuals, or even a corporation. Whatever the organization's structure, the results will largely depend on the capability, philosophy, experience, and effort of the General Partner. No single decision will have greater effect on your success or failure as a passive real estate investor than your selection of a General Partner. Again, I refer you to Part Three of this book for a detailed guide on this critical point.

UNDERSTANDING THE DIFFERENCES BETWEEN
PUBLIC AND PRIVATE LIMITED PARTNERSHIPS

If you are going to consider real estate limited-partnership investment seriously, it is important that you understand the two major
categories of partnerships: public and private. These terms derive
from the allowable method of offering the partnership interests for
sale, a distinction that in turn derives from the form of registration
or exemption with the federal Securities and Exchange Commission
and state securities bureaus.

Real estate limited-partnership interests are classified as securities, just as stock in a corporation is a security. Therefore, such
shares must either be registered or exempted before they can legally be offered for sale.

Registration is an expensive and extremely time-consuming process, so it is used only when necessary. Exemption from federal registration is granted to limited partnerships under Rule 147 (the
"intrastate exemption") when the property, the syndicator, General
Partner, and all limited partners are residents in a particular state.
Rule 146 (the "private placement exemption") exempts limited
partnerships on the condition that no more than thirty-five investors will be involved (investors meeting certain criteria don't count
in the limitation). Other requirements restrict advertising, assure
that all prospective purchasers are able to afford the risk involved,
and assure that prospects will receive complete information and
have an opportunity to ask questions regarding the terms and conditions of the offer. These rules are the major available exemptions
from federal registration. The securities must still meet the registration or exemption requirements of the state securities laws (otherwise known as "blue-sky laws," see page 93) in those states where
they will be offered.

Those limited-partnership offerings that have been exempted are
referred to as private limited partnerships, or sometimes as private
placements, due to the restrictions placed on the way they may be
offered for sale. Public limited partnerships, on the other hand,
have been registered with the SEC at the federal level, as well as
the various states in which they are to be sold. As you might assume,

they may be advertised in certain ways, and they are sold with less selectivity to a much broader public.

Beyond this definition, it is difficult to make absolute statements about the differences between public and private real estate limited partnership. There can be a great deal of variation within each group, although only certain differences are of interest to investors.

Public limited partnerships are usually offered in much smaller investment units and, therefore, are frequently and particularly attractive to investors of modest means. A typical public limited partnership might sell for $500 per unit, with a minimum of three to five units. On the other hand, depending on one's objectives, they may also be suitable for very large investors. Public limited partnerships are usually sold through Wall Street and local brokerage firms. This makes it easy to find and buy public partnerships, but does not encourage the personal contact with principals that large investors may desire.

Because of the cost and time involved in registration, public limited partnerships are frequently "blind pools." That is, the prospectus does not identify in advance the specific properties that will be involved. Instead, a partnership prospectus will usually specify objectives describing the general type of property to be purchased or developed after the investment funds are raised.

In a general way, it can be said that public limited partnerships tend to focus more on producing shelter to cover the cash flow from their investments, and relatively less on producing excess shelter for application to other taxable income earned by their investors. Once again, this tends to make the public partnerships more suitable for investors in somewhat lower tax brackets.

Private limited partnerships can be formed somewhat faster. They usually specify a particular property or properties that have been purchased or tied up in advance of the sale of limited partner interests. They may also be designed to achieve highly specific tax benefits of interest to a particular type of investor. While some cash flow may be involved in private placements, it tends to have less priority than the tax advantages. For tax benefits, private partnerships have a major advantage over public funds in that they may offer installment credit (*i.e.*, letting the investor put his money in overtime). This provides greater leverage and accordingly better tax benefits for investors.

Of course, both types of partnerships seek appreciation through the ultimate sale of the property at a favorable price, and with favorable tax consequences.

Both private and public real estate limited partnerships may be sold directly by the partnership as "issuer" if the partnership is not affiliated with a larger, more active syndicator. A larger organization may have its own licensed security broker staff, or it may sell through the local or regional brokers. Most public partnerships are sold through securities brokers such as the Wall Street brokerage firms. Today, with the increasing demand for high-grade real estate investments, private partnerships are also being sold by many of the large Wall Street brokerage firms.

It is important to understand that neither public nor private limited partnerships can be said to be better. Each serves the investor market well, and the key is to determine which type can best help you meet your particular investment objectives. We will consider this selection process further in Chapter 11.

CHAPTER 4

Is Limited-Partnership
Real Estate Investing for You?

I'D LIKE to answer the question posed by this chapter title by simply saying, "Sure it is!" Instead I have to point out that investing in real estate is very definitely not for everyone, and it is essential that each individual carefully consider its suitability before seriously undertaking to follow recommendations made throughout this book.

Through the preceding chapters you should have received enough basic knowledge to have a general understanding of the nature of real estate investment, and the special benefits it offers to many people who are currently suffering from the combined effects of inflation and excessive taxation. In this chapter we will look at a couple of specific investment case histories to see just what is reasonable to expect in terms of reward. Then we will look at the requirements both financially and emotionally. I hope that by the end of this chapter you will know if real estate investment is indeed right for you.

WHAT CAN YOU EXPECT AS A RETURN
ON REAL ESTATE INVESTMENT?

This is, of course, an impossible question to answer in any absolute sense, since each investment is separate and distinctly different. So I will not offer any averages or range of figures, but instead will present a few specific situations that I feel are fairly representative of programs with which I have been involved. In all of these cases I have changed the names of the property and the partnership out of respect to third parties involved in these transactions. If, as a result of this chapter and the rest of this book, you do decide to pursue real estate limited-partnership investments personally, you will surely be exposed to many more case histories from prospective General Partners, and this will allow you to develop your own level of anticipation.

Crestwood Commons—An Example of Tax Shelter with Economic Profit. Up to this point, we have been considering tax shelter as a concept. Now let's look at a real investment, and see how the concept can work in terms of real dollars. What follows are the facts concerning one of Hall Real Estate's limited-partnership ventures in effect from 1974 to 1976. Remember, this was a period of inflation, but nothing like the inflation experienced at the end of the decade and in 1980. This is a realistic example for a property of this type.

Crestwood Commons is an apartment project in a Detroit suburb.

It was a typical "turnaround" investment in that it was overbuilt for the area and had serious financial and operational problems that hampered the original developer and its second owner. By "overbuilt," I mean a project that has too high a cost and too many special features to be realistic for its time or location. This is usually the result of a builder's effort to erect a monument to his own ego. When a limited partnership can buy such a property at a price that reflects its operational problems, it offers special profit opportunities—if the problems can be solved and the property "turned around."

In the case of Crestwood Commons, we were able to turn its super-deluxe clubhouse from an operational drain to a money-producing asset. The clubhouse was so deluxe it had very high expenses, and its theoretical value in attracting renters was not enough to offset the costs. We decided to improve the clubhouse a bit more, but then convert it into a private health club with a stiff membership fee for nonresidents. This created a meaningful new source of income for the project. In addition, it gave a more dramatic value to the free memberships that were offered to residents (at no cost to the owners), and it ended up allowing us to increase occupancy while we increased rents.

The tax effects shown in Table 1 are not unusual. As a matter of fact, the only thing unique about this case history is that in less than three years we received an offer to buy the property, and it was too good to turn down. Thus, instead of its tax loss continuing at a declining rate for perhaps five or six years, this investment was unexpectedly wrapped up in the third year with the distribution of a handsome profit.

The sale was made on an installment basis, which returns the investment and profit over a period of years. As explained in Chapter 6, this avoids putting the investor in an artificially high tax bracket during the year of sale, and provides additional tax savings.

Table 1 illustrates the tax and financial gain for a hypothetical investor filing a joint return, having a taxable income of $60,000 per year, after taking the typical deductions for a family of four with a typical home and mortgage. I have selected the $60,000 rather arbitrarily, realizing that it may seem very high to some readers and low to others. In later examples, we will see the effect of other tax brackets on similar investments.

The total investment was $44,000 per limited-partnership unit. This sum was committed by each investor, but was paid through installments as indicated: $20,000 when the partnership was formed, $13,000 the second year, and $11,000 the third year. This is a fairly common arrangement in large private limited-partnership investments. It brings in money as required for prearranged payments on the property or to fund anticipated improvements or deficit operations. At the same time, it provides the partners with tax-shelter benefits from the total investment while they continue to have the personal use of some of their investment cash until it is required by the partnership.

The "cash distribution" line in the second year represents cash produced from operations in excess of the direct cost of operations and debt service (mortgage payments). As explained in more detail in the next chapter, this cash flow is tax-sheltered because it is more than offset by the "paper losses" generated by the investment. In general, these paper losses come from depreciation and other allowable bookkeeping expenses that are not, in fact, cash expenses.

TABLE 1
Crestwood Commons Investment Results

Item	Without shelter	With shelter
YEAR 1 (1974)		
Crestwood Commons investment	$ 0	$20,000
Crestwood cash distribution (tax-sheltered)	0	0
Taxable income after itemized deductions	60,000	60,000
Tax-shelter deduction	0	33,431
Net taxable income	60,000	26,569
Taxes payable	22,300	6,585
Taxes saved by shelter	$ 0	**$15,715**
YEAR 2 (1975)		
Crestwood Commons investment	0	13,000
Crestwood cash distribution (tax-sheltered)	0	2,196
Taxable income after itemized deductions	60,000	60,000
Tax-shelter deduction	0	32,696
Net taxable income	60,000	27,304
Taxes payable	22,180	6,729
Taxes saved by shelter	$ 0	**$15,451**
YEAR 3 (1976)		
Crestwood Commons investment	0	11,000
Crestwood cash distribution (tax-sheltered)	0	10,000*
Taxable income after itemized deductions	60,000	60,000
Tax-shelter deduction	0	1,135
Net taxable income	60,000	58,865
Taxes payable	22,120	21,518
Taxes saved by shelter	$ 0	**$ 602**

*Proceeds from sale—first installment

In the case of Crestwood Commons in the second year of the investment, there were additional paper losses of $32,696 per investment unit, and these provided the investor with a tax-shelter deduction that could be used to reduce taxable income from any other source. This, of course, provided the investor in our example with a cash saving in taxes paid that year of $15,451.

Table 2 provides a summary of the results of the Crestwood Commons investment over the total time from the first capital-investment payment to the receipt of the final installment of the sales proceeds. The subject of the taxes paid on the proceeds of an investment (Item 4) is somewhat complex, but is thoroughly explained in the next chapter. The method of computing rate of return (Item 7) is discussed in detail in Chapter 11.

As you can see, this was a very happy investment in terms of both shelter and ultimate profit. One of the interesting things about tax shelter, well illustrated in this case, is that the tax savings in the early years go a long way toward offsetting the cash involved in the investment. In this case, the shelter supplied 79 percent of the first-year investment installment, and over 100 percent of the second year's installment. In essence, this investment turned tax dollars into investment dollars, which in turn created an excellent profit. Part of the reason this works out so well is that the investors are able to spread their investment over a number of years.

Crestwood Commons is a good example of a balanced program in terms of shelter and profit objectives. There are investments that are much more thoroughly oriented to tax shelter, but these should be of interest only to investors who have large amounts of income in

TABLE 2
Summary of Crestwood Commons Investment Results
for Investor in 50 Percent Tax Bracket
(Including Period of Property Ownership
and Period of Sale Installments)

1. Total invested	$44,000
2. Total tax dollars saved on other income	31,768
3. Total cash received (includes distributions, sale proceeds, and interest on installments)	87,525
4. Total taxes paid by investor on Item 3	32,186
5. Net after-tax cash return (Item 2 plus Item 3 minus Item 4)	87,107
6. Net after-tax profit (Item 5 minus Item 1)	$43,107
7. Annual after-tax rate of return (using discounted rate-of-return method)*	31.9 percent

*See Chapter 11.

the highest tax brackets. I believe the orientation for most investors should be to balanced results. If there is not good reason to expect an ultimate profit, I would not suggest making an investment just for tax shelter.

Hall Sun-Key Associates—An Example of a Limited-Partnership Investment in Land. Hall Sun-Key Associates was a limited partnership organized to purchase and hold for later resale to a developer 26.21 acres of raw land on a beautiful island off the coast of Sarasota, Florida. The land was selected because it was viewed as extremely desirable for development within a few years, assuming favorable economic conditions.

Each of the fifteen limited-partnership units contributed $13,000 initially for the down payment and expenses, and was responsible for an additional $62,000 note to be paid at $4,000 per year (for mortgage payments) over nine years. At the end of that period, if the land had still not been resold, the balance of the note would be payable. While it was anticipated that the investment would be sold in three to five years, the investors did have to have staying power in case conditions did not allow a profitable sale at an early date.

The investment worked out very favorably. Only three of the semiannual investment contributions were actually made before a cash sale was concluded at an excellent profit.

Table 3 shows how the Hall Sun-Key investment worked out for the limited partners, assuming they were taxed in the 37 percent bracket (during the time of this investment about $25,000 gross income for a single taxpayer and $31,500 for a couple filing jointly).

TABLE 3
Summary of Hall Sun-Key Investment Results
for Investor in 37 Percent Tax Bracket

Total invested	$19,000
Total tax dollars saved on other income	1,648
Total cash received from sale	31,736
Total taxes paid by investor on sale	1,754
Net after-tax cash return	31,630
Net after-tax profit	$12,630
Annual after-tax rate of return (using discounted rate-of-return method)	38.04 percent

As a sidelight to the Hall Sun-Key investment, it should be pointed out that tax shelter played a very modest role because the investment covered raw land. No depreciation was involved, and the primary source of tax deduction was the interest on the mortgage. As a result, there was relatively little tax advantage, and most of the economic value was from the profit on sale. Thus, while an investor in a higher bracket would have fared better, the difference would have been slight. The key requirement in this kind of investment is the ability to meet the payments if the land is not sold as soon as anticipated. In other words, Hall Sun-Key might have been very suitable for a semiretired investor currently in a 37 percent tax bracket, but only one who had substantial savings that would assure the ability to make the semiannual cash contribution.

PUBLIC LIMITED PARTNERSHIPS

Because I am not in the public limited-partnership business, I do not feel it would be appropriate to include an identified case history. However, in Chapter 11 we do describe some data from partnerships that have been completely liquidated. Based on this data, we discuss the kind of returns you can expect from investments of this type.

DO YOU HAVE THE FINANCIAL AND EMOTIONAL STAYING POWER FOR SUCCESS?

In most investments, whether they be in the stock market or in active real estate ownership, the investor without financial or emotional staying power is in a weak position. Circumstances may create a need or a desire to sell out, and the timing may create a sizable loss. Thus, almost all types of investors are well advised to invest only money that is available over and above their anticipated needs for normal living expenses.

However, this approach is really not sufficient in considering the suitability of investing in a real estate limited partnership, because there are definite restrictions to the resale of a limited partner's interest. Real estate limited-partnership investments should only be made with funds that can be safely assumed to be completely un-available, even for an emergency.

There are two reasons why the resale of limited-partnership inter-est may be difficult. First, there is no established secondary market such as is offered by the stock market for the resale of listed corpo-rate stock. It should be noted that there are some funds being orga-nized and some just recently started that seek to provide a resale market for limited-partnership interests, but the market is still far from "liquid." In some cases the General Partner will make a sin-cere and active effort to locate a purchaser in case of an emergency need to sell, but there is no requirement to do so, and no assurance that he will be successful if he tries.

Secondly, if a purchaser is located by yourself or anyone assisting you, the purchaser must be qualified to make the investment in the same way you were able to make it—that is, in terms of net worth, income, and in some states, tax bracket as well. Since these qualifi-cations vary from state to state, they may in fact require more strin-gent qualifications than those you met.

If there is any question in your mind about your ability to get along without the funds that will be tied up in a limited partnership, just cut down on the number of dollars involved until you feel total confidence. Never allow yourself to be rushed into a decision. Your financial comfort should be a major criterion. If you aren't sure, just hold off. The partnership agreement does contain restrictions on transfer of interests, but it is usually possible to sell a unit with the consent of the General Partner. As a practical matter, most General Partners can accommodate you if it is absolutely necessary for you to sell your interest. However, it is more advantageous, financially, to hold on until the natural end of the partnership.

Besides being sure that you will not have financial pressure to cash in your limited partnership interest prematurely, you should also consider your emotional conditioning for long-term investment. If by nature or psychological conditioning you consider investing a kind of exciting game with lots of in-and-out action, you may have trouble with real estate limited partnerships. Real estate in any in-vestment format requires time for maturation. Your General Part-ner will be able to advise you of the time objectives of a specific investment. In general, assume five to seven years for most single-property programs. Blind-pool public syndications may well run eight to ten years since more properties are involved. If your mind is on an investment life of these lengths, any early sale with a good profit will simply be a pleasant surprise.

ARE YOU IN A HIGH ENOUGH TAX BRACKET TO BENEFIT?

This is a complex question, because what the proper tax bracket is depends on the specific objectives and potential of each investment. Many people have the idea that no one paying taxes below the 50 percent bracket should become involved in tax-advantaged investments. This is a complete misconception that dates back to the pre–1976 law, when many tax-shelter investments were in fact designed only for people with super incomes. Today there is a wide range of programs available, and those that offer moderate tax shelter coupled with good profit potential may be perfectly suitable for people in brackets as low as 32 percent, as long as they qualify in other respects.

In general, the question of your own tax bracket suitability is one you should consider with the help of your accountant or other tax advisor. As a rule of thumb, you can assume that any investment offering more than about 1.5-to-1 or 1.8-to-1 shelter is not advisable for an investor without sufficient income subject to 50 percent taxation. This means an investment where you will receive tax shelter of more than 1.3 times the amount of your cash investment during the years in which you make your capital contributions to the investment. For example, assume you invest $20,000 this year in XYZ limited partnership and receive $26,000 of tax loss at year's end (a 1.3-to-1 ratio of tax loss to investment). We would generally advise that you be in the 50 percent tax bracket for at least a substantial portion of the $26,000 of "tax write-off." Your highest tax bracket gets sheltered first, and then your savings diminish as your deductions shelter income in lower brackets. Assuming your entire $26,000 tax loss is in the 50 percent bracket, you will save $13,000 in income taxes.

The reason for not investing in higher shelter investments if you are in a lower tax bracket is not that there is anything inherently weak in such investments, but that because of their deep shelter they may create high recapture and tax-preference consequences that can be costly to an investor in a lower bracket. This is explained in detail in Chapter 5. It is possible that, after providing deep shelter advantages, the taxes on sale will push you into a higher bracket than you otherwise would experience on your ordinary income. The investor who is already in a 50 percent bracket will not suffer. The investor who would otherwise be substantially lower than 50 percent can in fact sustain excessive taxation that wipes out much of the benefit previously received.

The other important point to remember is that in all tax-advantaged investments, the higher the tax bracket of the investor, the more valuable the tax deferment or tax savings received. This adds motivation for the higher-income investor, but it does not necessarily mean that an individual in a moderate bracket should not participate. The really important criterion is the balance between the tax-shelter objective and the profit objective. If the tax shelter is moderate and the profit objective is strong, both higher- and lower-income investors will benefit.

In Chapter 6 there is a case history of a property called River View (p. 84–85). This was a limited-partnership investment actually sold only to investors in at least the 50 percent tax bracket, and from their point of view it was extremely successful. While it would not be suitable for investors in the 37 percent tax bracket based on our rule of thumb regarding the amount of shelter, Tables 4 and 5 pro-

TABLE 4
Summary of River View Investment Results for Investor in 50 Percent Tax Bracket

Total invested	$22,000
Total tax dollars saved on other income	$15,688
Actual and projected cash flow (includes distributions, sale proceeds, and interest on installments)	$53,800
Projected taxes	$16,323
Net after-tax cash return	$53,165
Net after-tax profit	$31,165
Annual after-tax rate of return (using discounted rate-of-return method, see Chapter 11)	23.42 percent

vide a direct comparison of the results in the two tax categories so you can compare the effects of tax bracket.

Notice that during the four years the property was owned and tax loss was being produced, the cumulative cost of the investment was much less for the 50 percent bracket investor than for the 37 percent. This, of course, came as a result of the value of the tax shelter. Had anything gone sour at this point, the 50 percent investor would have been far ahead of the 37 percent.

Then, in the fifth year, the property was sold on an installment contract, and the rest of the chart shows the effect of each investor receiving cash from the sale, and paying the appropriate taxes. At this point, the 37 percent bracket investor naturally had lower tax bills, and thus would have been able to keep more of the profit. Since most of this taxation is as a long-term capital gain, the 50 percent taxpayer is far better off than he would be with ordinary taxable income, but still he does pay a higher tax on the profit than someone in a lower bracket.

In the final analysis, the two investors would have practically identical net cash returns. However, on the basis of percentage return on the cash involved over time, the 50 percent bracket investor would be ahead (his 23.42 percent discounted rate of return versus the 20.02 percent for the 37 percent tax bracket investor).

The major point of this comparison is to stress the fact that when appropriate profit objectives are involved, taxpayers well below the 50 percent bracket can benefit from real estate limited-partnership

TABLE 5
**Summary of River View Investment Results
for Investor in 37 Percent Tax Bracket**

Total invested	$22,000
Total tax dollars saved on other income	$11,609
Actual and projected cash flow	$53,800
Projected taxes	
(includes distributions, sale proceeds, and interest on installments)	$12,077
Net after-tax cash return	$53,332
Net after-tax profit	$31,332
Annual after-tax rate of return	
(using discounted rate-of-return method)	20.02 percent

investment. If you fall into a lower tax bracket, be very selective in choosing programs and emphasize the real profit potential in the investment rather than the tax aspects alone.

Suitability Regulations. As you start to examine specific limited partnerships, you will find that they have clearly defined suitability requirements established by the sponsor, usually with the approval of the state securities bureaus involved.

The establishment of specific suitability criteria is tied directly to the risk involved, and also reflects the amount of tax shelter involved. Therefore, while you might be tempted to try to stretch your suitability, it would be ill advised. If you find that you do not truly meet the requirements for a particular investment, pass on that one, and find one for which you do qualify.

Many of the public limited partnerships with investment minimums of $5,000 or less have suitability standards along the lines of "A net worth (exclusive of home, home furnishings, and automobiles) of at least $20,000." For the investor who is not employed, the same partnership might simply require a net worth in excess of $75,000. These are reasonable requirements, and they should not exclude any potential investor who in fact can meet the personal standards I have suggested in terms of investing only with dollars not needed for other purposes.

WHAT KIND OF PEOPLE INVEST IN
REAL ESTATE LIMITED PARTNERSHIPS?

I am frequently asked this question, and the only answer I can give is, "All kinds."

One of my first outside investors when I was getting started was a graduate student at the University of Michigan. Like most graduate students he was living in less than the lap of luxury, but he did understand business and he wanted to participate. He got together $2,500 to help me purchase a seven-unit apartment building. Happily, he ended up with a good profit for his faith.

Today there are many thousands of small investors like that grad student who are participating in real estate limited partnerships, either through small sponsors like myself some years ago, or through the brokerage firms that sell public limited partnerships.

My own business has changed in recent years, and this has created a change in the type of investors we work with. We have moved into larger and larger properties, most of which require cash investments between $1 and $5 million. Since we work through private limited partnerships we are restricted, in most cases, to a maximum of thirty-five investors per program. This means that a typical investment unit will require $50,000 to $150,000, usually paid in installments over at least three to six years. As a result, we only accept new investors who meet rigid qualifications.

Still, we do work with people from many backgrounds and in many kinds of careers. There are a great many professionals, including accountants, attorneys, physicians, and dentists. Independent businessmen rate high on our client list. We are especially proud to be associated with the chairmen, presidents, and other high executives of some of the largest corporations in the country. These men certainly have the business acumen to play an active role in managing their investments, but they choose to become limited partners because they recognize the value of the expertise we supply.

A VERY PERSONAL DECISION

Ultimately, the question of whether real estate limited-partnership investing is right for you can only be answered by you. As you read on, you will learn more about the way limited partnerships operate, about the ins and outs of tax shelter, and about how to analyze specific investment opportunities. By the end of the book, you will be able to make your decision easily—and what's more, you will be ready to make your first move toward becoming a limited partner.

Part Two

TAX AND LEGAL ASPECTS OF REAL ESTATE INVESTMENT

Why Tax Shelter Can Be the Cornerstone of Your Economic Survival

MOST taxpayers are discovering that as they work harder and earn more, they pay a greater percentage in taxes, only to find that what is left will buy less because of inflation. More and more people are being forced to the decision that their only way to survive is to reduce their standard of living. This is the opposite of everything our country has stood for. It is acceptance of defeat instead of belief in opportunity. If we allow this negative approach to become widespread, we curtail the motivation that has made this country the most productive and fruitful in the world.

Thus, this chapter does not deal with economic survival in the sense of just staying alive. It deals with survival in the sense of maintaining upward mobility and of working hard in order to earn the right to live better than you did before. It deals with keeping enough of your earnings to build a better future.

TAX-DOLLAR POWER

The primary reason that tax shelter can be the cornerstone of your economic survival is that tax dollars can be given investment power. This is a concept that many taxpayers have never been introduced to, and it is at the heart of understanding the intelligent use of tax shelter.

At present, the average taxpayer thinks of his income-tax dollars as a portion of his income that is beyond his control. He has been brainwashed into thinking he has no choices about his tax obligations: "This is what you made last year, this is what you owe in taxes!"

The fact is, the very government that takes and spends all of your tax dollars has provided you with a choice. Through legitimate tax-shelter investment, the government has ordained that you can keep some of your tax dollars. No, you can't just spend these dollars as you might desire, but you can invest them in real estate to build your net worth, and eventually this will produce profit to be spent like any other dollars you earn.

The options provided by the government are fairly simple. Pay every dollar possible in taxes, or put some of those dollars to work in legitimate tax-sheltered investments for your own economic benefit. Either pay your tax dollars to the IRS, or produce tax-dollar power for yourself.

The kind of economic survival you achieve is really up to you.

TAX SHELTERS ARE INVESTMENT INCENTIVES AND ARE YOUR LEGAL RIGHT

In Chapter 2, I briefly introduced the concept of tax shelters, and touched on the fact that they are not "loopholes" in the law. This is such an important concept it bears some elaboration before we go into more detail on how tax shelters can work for you.

Over the years, as our Internal Revenue Code has been developed by Congress and the IRS, there have certainly been errors and omissions that created unintended opportunities for some taxpayers. These may properly be referred to as "loopholes." Historically, such opportunities have proved short-lived. As soon as the IRS realizes the error, it recommends a change in the code, and in due time most loopholes are plugged.

Since tax-shelter opportunities have been a part of the federal tax laws for many years, they can hardly be referred to as loopholes. Still, there are many individuals who feel it is unethical or even illegal to take advantage of tax shelter. There is no law, and no moral code I'm aware of, that says we should each pay the most taxes possible. On the contrary, Congress is fully aware of the benefits created by tax shelters. Public hearings bring out both sides of the question, and the issues are debated with great emotion.

In a famous court case in the Second Circuit Court in 1934, Judge Learned Hand said,

Anyone may so arrange his affairs [so] that his taxes shall be as low as possible; he is not bound to choose that pattern which will best pay the Treasury; there is not even a patriotic duty to increase one's taxes.

One of the reasons that tax shelter has become questionable in the minds of some people is that tax laws are particularly subject to interpretation, and this quite naturally leads to gimmick applications and abuses. Some of the schemes that have been used have given the entire idea of shelter a bad name. Those investments that are commonly referred to as "exotic shelters"—such as investments in bibles, cemetery plots, recordings, flowers, art, and buffalo herds—are highly questionable. Our purpose here is to discuss only absolutely legitimate tax-advantaged investments. Our goal is to pay the government all the tax the law requires, but not to pay more than is necessary.

Politically there has been a great deal of negative outcry concerning tax shelter. After all, shelters have helped the rich stay rich, and many people in this country simply don't like that. Then, due to stepped-up inflation in recent years, many more people have been pushed into higher income brackets, and even the not-so-rich discovered they could profitably use tax shelters.

In response to growing political pressure, Congress in 1976 and again in 1978 passed tax-reform acts. Many forms of tax-shelter investment were curtailed. Real estate was given the greatest continuing tax benefits for limited-partnership investors. This was not an error or accident. It was the result of knowledgeable and carefully considered Congressional decisions.

The simple fact is that real estate tax shelter exists because it serves a social purpose. On the one hand, a large segment of our population wants and needs good rental housing at a price it can afford. On the other hand, construction prices have skyrocketed, and desirable land is becoming limited. If tax-shelter incentives were not available, investors would not be attracted to housing unless they could earn a much larger operating profit than rents return at present. This would change the economics of housing, raise rents substantially, and effectively put decent housing out of the reach of millions of Americans.

For these reasons the tax-shelter aspect of real estate investment has become public policy. It is an incentive to encourage capital formation in a field that desperately needs capital if it is to meet the demands of our society.

HOW TAX SHELTERS WORK

In all of its infinite detail, tax shelter is a highly complex subject. That's why investors are well advised to work with a knowledgeable accountant or tax attorney, and to select limited partnerships that are supported by proven tax expertise. While the intelligent investor need not try to become an expert, it is important to understand the concepts and basic ways in which shelter works.

A legitimate tax shelter is an investment designed to provide the investor with a profit, plus tax losses that may be used to reduce the tax otherwise due on ordinary taxable income or other personal investment gains.

While we are concentrating here on the shelter aspect of an investment, let me underscore the idea that a tax shelter investment should first and foremost envision a profit. There have been investments designed entirely for their shelter value, with little or no chance of ever producing a profit *per se*. These are frowned on by the IRS, and in any event should be highly suspect on economic grounds. My own feeling is that no investment should ever be considered unless its ultimate purpose is to produce a worthwhile profit. Tax-shelter values should, of course, be considered a part of the total profit picture.

The degree of shelter varies widely from investment to investment. In some instances an investment may be designed to produce little or no operating income, so virtually all the tax shelter produced is available to offset unrelated and taxable income. In other cases, the shelter may just cover the cash distribution from the investment, or it may do that and leave additional shelter for other use.

It is usually confusing to new investors to learn that an investment can at the same time produce cash distributions and tax losses, but that is the case in real estate. The reason is that "paper" losses are generated through depreciation and accrued expenses, which are not paid for in cash at the time the deductions are taken. Thus, these "losses" do not reduce cash that may be produced through operations.

A Paper Loss: Depreciation. The centerpiece of real estate tax shelter is the tax deduction you receive for depreciation of the property in which you have invested.

Depreciation is simple in theory, though its applications may be quite complicated. The tax code recognizes that income-producing machinery and buildings have a limited useful life. They must be replaced eventually. Therefore the code allows a deduction for depreciation against the taxable income the investment produces.

Often, this deduction is greater than the taxable income from the property. In that case, you have a tax loss you can apply against your taxable income from other sources.

In a typical nonshelter investment like manufacturing, as a machine is depreciated it is in fact wearing out or becoming obsolete, and at some point it must be replaced. Hopefully, the tax savings realized through depreciation will pay for a replacement machine.

In the case of real estate, though, the property often appreciates in value while it is being depreciated on paper.

There are four other simple points to be made about depreciation. After that, we will consider the complications.

First of all, your benefits from depreciation are increased by leverage. As you probably know, most real estate is heavily financed. The cash investment may amount to no more than 20 to 40 percent of the cost of the property. Depreciation is credited against the total cost of the property, not just against the amount of the partnership investment. If the property has been purchased with, say, 66 percent or 75 percent financing, then depreciation will be credited against two or three times the amount you have invested.

Secondly, depreciation is a paper expense, an accounting entry— not a cash outlay. It is possible for a property to show a tax loss because of depreciation and yet have a substantial untaxed cash flow. Cash flow is a vitally important concept in real estate. Real estate professionals never look at the net earnings of a property or a real estate corporation. They look at the cash flow—or, better yet, at cash flow plus tax losses.

Thirdly, it is possible under some circumstances to enjoy tax deductions from depreciation that are greater than your investment without liability on the investment's indebtedness. Only in real estate investment is this permitted.

And finally, the depreciation deductions are not a giveaway. The IRS reclaims them at the time the property is sold. But even at that point you enjoy favored tax treatment.

Capital-Gains Treatment. Providing the property has been held more than a year, the difference between the sales proceeds and its straight-line depreciated value (that phrase will be explained in more detail below) will be treated as long-term capital gain. That means it will be taxed at only 40 percent of your ordinary tax rate. Technically, the correct way to express this is that 60 percent of the gain is excluded from taxation.

In effect, then, you have borrowed 100¢ dollars that would have been used for tax payments, and repaid them, years later, with 40¢ dollars and no interest. In addition, any profit you make above the original investment will also be taxed at that 40 percent of ordinary rate.

This is not yet the whole story of tax shelter. But let's pause long enough to see how these basic aspects of tax shelter add up. Let's assume that you bought a building (without partners, for the sake of simplicity) for $120,000 with a $100,000 mortgage and a $20,000 cash investment.

Average annual cash flow from operations after paying interest and all other cash expenses	$1,000
Annual depreciation on $120,000 property	(8,000)
Annual depreciation remaining after offsetting cash flow for tax purposes	($7,000)

This means that your $1,000 cash flow is tax-free and you have an additional $7,000 tax deduction, which can reduce otherwise taxable income from your salary or any other source. Assuming that this other income would be taxed at 50 percent, you realize a savings of $3,500. Altogether, you have received *after-tax* cash benefits of $4,500 annually.

Depreciation. President Reagan's Economic Recovery Tax Law of 1981 dramatically changed the rules regarding depreciation of real estate. Under the old law, depreciation was based on the estimated useful life of the property. This resulted in uncertainty about what the correct life was. There were many Internal Revenue audits relating to this issue. Generally, new residential and commercial real estate was depreciated on lives from thirty to forty years, although the Internal Revenue Service often required longer lives.

The new law eliminates these problems by assigning generally a fifteen-year life to real estate. This results in significantly higher depreciation deductions. Depreciation may be taken on a straight-line basis, which means that the property is depreciated one fifteenth each year. The new law also provides that real estate may be depreciated on an accelerated rate of 175 percent of the straight-line rate. This applies to new or used property acquired after December 31, 1980. Certain low-income residential properties may be depreciated on a 200 percent accelerated basis.

As an example, assume a property has a depreciable basis of $120,000. Under the straight-line method, you would depreciate the property $8,000 per year ($\frac{1}{15}$ × 120,000). Under the 175 percent declining balance method, you would be able to depreciate the property in the first full year by $14,000 (175 percent × $\frac{1}{15}$ ×

120,000). However, in the second year you would subtract the prior depreciation deduction. Therefore, the depreciation in the second year would be $12,367 [175 percent $\times$ $\frac{1}{15}$ $\times$ (120,000 − 14,000)]. This process would continue for each succeeding year. Eventually the annual depreciation would diminish below the straight-line rate. At that point you would switch to depreciating the then current balance over the remaining life on a straight-line basis. Therefore, over the fifteen-year period, the property would be depreciated the full $120,000 in each case. Over five years, the accelerated deductions would be $55,476 compared to $40,000 by the straight-line method.

If this sounds too good to be true, in certain respects it is. It can turn around and bite you in several ways. First, the amount of excess depreciation is a tax preference item. In the example above, the extra $6,000 in the first year is a tax-preference item. If your tax preferences add up to more than $10,000, or half your regular tax (whichever is greater), in any year, the excess is subject to a fifteen percent minimum tax, which is added to your regular tax.

And Then There Is Recapture. Recapture is the one price of accelerated depreciation that every investor must pay. When property that uses accelerated depreciation is sold there are two distinct rules regarding the treatment of the gain on sale. For residential real estate, only that portion of depreciation taken in excess of straight-line will be taxed as ordinary income. The rest will be capital gain. For nonresidential property, all depreciation will be recaptured as ordinary income if accelerated depreciation was used. This makes apartment houses far and away the best tax shelter in real estate today.

Recapture is not all bad, as long as you avoid, or can afford, the hazards I have enumerated. Really, it is a problem only if it is not expected or planned for. True, you do not actually save any taxes on recapture items. You eventually pay the tax in full. But you have succeeded in *deferring* the tax payment. You have in effect had an interest-free loan from the federal government.

To illustrate this, let's say you bought a property in 1975, and your tax loss applicable to ordinary taxable income that year was $5,000. Assuming you were in the 50 percent marginal tax bracket in 1975, your actual tax due would have been reduced by $2,500.

In 1990 the property is sold, and that $5,000 of loss is now taxable as ordinary income. Assuming you are still in the 50 percent bracket, you would now owe $2,500 in income tax. In effect, you have deferred payment of the 1975 tax until 1990. For fifteen years you have had the use of the money that would otherwise have been in the government treasury, and you haven't had to pay a penny of interest! A very valuable benefit indeed.

The choice of accelerated or straight-line depreciation, or maximum deferral as against minimum recapture, is a complex issue that should be analyzed in advance of a particular investment in which either may be involved.

Conversion. As you can see, there are two distinctly different ways in which tax shelter serves investors: deferral and conversion. Recapturable items—the use of accelerated depreciation—are in the deferral form. Investment with straight-line depreciation, converting 100¢ tax liabilities to later 40¢ liabilities, is in the conversion form, though it contains a lot of deferral too.

Another method of conversion revolves around the timing of your tax-loss deductions and your gain on sale and recapture. If you create deductions during the years when you are earning at your highest potential, you are, of course, deferring high-bracket taxes. If you are then able to pay back these tax losses when you are in a substantially lower tax bracket, perhaps after retirement, you can create a significant saving of tax dollars, in addition to the advantages of deferral.

This technique does require a high degree of expert analysis in order to select the limited partnerships that will help achieve your conversion desire. Let's suppose you are a moderately high-earning executive, aged fifty-four, and plan to retire at sixty-five with a fairly healthy pension plus investments. You are currently paying a top tax of 50 percent because of your earned income, plus investment and interest income. Your accountant calculates that after retirement, because your pension will only partially replace your present salary, you will probably drop to a 40 percent income tax bracket.

You now plan to invest an average of $15,000 per year in real estate limited partnerships that offer fairly heavy shelter, a considerable portion of which will not be subject to recapture as ordinary taxable income when the property is sold. Of course, you cannot control the time of the sale, as this is the responsibility of the General Partner. However, different kinds of property do tend to fall into different normal holding periods. You will select partnerships purchasing properties that will probably be held for ten or more years, until after your retirement.

With this kind of program you will receive extremely valuable tax deferment during your high-income years, and very favorable tax consequences when the investments are sold and the profit is taken. Furthermore, you will be making the investments during the years when you can most easily afford to reduce your cash flow, and you will be receiving profits later when you will need additional cash flow to supplement your retirement income.

To analyze the favorable tax impact, let's say you invested $150,000 over the ten-year period, and you received $225,000 of tax shelter prior to your retirement. Considering your 50 percent tax bracket, this saved you from immediate tax payments of $112,500 over the ten years. You had the full and free use of this money during that time—or another way to look at it, you paid for a large portion of the $150,000 investment through "tax-dollar power."

Now, what will happen when the limited partnerships in which you invested sell their properties and pass on the proceeds to you? The details of this kind of tax calculation are presented in the next section of this chapter. For now, let's just concentrate on the results. Essentially, the tax loss you have been enjoying now becomes subject to taxation (there is, as they say, no such thing as a free lunch). However, the taxation is much more favorable than it would have been when the tax was due originally.

First of all, we'll assume about $11,000 of the $225,000 would normally be "recaptured" by being subject to your full ordinary income rate of 50 percent. However, you are now retired, so your full ordinary income rate has dropped to 30 percent. On the recapture you will pay about $3,300 rather than the $5,500 due if you were still in your high earning bracket. You have saved $2,200 simply through good investment and tax planning.

The balance of the $225,000 is taxable as long-term capital gains.

In other words, 60 percent of the amount is not taxed at all, and the balance is taxed at your present ordinary income rate. This works out to a tax of $25,680. Add up the two tax items, and the total is $28,980.

To put all of this into perspective:

- Over ten years of investment during your high-income years, you invested $150,000. You received $225,000 of tax loss over the ten years, and this reduced your cash tax payments by $112,500.
- As the properties were sold over succeeding years, your tax payments on the previously tax-sheltered amounts received the benefit of long-term capital gain and of your lower retirement income-tax bracket, and thus amount to only $28,980.
- Your net cash tax saving amounts to $83,520.
- All of the above deals only with potential tax benefits. In an actual investment program, profit on sale would be a major objective. The results would presumably include the return of your $150,000 invested capital plus a substantial profit from appreciation of the real estate, in addition to the tax benefits.

TAX BASIS

When you start to discuss tax-shelter investment with your accountant, you may have trouble with the concept of "tax basis." This is the key item in computing the ultimate gain or loss on a sale from a tax point of view. It can be somewhat confusing in that a tax basis has only a limited direct relationship to how much money you invest in a limited partnership, and how much profit you make on the investment from your personal point of view. Essentially, the difference between what you receive when the property is sold and the tax basis is the amount that is taxable either as capital gain or as ordinary income.

Tax basis starts out as the amount of debt to which your property is subject, plus the amount of investment you have put into the property. For instance, if you bought a building (again, without partners, for the sake of simplicity) for $100,000 with a $75,000 mortgage and a $25,000 cash investment, your tax basis in the property would be $100,000. Thereafter, your tax basis would be increased by the amount of any taxable income the property earns and would be decreased by the amount of any cash distribution or any tax deductions taken.

Let's assume that in the first year of your ownership you realize 10 percent of your $25,000 investment as cash flow from operations. This does not affect your taxable income whatsoever because it is offset by tax loss. It does affect your tax basis—as does the tax loss you receive.

Let's assume during this same year, on this same building, you have a tax loss of $5,000. Your tax basis is now $92,500 ($100,000 minus $2,500 cash flow and $5,000 tax loss). In a normal investment held over a number of years, the tax basis will be adjusted in the same fashion each year. Of course, as a limited partner, your personal tax basis is established simply by calculating your share of the total. This information is provided to you each year by the General Partner.

Now, let's return to our example, and follow through to see the consequences of tax basis. We will assume the building is now sold at the end of a year of ownership for exactly what you paid for it, and the mortgage has not been reduced at all. You will be relieved of the mortgage obligation, and you will receive $25,000 in cash. You will owe tax on the difference between your present tax basis of $92,500 and your sale proceeds of $100,000, or $7,500 of gain. True, you sold the property for the same amount as you paid for it, so from that point of view you may feel you did not make a "profit." Nevertheless, from the tax point of view, as related to your tax basis, you did make a "gain."

If the property were held for even a day over one year, most, if not all, of that gain would be taxed as long-term capital gain, so you would pay tax on only $3,000 of gain (40 percent of the $7,500).

To summarize, as a result of this brief investment you received a cash profit of $2,500 (the cash flow received) and were able to deduct $5,000 in losses, and pay tax on only $3,000 in gain on sale. In other words, you made a $2,500 cash profit and realized a net

$2,000 tax loss. That's not bad, for a purchase and resale at the same price. The tax loss is calculated as follows:

Tax shelter	$5,000
Long-term capital gain on sale (40 percent of $7,500 tax gain)	–3,000
Net tax shelter	$2,000

To a taxpayer in the 50 percent bracket, the $2,000 in tax shelter is worth $1,000 in cash.

Tax basis has another important effect in limited-partnership investments in that you can deduct tax losses only to the extent you have tax basis. While basis, as we've described it above, comes from your actual dollar investment plus the partnership's debt, it actually gets a little more complicated. In order for debt to be used to extend the amount of your basis above your original investment, it must either be debt for which you are personally liable, or debt for which no one including the General Partner is liable. Since you don't want to incur personal liability, it is important that the partnership be "subject to" enough debt on which no one is personally liable to give you sufficient basis to take your partnership losses. In other words, the most desirable arrangement to create tax basis is when most or all of the debt involved is secured by the property alone, and not by the personal liability of the General Partner or limited partners.

SPECIAL TAX RISKS INHERENT IN TAX-SHELTER INVESTMENT

There are normal business risks in any investment. As I have stated before, I do not see real estate investment as particularly risky; as a matter of fact, I view it as conservative and low-risk, as long as the proper knowledge, expertise, and staying power are involved. This is not to say that certain types of real estate are not highly risky.

At this point I want to bring your attention to such potentially serious risks—or perhaps I should say shocks—that can hit tax-shelter investors (in real estate or any other field) if they lack knowledge of possible tax consequences tied to tax shelter under certain conditions. There are two specific situations to be considered: recapture on a negative capital account, and the tax effect of foreclosure.

Recapture on a Negative Capital Account. This is the second meaning of the word *recapture*. When we use the term "negative capital account," we mean an investor has taken more tax losses than the amount of capital originally invested. To illustrate this, let's go back to the example of a $25,000 cash investment on a $100,000 property. We'll assume this time that the property was held for eight years, and during that time $35,000 of tax loss was taken, and no cash flow was realized.

Now, assume a sale at a price sufficient to repay the investor his $25,000—in other words, just enough to get back the original cash investment while being relieved of the mortgage. That would not strike the average investor as a profitable deal, and he might even assume that no tax would be due. Not so.

Because of the decreased tax basis, and recapture requirements, the investor would have to pay tax on the return of all of his original money, *plus* an additional $10,000 of negative capital. This can come as a big shock, as the investor ends up owing a significant amount of tax out of the money that he views as his own returned capital. The point, of course, is that the investor has received the benefit of $35,000 in tax loss; he had this to use in varying degrees over a period of eight years.

This kind of financial shock should never occur. The investor has a responsibility to realize there will be a tax liability in connection with the advantage of tax losses. A concerned General Partner will try to help inform his investors regarding the basic ways the tax law affects their investments. Proper planning will alleviate the shock, and will make this type of end result just a part of an overall happy experience. If an investor plans for recapture of the type described above, he will simply consider a portion of his tax-loss benefit an interest-free loan, and he will know that he will have to repay it on sale.

You may be wondering why this example does not include a profit on the sale after eight years, when in fact all of the case histories I have shown do include a very nice profit over the purchase price.

Obviously, this was an example to illustrate the point of what *can* happen. It should reinforce the importance of selecting real estate investments that are profit-oriented, not just focused on tax shelter. It should also remind all real estate investors that no results are certain, and the only protection against financial shock is to stay constantly aware of each investment's condition over its life.

The Tax Effect of Foreclosure. Foreclosure on an investment property is, of course, the worst result possible. It might be compared to the bankruptcy of a corporation in which you are a shareholder, but in fact because of the tax consequences it can be worse.

During my fourteen years of involvement in real estate investment, I have never experienced a foreclosure, and I have no intention of allowing one to happen. Still, they are possible. Therefore, you must understand the consequences and, even more important, what defensive measures can be taken.

When a property is foreclosed, it is treated for tax purposes as a sale at the amount of the mortgage owed on the property. If, through tax loss while owning the property, the tax basis has been reduced below the mortgage, the investors end up with a tax liability even though they received no cash from a sale!

As you probably now realize, this situation occurs only when you have received considerable benefits from tax loss while holding the property. The problem of tax liability without enough cash-from-sale-to-cover can also occur without foreclosure. In a situation where you have taken large deductions in the early years and then sell the property, you may not receive enough cash from a sale to pay your tax liability.

Either of these situations usually occurs in properties owned by new-construction partnerships where high amounts of accelerated depreciation were taken during the period of ownership. Such partnerships provide tremendous tax shelter to the investors, who are usually people with extremely high incomes. They are generally advantageous, but the risk in the event of foreclosure is enormous.

The possibility of special tax risks should not deter a conservative person from entering into real estate limited-partnership investment. Rather, he or she should select those with a degree of tax shelter that suit their economic position, remembering that properties with heavily accelerated depreciation do have more ultimate risk. I have worked out a plan to recognize and actually fund these risks so there can be no surprises or financial debacles. This plan is detailed in Chapter 13 in the section "How Planning Can Eliminate the Tax-Preference Shock Syndrome." I urge you to study it and apply it to your investment planning.

REDUCING WITHHOLDING TAX

If you are a self-employed taxpayer and have just entered into a tax-shelter investment, you can reduce your quarterly estimated tax payments based on the estimated tax loss from your investment. If you are a salaried employee, you can reduce your tax withholding by claiming the maximum number of exemptions available to you. These options allow you to obtain a lot of the financial benefit of your tax shelter immediately instead of waiting until tax year is over.

In fact, if you have not paid taxes during the current year, and by virtue of your tax shelters will not be paying taxes in the next year, you can totally eliminate withholding by filing a Form W4E.

It is important to note that it is a criminal offense to falsely file this form just to reduce withholding. You must be reasonably certain you will not owe taxes at all in the next year. In general, we do not advocate tax sheltering yourself to a zero tax bracket. The higher the bracket, the more valuable the shelter, and low-bracket sheltering can be of questionable value.

Why Real Estate Is the Super Tax Shelter

ONCE you become familiar with the concept of investing in tax shelters and start to inquire about opportunities, you will be amazed at the many different kinds of deals available. It is not in the scope of this book to discuss the merits or disadvantages of various kinds of shelter investments other than real estate. However, since you will ultimately have to choose your own type of investment, it is important that you understand the unique advantages that make real estate probably the most outstanding type of tax shelter for most investors.

ECONOMIC INVESTMENT STRENGTH

Whenever you are making an investment with tax-shelter objectives, it must stand up to your analysis as a straight economic investment as well. After all, you are investing after-tax cash dollars, and you want to come out with a profit in after-tax cash dollars. Just playing games with tax deferment is not likely to be profitable in itself. As I have already pointed out, an investment that creates an economic loss after providing deep shelter may in fact end up costing the investor hard dollars. At best, that type of investment may be of only marginal benefit compared to what is available in good real estate.

One of the most important comparative strengths of real estate investment is that it frequently offers superior economic profit objectives over and above the tax advantages. Real estate values tend to increase with inflation, and therefore they can create considerable profit over the holding period. Real estate values tend to react very positively to creative improvements such as physical upgrading, better marketing, improved management, or higher utilization. Underproductive real estate, which is nonetheless in a good location ahead of its time, will benefit simply by the passage of time and the development of the surrounding marketplace.

All of these possibilities merely indicate why real estate investments do tend to have sound economic value. When you select an investment that combines excellent economic growth potential with excellent tax shelter, it quickly moves into the super value category. However, super value is not automatically created by all real estate investment. It requires careful and knowledgeable selection.

LEGISLATIVE ADVANTAGES PROVIDED FOR REAL ESTATE INVESTMENT

The Tax Reform Act of 1976 as modified by the Revenue Act of 1978 restricts the amount of tax-loss deduction a limited partner can take to the amount of money "at risk." This means that in most cases the investor's deductions can only be as large as the investment of his own money and/or personal notes, and any borrowed money for which he is personally liable. He cannot include funds borrowed by the partnership for which he is not personally liable (nonrecourse loans). Naturally, this new law severely limits the tax advantages and the leverage which were available prior to 1976. This is true of all shelter investments *except real estate!*

Real estate investments were specifically exempted from the "at risk" regulations. There are effectively no limits on the amount of tax-loss deduction from a real estate investment as long as the expenses involved are for proper and allowable purposes. This makes real estate unique, and the outstanding opportunity among tax shelters.

Recent tax laws, as well as legislative history, also encourage oil and gas exploration, and venture-capital investment, but these areas do not have the advantage of freedom from the "at risk" shelter limitation.

On the other hand, certain "exotic" shelters that were once allowed—such as motion pictures, books, lithographs, commodities, and cattle—are being vigorously attacked by the IRS. Promoters are very clever in studying each new legislative move, ignoring the obvious intent of Congress and developing gimmicks to try to apply the advantages intended for one kind of investment to others that the law was not intended to benefit. On such exotic shelters, I can only say, "Beware." In the final analysis, the IRS usually wins in these situations, and the result can be costly to ill-advised investors.

THE VALUE OF LEVERAGE

Simply defined, leverage is the use of borrowed money to finance an investment. It is basic to many investment strategies, but it is particularly available and valuable in real estate. The use of borrowed money in excess of personal funds can benefit an investment in three ways:

· Less cash is required.
· The potential rate of return on the cash invested is greatly increased.
· The tax loss is substantially increased (subject to the "at risk" limitation from which real estate is exempt).

Leverage is a built-in advantage in virtually all real estate investments. The details will vary, but in limited-partnership programs it is normal for the partnership to borrow a major portion of the purchase price, usually 60 to 80 percent. This may be through financing supplied by the seller, or through a new mortgage arranged by the limited partnership, or by taking over an existing mortgage, or some such combination. As you know, the limited partners have no personal liability for such loans to the partnership.

Real estate is unique in that it allows for higher percentages of borrowed money than can usually be obtained for most other investments. The reason is that real estate has a relatively dependable innate value, and in all respects is viewed by lenders as a desirable long-term security for loans. Few if any other investments can provide as much borrowing power, and therefore as much leverage.

During inflationary times, borrowing power is the key to keeping ahead of inflation. Financing allows you to control real estate assets worth three to four times your cash investment, with the repayment scheduled over many, many years. This makes inflation a benefit since the debt will be paid off with dollars worth less than they were when you made the investment.

Again, because your investment controls about three or four times as much asset value as the cash involved, the resulting tax shelter is also increased. As discussed in the preceding chapter, shelter results from paper losses, not operating losses. The greater the value of the property, and the larger the amount financed, the greater the tax shelter produced.

Finally, the profit realized from the sale of a successful invest-

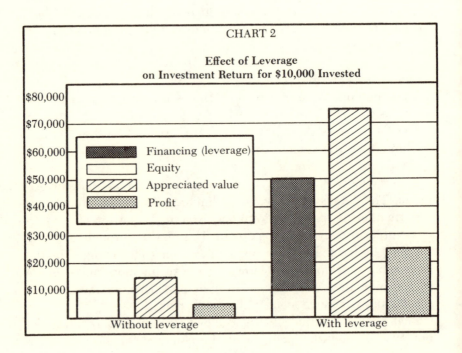

CHART 2

Effect of Leverage
on Investment Return for $10,000 Invested

ment is also enhanced by leverage. Chart 2 shows the effect of typical 75 percent financing (3-to-1 leverage) on the profit percentage realized when the investment is sold.

TAX LOSS PROVIDES CURRENT RETURN

Many investors like a good, stable cash flow while they are holding an investment, and they tend to look for real estate that will provide this. Current cash return from a real estate investment is not always a reasonable expectation, as each aspect of an investment must be balanced against the others. High leverage tends to maximize shelter and ultimate investment profit, but it jeopardizes the reliability of cash flow. No matter how carefully cash-flow projections are made, the slightest negative change in operations can dramatically reduce actual cash flow.

With high leverage, there is automatically a high debt-service requirement. Thus, if occupancies go down just slightly, or expenses go up just a few percentage points during any given period, the entire cash flow can be wiped out for the time being. Quite simply, that uncertainty is the price of having high leverage. But then, it is offset by high tax shelter, which provides current economic benefits, and by higher profit potential when the property is sold.

Leverage is generally higher in private limited partnerships than in public offerings, and this accounts for some of the fundamental differences previously pointed out.

It is my strong belief that cash flow should not be viewed as the current return from most private limited-partnership real estate investments. It should be looked upon as a potential bonus, rather than as a dependable source of monthly or quarterly income. When this point of view is accepted, the potential vagaries of cash flow will not create any burden or disappointment for the investor. The arrival of a distribution check should be a pleasant occasion; its absence should never be a hardship.

The current return that can and should be counted on from private real estate limited partnerships is the value of tax shelter to the investor. As you now know, this can be considerable as it turns current tax-payment dollars into available cash. Deferment and conversion can be projected with excellent dependability, and when the investor plans the use of shelter intelligently it has outstanding current value.

THE IMPORTANCE OF PROPERTY MAINTENANCE INSTEAD OF CASH-FLOW MAINTENANCE

Obviously, many private real estate limited partnerships are designed to provide a variety of balanced benefits to the investors. A reasonable degree of cash flow is often projected along with tax shelter and ultimate profit from equity build-up and value appreciation. If no unanticipated physical or economic difficulties occur throughout the operating period, the projections will become reality. However, when unexpected problems arise, the General Partner must make a tough decision: either let the property deteriorate in order to maintain projected cash flow, or use available funds to keep the property in A-1 condition while cutting or even eliminating cash-flow payments.

In our management of limited partnerships at the Hall Real Estate Group, there is no question as to the right decision. As I pointed out in Chapter 4, successful real estate investment requires staying power. The most important profit is that which can be realized when the property is sold. But that profit is earned only when the property is maintained in top condition, whether current operations can afford it or not. Thus, we try to make sure that our investors understand the value of shelter as current income and are aware of the benefits of spending what is necessary to keep their property in top shape.

RIVER VIEW ASSOCIATES—A CASE HISTORY

River View Associates, a fairly typical limited partnership syndicated by the Hall Real Estate Group, was concluded by a sale in 1980. Its financial history illustrates several of the special opportunities that make real estate the super tax-shelter value.

River View Apartments is a property with 174 rental units. The total purchase price was $2 million, of which $282,000 of investor funds was used as equity. Therefore, the leverage was six to one.

Each investment unit amounted to $22,000, paid in installments over four years, which provided capital for the down payment as well as funds for other partnership needs. During that time, the cash flow per unit amounted to a total of only $1,600. Unexpected increases in utility costs, plus the cyclical nature of the area's economy, created temporary reversals. We had to decide between maintenance and cash flow, and we chose not only to maintain, but actually to improve the project.

On the surface, the $1,600 cash flow over the first four years doesn't seem very impressive. But to get the whole picture, examine Table 6, which includes the tax-loss values received during the same four years. Then note how the cash flow improved in the fifth year as a result of our staying power. Some owners might have decided to push the cash flow up during the lean periods by deferring maintenance and replacements, in a sense "milking" their own property. This would have reduced the tax-shelter benefits to the investors during those years, and we believe it would also have been a short-sighted philosophy from the viewpoint of ultimate profit.

The final proof of the wisdom of our course came when the property was sold in 1980 at an outstanding profit, on an installment basis. When all of the sale proceeds are received and the tax consequences paid, an investor in the 50 percent bracket will show a 23.42 percent average *annual after-tax* profit on all the money in-

TABLE 6
River View Associates

Year	Investment	Cash flow	50% tax bracket		37% tax bracket	
			Tax saving	Annual economic benefit	Tax saving	Annual economic benefit
1975	$6,500	$ 0	$3,524	$3,524	$2,608	$2,608
1976	7,500	200	5,848	6,048	4,328	4,528
1977	5,500	600	4,066	4,666	3,009	3,609
1978	2,500	800	1,987	2,787	1,470	2,270
1979	0	1,167	263	1,430	195	1,362

vested during each of the years involved, including the period of installment payments. To achieve a comparable return without the tax benefits would require a yield of over 46 percent per year before taxes!

THE SPECIAL TAX BENEFIT OF AN INSTALLMENT SALE

Installment sales of property have for many years offered real estate investors the opportunity to defer some of the tax consequences of a sale. However, in the past there were a number of gray areas and requirements a General Partner had to contend with in trying to use an installment sale most advantageously.

The Installment Sales Revision Act of 1980 has simplified and liberalized installment-sale tax treatment. Essentially, the new law eliminates the previous requirement that a buyer receive less than 30 percent of the total as an initial payment. It also eliminates the requirement to have at least two payments in an installment sale.

Now, if a payment is deferred at all, the sale is treated as an installment sale. This makes it very simple to split the tax consequences over two years, which of course is beneficial to the investors in terms of avoiding artificially high taxable income in any one year. It also gives the General Partner clear options that can be used to aid the tax planning of investors or defer some of the taxation on gain received by the investors from the sale.

One of the major benefits of an installment sale is that it can defer a major amount of the tax due on early payments until later payments, or even until the final payment is made. This has the same benefit as deferral through shelter: free use of the tax that will ultimately be due. Essentially it provides an interest-free loan from the government.

This benefit is due to the fact that all cash received in installments is treated for tax purposes as a percentage of the total purchase price, not as a percentage of the total cash proceeds. Thus, particularly when a substantial existing mortgage is involved, the seller can get an excellent tax deferral through installments.

To illustrate this advantage, let's assume a partnership is selling a property under the terms shown below. As partner, you will, of course, receive your proportionate share of proceeds and taxation.

Sale price		$1,000,000
Consisting of:		
Cash		400,000
Existing mortgage		600,000
Tax basis		600,000
Taxable gain		400,000

The $400,000 cash is to be paid in three annual installments—the first year $200,000, the second and third years $100,000 each. The purchaser will supply the funds to make the mortgage payments, and the mortgage will be assumed when the cash installments are completed.

The first year the partnership receives $200,000, which is 50 percent of the total taxable gain. However, only $80,000 is subject to taxation in the first year of installments. This is based on the fact that the $200,000 payment represents only 20 percent of the total sale price. Thus, tax is due on 20 percent of the $400,000 gain, or $80,000. A similar deferral will be received on a portion of the payment received in the second year.

When the entire installment sale is paid off, the total $400,000 of gain will be taxed, but meanwhile the partners received a valuable deferral during both the first and second years.

While all real estate sales are not made on an installment basis, it is a common method of payment. It provides a cash-flow benefit to the purchaser, which may well help make the sale. At the same time, the seller also benefits from tax deferral, making the installment arrangement economically beneficial for him too. A point of caution, however: any tax-preference items on installment sales to be recaptured at sale are taxed at ordinary income rates first, rather than as long-term capital gains.

THE IMPORTANCE OF CAPITAL-GAINS TAXATION

In the last chapter, we discussed conversion as one of the benefits of tax shelter. The ability to defer tax payment on ordinary income earned today, and then convert that income to a capital gain in the future, is a key to successful tax planning through real estate investment. The fact that long-term capital gains provide a 60 percent exclusion from taxation gives a high-bracket taxpayer a big break in maintaining purchasing power.

In the example of an installment sale above, it is safe to assume that capital-gains treatment would apply, and this would eliminate 60 percent of the taxable gain. Therefore, on the $200,000 of gain received the first year, the partners would be taxed only on their proportionate share of the $80,000 installment gain, less the 60 percent exclusion resulting in $32,000 at that time!

Real estate is particularly suited to produce capital-gains profits, which are economically desirable in their own right, and which provide the high after-tax return that makes a big difference in beating inflation.

STEPPED-UP BASIS FOR ESTATE TAX

In terms of long-range planning, real estate has a unique and extremely advantageous estate-tax benefit. While no one likes to think about death, it is one of the things that has been said to be inevitable, so estate planning becomes extremely important if you want to preserve your wealth for the good of your heirs. Here again, real estate investment can make a unique contribution because a very favorable treatment is provided for estate tax valuation on the death of a real estate investor.

As demonstrated in the previous chapter, real estate that has been owned for some time will probably have a significantly lower tax basis than the market price at which the property can be sold. The difference between the basis and the sale price is, of course, the amount subject to taxation at the time of a sale. It would seem reasonable to expect the tax basis of an investment to stay with the property when the owner dies.

Instead, on the death of the owner, special treatment is given to the basis. The actual basis developed during the period of ownership is ignored, and a "stepped-up basis" is established equal to the estate valuation amount for the property. This, of course, should be the same as the market value at the time of death. Therefore, there would be no taxable gain if the estate chooses to sell the property at the amount of the stepped-up basis. If the heirs choose to hold on to the property, they are in effect starting over with the newly established basis equal to the present market value.

To provide an example of stepped-up basis, assume a limited-partnership investment was made several years ago in which the individual put in $30,000 and the partnership's financing applicable to his unit of investment was $90,000. Thus, the original tax basis was $120,000.

During the years the investment was held, tax loss of $41,000 was realized and, in addition, cash flow from operations amounting to $8,000 was received. As you recall from Chapter 5, these amounts are deducted from the original tax basis. Thus, the present tax basis is $71,000. If the property was sold, the difference between the $71,000 and the price at which the property was sold would be the investor's taxable gain. Most of this would be taxable at the favorable capital-gains rate.

For the sake of our illustration, the investor dies at this time, and the limited-partnership interest goes to his estate. In terms of estate taxes, if any are involved, the investment would, of course, be taxed at its present market value. However, the heirs now own the limited partnership with a stepped-up basis equal to the present market value, and when the property is sold, their taxable gain will be figured from that point.

Let's assume that the present market value of the property represented by the partnership unit is $130,000. The taxable gain on the sale would have amounted to $59,000. Instead, the tax basis of the investment is now considered $130,000 by the IRS, and if the property were sold for that price there would be no taxable gain for the heirs or estate. If, on the other hand, the investment were held for an additional period of time and eventually sold for, let's say, $160,000, the taxable gain on sale would be $30,000. If there were no step-up in basis, the taxable gain on a sale at $160,000 would be $89,000. Because of the stepped-up basis, real estate investments are often very good for older investors who need current tax shelter and are trying to plan an orderly estate.

THE ECONOMIC RECOVERY ACT OF 1981 AND CONGRESSIONAL PLANS FOR FUTURE REAL ESTATE INVESTMENT TAXATION

Many people in the tax-shelter industry, including myself, used to worry a great deal about literally being legislated out of business. As each session of Congress began, we wondered how much the next tax-reform act would hurt us. Even with the election of Ronald Reagan in a Republican landslide, the antitax-shelter talk by certain Democratic liberals cannot be said to be a dead issue. But a dramatic shift seems to be taking place. For the first time in over a decade, the predominant tax-reform discussions from most members of both parties are centered around how we can improve the tax incentives for capital formation; not how they can be curtailed.

The fact that our country now has an administration pledged to control inflation and rebuild our productive capacity has created a political climate advantageous to real estate investors. Even if a surprisingly healthy economy is achieved soon, an event that would reduce the need for inflation-fighting investments, I do not expect real estate to lose its dramatic investment value. Remember, the fundamental importance of providing reasonably priced housing and commercial facilities will not change. The need will continue to exist, and when investors meet a need, they are rewarded.

The Economic Recovery Act of 1981 made real estate investors major beneficiaries of Congress's attempt to reindustrialize America and meet the severe needs for investment in real estate.

The shorter depreciation schedule will produce materially higher tax losses for real estate investors. This should make many properties more attractive to investors, and therefore, more profitable when present owners decide to sell. New investors will directly benefit from the shorter depreciation life allowed on real property purchased after December 31, 1980.

The second key benefit lies in the taxes paid when the property is sold. Since the maximum capital-gains tax is reduced from 28 percent to 20 percent, after-tax profits on the sale of properties will increase substantially. This change will benefit both current and future real estate investors.

These changes show a trend toward keeping real estate as a favored form of tax shelter. The direction in the future could possibly lead to even lower capital-gains rates. There are those in Congress who are advocating no capital-gains tax at all as an incentive for investment. Whatever the exact form of future tax legislation, it's safe to say it will likely be favorable to real estate. The ability to receive current ordinary income losses and, down the line at sale, convert those losses into a capital gain while investing in a good economic investment, gives real estate a uniquely favorable position in the financial world.

IRS Practices and Pitfalls

THE Internal Revenue Service is charged with the awesome task of collecting over $322,990,000,000 annually in tax revenues from the people and businesses of the United States. When you consider that there are over 93,350,000 taxpayers, and the system expects them to voluntarily declare their proper income, exemptions, and deductions, then properly compute their tax and file on time, it is obvious that enforcement is a monumental job.

Our tax-collection system is far from perfect, and far from a science. Still, it is the best we have, and it is considered by many to be the most efficient in terms of cost per collected dollar of any in the world.

THE IRS POSITION ON TAX SHELTERS

It is difficult to provide a single description of the IRS position on tax shelter. As a result of the nearly impossible job the IRS has to do, its attitudes swing through an entire spectrum from paranoid to aggressive to quite reasonable and realistic.

Obviously, the Internal Revenue Service realizes that many people are committed to using every possible means (and some which are clearly impossible) to avoid paying taxes. Since the law is by its nature complicated and convoluted, the relationship can become a contest or a game: the IRS versus the Taxpayer. Or perhaps, from the point of view of the government, the Taxpayer versus the IRS.

So there is little wonder that the IRS sometimes displays paranoid feelings—especially when you consider that this has to be the agency that tops almost everyone's "least desired" list—and in its public posture frequently becomes quite aggressive. Jerome Kurtz, when he was the IRS Commissioner, made public statements that were widely considered to be negative to tax-shelter investment. For example, he was quoted in a *Time* magazine article as saying, "Those people investing heavily in abusive tax shelters are looking for trouble with us."

The question is, exactly what did Mr. Kurtz mean? I suspect he meant exactly what he said: "Abusive" shelters, those that abuse the intent of current legislation, are going to be cracked down on in the future. My own major discomfort remains the lack of evenhandedness in the attitudes portrayed to the public concerning tax shelter. I can understand and agree with the warnings concerning abusive and exotic and overly aggressive shelter investments. On the other hand, I believe the IRS should also provide some guidance to help investors realize there is an area of legal, acceptable, and desirable tax shelter that is not frowned upon by the IRS. This may be unrealistic because the IRS is primarily concerned with the collection of tax revenue.

Tax-Shelter Abuses of Particular Concern to the IRS. In recent years, IRS statements have made it fairly clear that they are focusing their attention on certain types of shelter programs, especially those investments that have no economic viability and are designed merely to reduce tax payments by individuals. Very few real estate limited partnerships fall into that category.

Additional IRS targets include those partnerships that produce excessive losses, and those that maneuver to charge off doubtful front-end fees. Unfortunately, there is no absolute definition of "excessive losses." The notion ties back to the pre–1976 era when losses of 300 to 400 percent of investment were regularly achieved. Today, this is not normal, and certainly not available in legitimate real estate ventures.

Tax Shelter Is Not Necessarily a Red Flag for Audit. The IRS has various methods, some by random selection and others by category grouping, to choose who gets audited each year. One of the prime methods of classifying returns for audit is by scoring them. This is through what is called the DIF System. Although the exact scoring mechanism is a highly guarded secret of the Internal Revenue Service, it is well known that certain items will score high enough to trigger an audit. For example, a taxpayer earning $100,000 per year and contributing $5,000 to a charity is less likely to have that item create an audit than a taxpayer earning $15,000 contributing $2,000 in used clothing to a charity. Other items such as deductions for home offices and casualty losses are very likely to trigger audits. As a general position, the higher your tax bracket, the more likely you are to be selected for audit.

Among limited-partnership investors affiliated with Hall Real Estate, we have some who are audited every year, and others who have never been audited over many years of investing in shelter. Just because you have a tax-shelter investment does not mean you are going to be audited.

Perhaps the most important point to understand is that if an audit does occur it will probably not be as devastating as you might anticipate. It is generally time-consuming, and it can be expensive because of the probable involvement of your accountant or attorney. Beyond that, as long as you maintain proper records and full information concerning all deductions, you should have nothing to fear. Philosophically, I suggest you take all deductions your professional consultants feel you are legally entitled to, and no more. Being overly aggressive on your tax-reporting is not advantageous in the long run, and with proper planning it should not be necessary.

THE RELATIONSHIP BETWEEN PARTNERSHIP AND INDIVIDUAL AUDITS

You can be an investor in a limited partnership that is audited and still not have your personal return audited. The two do not go hand in hand. The partnership tax return is an informational filing, with the individual partners as the taxpayers. The partnership may well be audited as a check on the accounting practices and tax methods followed in preparing the partnership return, but that would not mean that every partner would also be audited. Unless the IRS takes exception to something they find in the partnership audit, it is likely that no further action will result.

When a partnership is audited, your General Partner should take the responsibility to support the deductions that were taken. This is an important reason to select a General Partner with proper tax experience and knowledge. When the audit procedure is completed, the agent comes up with initial findings, and the General Partner will communicate with you concerning the impact of the findings.

If the findings are of little or no consequence, the General Partner may accept them after appropriate negotiation at the agent level. In many cases where the findings are unacceptable to the General Partner, he may appeal them. The appellate level is administrative rather than judicial, but it is generally where most disputed tax audits are settled.

If the partnership cannot settle its case at this point, it must go to court, a process that may take two to five years. The IRS has numerous cases pending at all times, and while yours may be of utmost importance to you, it is just a matter of numbers to the IRS. If your case can produce a large amount of additional tax income, and if the IRS feels it is in a strong legal position, it may take a very tough attitude and offer no settlement or a very low value settlement before court, but this is not usually the case.

There is a risk to both parties in going to court, and certainly the IRS is overburdened with court cases. Therefore, negotiation generally produces equitable settlements. Particularly when the issue has to do with valuation or depreciation, the courts recognize it as a matter of opinion rather than law, and they urge settlement rather than trial. The important thing for the investor to understand when a tax audit raises serious questions is that the matter probably will not be settled in a hurry, and that it probably will be settled eventually and fairly through negotiation. If the process of audit and appeal continues for more than three years, you will be asked by the IRS to file an extension form to keep your tax return for the year in question open beyond the statute of limitation. Officially, this is voluntary, but in fact if you do not comply, the IRS can move to collect whatever the questioned tax is from you immediately without waiting for the ultimate decision. Therefore, the realistic position is for you to file the extensions as requested. In fact, these extensions do you no harm. They do not in themselves mean that you will be audited at a later date, and they do not remove any of your options after the partnership matter has eventually been settled.

Individual Partners Are Not Forced to Accept Partnership Settlements. When the partnership matter is settled, you have the right to accept or reject it as an individual. You should have been kept up to date by your General Partner, so the nature of the settlement should not come as a surprise. Assuming you have been satisfied with the General Partner's effort all along, it is usually an unwise move to decide to reject the settlement and fight on alone. Of course, in a specific situation, your deciding in the alternative would depend on the advice of your professional consultants. In general, however, the cost of continuing on your own will exceed the potential value.

Following the settlement, whatever adjustment has been agreed to will be made by the IRS on your individual tax return, and you will be billed for the additional tax due, plus interest from the date the tax would have been due some years earlier.

While no one ever enjoys a tax adjustment, it is important to realize that if you had not taken the deductions that you are now agreeing to lower somewhat, you would never have had a chance to get them in the first place. Philosophically, deductions that are within reasonable and well-advised limits must be looked at in the tradition of nothing ventured, nothing gained.

All of this detailed description of a partnership audit, and its potentially negative result, should not be taken as an indication that every limited partnership is audited. Far from it. The more exotic, unusual, and obviously aggressive shelter investments are far more likely to be audited, as are the individual partners in such schemes. Normal, generally acceptable shelter investments are probably audited no more than other common business ventures. Furthermore, in many cases an audit will result in no change.

Individual Audits Do Not Affect Partnership Returns. Just as an audit of a partnership does not necessarily trigger audits of the individual partners the reverse holds true. If you are audited as an individual, it does not necessarily mean your partnerships will be audited.

In fact, an agent conducting an individual audit is a completely different person, trained in a different way, from a partnership auditor. Typically, the individual auditor will examine the K-1 form, which is your part of the partnership informational return. This supplies the numbers you will put into your personal tax return each year. If the numbers match up, and the agent sees that your partnership deductions are taken from the partnership's books as reported, that aspect of your audit will probably end right there.

To summarize, if you are an investor in a tax-shelter partnership, that fact has very little bearing on whether you, personally, or the partnership will be audited. If either is audited, that event will have very little bearing on whether the other will be audited. If adjustments are made in connection with the tax-shelter investment, it is likely those adjustments will be items you otherwise would not have been entitled to if you had not tried to take those deductions. In short, I know of no situation in which a taxpayer puts himself in a position of broad tax jeopardy simply by investing in a realistic tax shelter.

THE NATURE OF TAX-LAW RISKS

Whenever you consider a tax-shelter investment, it is important to ask your personal financial advisor exactly what the risks are. Also, carefully study and analyze the risk section of the prospectus supplied to you. As long as you are acting in good faith and dealing with reputable people. your risks should be minimal. Nevertheless, it is important that you understand the difference in degree of risk from one investment to another. In many more aggressive shelters there is a certain degree of risk built in. If you understand this, you can make your decision accordingly and accept in advance the possibility of losing a portion of the shelter on audit. This is quite different from being involved in a potentially fraudulent transaction that can create a high degree of liability.

One good rule of thumb: if your first reaction to a proposition is that it sounds too good to be true, check it out carefully with professionals you can trust. It may indeed be too good to be true, and too good to be legal.

Special Deduction Problems in Real Estate Investment. In general, real estate limited-partnership investment is less subject to IRS attack than many other forms of investment, because, as noted before, real estate is the one product specifically exempted from the "at risk" regulations. Nevertheless, several changes created by the 1976 and 1978 legislation are still producing differences of opinion, and therefore leave areas of risk.

The area that the IRS has been attacking most vigorously in recent times is preopening costs associated with new construction. These include the cost of investigating the feasibility of a project, costs incurred in building and preparing the project for occupancy, and costs of securing tenants before the project is completed and ready for occupancy.

These costs used to be deductible, but have recently been held to be organizational costs, which should be capitalized and written off over a five-year period. In certain circumstances, they must be written off over the life of the project. At this moment, the proper position of certain of these expenses is still subject to interpretation. Therefore, when considering investment in new construction, it is wise to check the syndicator's position carefully with your own professional advisor. If the syndicator plans to deduct any preopening costs, be prepared for a potential adjustment by the IRS later.

Syndication Costs. Syndication costs, which include a broker or dealer fee and in some cases a General Partner fee, are not deductible whatsoever. It used to be that many General Partners did deduct their fee for organizing the partnership as an expense in order to create additional tax loss. The IRS and the courts have held this is not in accordance with the tax code. Expenses to the General Partner or his affiliates can be deductible, but the test is that these expenses must be ordinary and necessary to the partnership.

In many cases a General Partner's services are organizational in nature, and therefore would not be deductible for putting together the syndication. If, however, the General Partner is performing highly specific functions relating to the property after the partner-

SCHEDULE K–1
(Form 1065)
Department of the Treasury
Internal Revenue Service

Partner's Share of Income, Credits, Deductions, etc.—1980

For calendar year 1980 or fiscal year
beginning ...., 1980, and ending ...., 19........
(Instructions for partners attached. Complete for each partner—See instructions on
back of Copy B)

Partner's identifying number ▶ 999-99-9998	Partnership's identifying number ▶ 72-314561
Partner's name, address, and ZIP code Sam Taxpayer Inflation City U.S.A.	Partnership's name, address, and ZIP code Real Estate Shelter Associates Village of Tax Reduction U.S.A.

		Yes	No				Yes	No
A	(i) Date(s) partner acquired any partnership interest during the year ▶ June 1, 1980			F	(i) Did partnership interest terminate during the year?			X
	(ii) Did partner have any partnership interest before 1/1/77?		X		(ii) Did partnership interest decrease during the year?			X

B Is partner a nonresident alien? . . . . No: X
C (i) Is partner a limited partner (see page 2 of Instructions)? . Yes: X
  (ii) If "Yes," is partner also a general partner? . . . . No: X
D (i) Did partner ever contribute property other than money to the partnership? . No: X
  If "Yes," enter:
    a Basis to partnership of contributed property (other than money) at time(s) of contribution to the partnership . . $................
    b Value of contributed property in "a" above as reflected in the partner's capital account $................
  (ii) Did partner ever receive a distribution other than money from the partnership? . . . . No: X
  If "Yes," enter:
    a Basis to partnership of distributed property (other than money) at time(s) of distribution to the partner . . $................
    b Value of distributed property in "a" above as reflected in the partner's capital account $................
E Was any part of the partner's interest ever acquired from another partner? . X

G Enter partner's percentage of:
	(i) Before decrease or termination	(ii) End of year
Profit sharing	........%	....5....%
Loss sharing	........%	....5....%
Ownership of capital		....5....%
Time devoted to business		...none....%

H IRS Center where partnership filed return ▶ Cincinnati, Ohio
I What type of entity is this partner? ▶ Individual
J Partner's share of liabilities (see page 7 of Instructions):
	(i) Incurred before 1/1/77	(ii) Incurred after 12/31/76
Nonrecourse . . $................		$...140,000......
Other . . . $................		$...none......

K Enter total amount of liabilities other than nonrecourse for which the partner is protected against loss through guarantees, stop loss agreements, or similar arrangements of which the partnership has knowledge:
  Incurred before 1/1/77 . . . . . . $................
  Incurred after 12/31/76 . . . . . . $................

L Partner's share of any pre-1976 loss(es) from a section 465(c)(1) activity (i.e., film or video tape, section 1245 property leasing, farm, or oil and gas property) for which there existed a corresponding amount of nonrecourse liability at the end of the year in which loss(es) occurred . . . . $................

M Reconciliation of partner's capital account:

a. Capital account at beginning of year	b. Capital contributed during year	c. Ordinary income (loss) from line 1b	d. Income not included in column c, plus non-taxable income	e. Losses not included in column c, plus unallowable deductions	f. Withdrawals and distributions	g. Capital account at end of year
none	20,000	(32,000)			500	(12,500)

a. Distributive share item	b. Amount	c. 1040 filers enter the amount in column b on:
1 a Guaranteed payments to partner: (1) Deductible by the partnership . .		Sch. E, Part III
(2) Capitalized by the partnership		Sch. E, Part III
b Ordinary income (loss)	(32,000)	Sch. E, Part III
2 Additional first-year depreciation (Basis ....)		Sch. E, Part III
3 Gross farming or fishing income		Sch. E, Part IV
4 Dividends qualifying for exclusion		Sch. B, Part II, line 3
5 Net short-term capital gain (loss)		Sch. D, line 3, col. f or g
6 Net long-term capital gain (loss).		Sch. D, line 10, col. f or g
7 Net gain (loss) from involuntary conversions due to casualty or theft . . .		Form 4684
8 Other net gain (loss) under section 1231		Form 4797, line 1
9 Net earnings (loss) from self-employment		Sch. SE, Part I or Part II
10 a Charitable contributions: 50% ...., 30% ...., 20%		Sch. A, line 21 or 22
b Other itemized deductions (attach list)		See Sch. A
11 Expense account allowance		
12 Jobs credit		Form 5884 Form 1040, line 61, add words "from 1065"
13 Taxes paid by regulated investment company		
14 a Payments for partner to a Keogh Plan (Type of plan ▶................) .		Form 1040, line 26
b Payments for partner to an IRA		Form 1040, line 25
c Payments for partner to Simplified Employee Pension (SEP)		Form 1040, line 26

			Form 1116
15 a	Foreign taxes paid (attach schedule)		(Enter on applicable lines of your return)
b	Other income, deductions, etc. (attach schedule)		
16	Oil and gas depletion. (Enter amount—not for partner's use ▶................)		For IRS use only.
17	Specially allocated items (attach schedule): a Short-term capital gain (loss)		Sch. D, line 3, col. f or g
b	Long-term capital gain (loss)		Sch. D, line 10, col. f or g
c	Ordinary gain (loss)		Form 4797, line 9
d	Other		Sch. E, Part III
18	Items of tax preference: a Accelerated depreciation on real property—		
	(1) Certified historic structure rehabilitation (167(o) or amortization under 191) . . .		Form 4625, line 1(a)(1)
	(2) Low-income rental housing (167(k))		Form 4625, line 1(a)(2)
	(3) Other government-assisted low-income housing		Form 4625, line 1(a)(2)
	(4) Other real property	1,283	Form 4625, line 1(a)(3)
b	Accelerated depreciation on personal property subject to a lease		Form 4625, line 1(b)
	Amortization: c................, d................, e................, f................		Form 4625, line 1(c) thru (f)
g	Reserves for losses on bad debts of financial institutions		Form 4625, line 1(g)
h	Depletion (other than oil and gas)		Form 4625, line 1(i)
i	(1) Excess intangible drilling costs from oil, gas, or geothermal wells . .		See Form 4625 instr.
	(2) Net income from oil, gas, or geothermal wells		
19	Interest on investment indebtedness: a Investment interest expense—		
	(1) Indebtedness incurred before 12/17/69		Form 4952, line 1
	(2) Indebtedness incurred before 9/11/75, but after 12/16/69		Form 4952, line 15
	(3) Indebtedness incurred after 9/10/75		Form 4952, line 5
b	Net investment income (loss)		Form 4952, line 2 or line 10(a)
c	Excess expenses from "net lease property"		Form 4952, lines 11 and 19
d	Excess of net long-term capital gain over net short-term capital loss from investment property		Form 4952, line 20
20	Property qualified for investment credit:		

New property	a 3 or more but less than 5 years		Form 3468, line 1(a)
	b 5 or more but less than 7 years		Form 3468, line 1(b)
	c 7 or more years		Form 3468, line 1(c)
New commuter highway vehicle	d 3 or more years		Form 3468, line 1(d)
Qualified progress expenditures	e 7 or more years		Form 3468, line 1(e)
Used property	f 3 or more but less than 5 years		Form 3468, line 1(f)
	g 5 or more but less than 7 years		Form 3468, line 1(g)
	h 7 or more years		Form 3468, line 1(h)
Used commuter highway vehicle	i 3 or more years		Form 3468, line 1(i)
21 a	Credit for alcohol used as fuel		Form 6478, line 15
b	Nonconventional source fuel credit		
c	Unused credits from cooperatives		

22 Property used in recomputing a prior year investment credit (enter on corresponding line of Form 4255):

Description of property (also state whether new or used)	(1) Rate	(2) Date placed in service	(3) Cost or basis	(4) Estimated useful life	(5) Applicable percentage	(6) Original qualified investment (column 3 × column 5)	(7) Date item ceased to be investment credit property	(8) Period actually used	(9) Applicable percentage	(10) Qualified investment (column 3 × column 10)
A										
B										

Instructions
for the Partnership

Complete Schedule K-1 (Form 1065) for each partner. File Copy A with Form 1065 and send Copy C to the appropriate partner. Schedule K-1 and Schedule K have the same line numbers to make it easier for the partnership to prepare Schedule K-1. (In addition, Schedule K-1 has questions A through L, item M, and line 22.) Refer to the Schedule K instructions before preparing Schedule K and

Schedule K-1, especially the instructions for line 15b. Also, refer to the instructions for the lettered items at the top of Schedule K-1. Additional copies of Schedule K-1 are available from your District Director. The total amount of the distributive share items (column b) reported on each line on all of the partners' Schedules K-1 should equal the amount reported on the same line of Schedule K (Form 1065). Similarly, the total of the amounts reported in each column of item M of all the partners' Schedules K-1 should equal the amounts reported in the same column in Schedule M of Form 1065.

Substitute forms.—Prior IRS approval is not required for (a) a substitute Schedule K-1 that shows only the line items required for use by a taxpayer if those line items have the same numbers and titles and are in the same order as on the comparable IRS Schedule K-1; and (b) a substitute Schedule K-1 that is an exact facsimile of an IRS Schedule K-1. Other substitute Schedules K-1 require prior approval. You may apply for approval of a substitute form by writing to: Internal Revenue Service, Attention TX:R, 1111 Constitution Avenue, NW., Washington, DC 20224.

SCHEDULE E
(Form 1040)

Department of the Treasury
Internal Revenue Service

Supplemental Income Schedule

(From pensions and annuities, rents and royalties, partnerships, estates and trusts, etc.)
▶ Attach to Form 1040.   ▶ See Instructions for Schedule E (Form 1040).

1980

16

Name(s) as shown on Form 1040   **Sam Taxpayer**   Your social security number **999 99 9998**

Part I   **Pension and Annuity Income. If fully taxable, do not complete this part. Enter amount on Form 1040, line 17.**

For one pension or annuity not fully taxable, complete this part. If you have more than one pension or annuity that is not fully taxable, attach a separate sheet listing each one with the appropriate data and enter combined total of taxable parts on line 4.

1a Did you and your employer contribute to the pension or annuity? . . . . ☐ Yes ☐ No

  b If "Yes," do you expect to get back your contribution within 3 years from the date you receive the first payment? . . . . . ☐ Yes ☐ No

  c If "Yes," show: Your contribution ▶ $................................, d Contribution received in prior years . . . . . ▶ | 1d |

2   Amount received this year . . . . | 2 |

3   Amount on line 2 that is not taxable . . . . . . | 3 |

4   Taxable part (subtract line 3 from line 2). Enter here and include in line 18 below . . . . . . | 4 |

Part II   **Rent and Royalty Income or Loss. If you need more space, attach a separate sheet.**

5a Are any of the expenses listed below for a vacation home or similar dwelling rented to others (see instructions)? . ☐ Yes ☐ No

  b If "Yes," did you or a member of your family occupy the vacation home or similar dwelling for more than 14 days during the tax year? ☐ Yes ☐ No

6a Did you elect to claim amortization (under section 191) or depreciation (under section 167(o)) for a rehabilitated certified historic structure (see Instructions)? . . . . ☐ Yes ☐ No

  b Amortizable basis (see Instructions) ▶

(a) Property code (describe in Part V)	(b) Total amount of rents	(c) Total amount of royalties	(d) Depreciation (explain in Part VI) or depletion (attach computation)	(e) Other expenses (explain in Part VII)	(f) Net loss	(g) Net income
Property A .						
Property B .						
Property C .						
7 Amounts from Form 4835 . .						
8 Totals . .					( )	

9 Total rent and royalty income or (loss). Combine amounts in columns (f) and (g), line 8. Enter here and include in line 18 below . . . . | 9 |

Part III   **Income or Losses from—**

(a) Name	(b) Employer identification number	(c) Net loss	(d) Net income
Partnerships			
Real Estate Shelter Assoc.	72-314561	(32,000)	

10 Add amounts in columns (c) and (d) and enter here . . . . | 10 | (32,000) |

11 Combine amounts in columns (c) and (d), line 10, and enter net income or (loss) . . . . . | 11 | (32,000) |

12 Additional first-year depreciation (see instructions for limitations) . . . . | 12 | ( ) |

13 Total partnership income or (loss). Combine lines 11 and 12. Enter here and include in line 18 below . . . . | 13 | (32,000) |

Estates or Trusts			

14 Add amounts in columns (c) and (d) and enter here . . . . | 14 | ( ) |

15 Total estate or trust income or (loss). Combine amounts in columns (c) and (d), line 14. Enter here and include in line 18 below . . . . | 15 |

Small Business Corporations			

16 Add amounts in columns (c) and (d) and enter here . . . . | 16 | ( ) |

17 Total small business corporation income or (loss). Combine amounts in columns (c) and (d), line 16. Enter here and include in line 18 below . . . . | 17 |

Part IV

18 **TOTAL** income or (loss). Combine lines 4, 9, 13, 15, and 17. Enter here and on Form 1040, line 18 . ▶ | 18 | (32,000) |

19 Farmers and fishermen: Enter your share of gross farming and fishing income applicable to Parts II and III . . . . | 19 | **E** |

Part V **Property Reported in Part II**

Property Codes	Kind and location of property
A	
B	
C	

Part VI **Depreciation Claimed in Part II. If you need more space, use Form 4562.**

(a) Description of property	(b) Date acquired	(c) Cost or other basis	(d) Depreciation allowed or allowable in prior years	(e) Depreciation method	(f) Life or rate	(g) Depreciation for this year
Total additional first-year depreciation (Do not include in items below. See instructions for limitations.)——▶						
Property A						
Totals (Property A)			. . . .			
Total additional first-year depreciation (Do not include in items below. See instructions for limitations.)——▶						
Property B						
Totals (Property B)			. . . .			
Total additional first-year depreciation (Do not include in items below. See instructions for limitations.)——▶						
Property C						
Totals (Property C)			. . . .			

Part VII **Expenses Claimed in Part II**

Expenses (Description)	Properties		
	A	B	C
Taxes			
Insurance			
Interest			
Commissions			
Other (list) ▶			

Form **4625**
Department of the Treasury
Internal Revenue Service

Computation of Minimum Tax—Individuals

▶ See instructions on back.
▶ Attach to Form 1040.

1980
30

Name(s) as shown on Form 1040

Sam Taxpayer

Your social security number

999 99 9998

File this form if the total of tax preference items (line 2) is more than $10,000 ($5,000 if you are married filing separately) even though you owe no minimum tax, **OR** if you have any minimum tax liability deferred from an earlier tax year until this year. If this is a short-period return, see instructions for line 7.

1 Tax preference items:

(Note: Adjusted itemized deductions and capital gains are now tax preference items for the alternative minimum tax. See Form 6251.)

(a) Accelerated depreciation on real property—		
(1) Certified historic structure rehabilitation (167(o) or amortization under 191)	1a(1)	
(2) Low-income rental housing (167(k))	1a(2)	
(3) Other real property	1a(3)	1283
(b) Accelerated depreciation on personal property subject to a lease	1b	
(c) Amortization of certified pollution control facilities	1c	
(d) Amortization of railroad rolling stock	1d	
(e) Amortization of on-the-job training facilities	1e	
(f) Amortization of child care facilities	1f	
(g) Reserves for losses on bad debts of financial institutions	1g	
(h) Stock options	1h	
(i) Depletion	1i	
(j) Intangible drilling costs	1j	

2 Total tax preference items. Add lines 1(a) through 1(j) — **2**

3 Amount from Form 1040, line 47* — 3

4 Tax from recomputing prior-year investment credit — 4

5 Tax on premature redemption of Individual Retirement Bond(s) — 5

6 Add lines 3 through 5 — 6

7 Enter the larger of: (a) one-half of the amount on line 6, or (b) $10,000 ($5,000 if you are married filing separately) — **7**

8 Subtract line 7 from line 2 (If line 7 is more than line 2, enter zero) — **8**

9 Multiply amount on line 8 by 15% — **9**

10 Enter any 1980 net operating loss carryover to 1981 (attach statement showing computation) — 10

11 Multiply amount on line 10 by 15% — 11

12 Deferred minimum tax. Enter the amount from line 9 or line 11, whichever is smaller — **12**

13 Minimum tax. Subtract line 12 from line 9 — **13**

14 Enter minimum tax deferred from earlier year(s) until this year (attach statement showing computation) — **14**

15 Total minimum tax. Add lines 13 and 14 — **15**

16 Excess tax credits. If Form 1040, line 47, is more than zero, this section will not apply; skip lines 16(a) through 17 and enter the amount from line 15 on line 18.

(a) Credit for the elderly	16a	
(b) Credit for political contributions	16b	
(c) Credit for child care expenses	16c	
(d) Residential energy credits	16d	

17 Add lines 16(a) through 16(d) — **17**

18 Subtract line 17 from line 15. If line 17 is more than line 15, enter zero. Enter here and on Form 1040, line 49a — **18**

*Do not include any tax from Form 4970, Form 4972, Form 5544, or any penalty tax under sec. 72(m)(5).

Form **4625** (1980)

Instructions

(Section references are to the Internal Revenue Code unless otherwise specified)

Line 1. Tax preference items.—

(a) Accelerated depreciation on real property.—

On the appropriate line(s), enter the amount you get (never less than zero) by subtracting the depreciation that would have been allowable for the year if you had used the straight-line method, from the depreciation actually allowable. Figure this amount separately for each property.

Note: *If you amortized certain rehabilitation expenditures for certified historic structures or other section 1250 property over a 5 year period, enter the amount you get by subtracting the straight-line depreciation over the normal useful life of the improvement, from the amount of this amortization.*

(b) Accelerated depreciation on personal property subject to a lease.—Enter the amount you get (never less than zero) by subtracting the depreciation that would have been allowable for the year if you had used the straight-line method, from the depreciation actually allowable. Figure this amount separately for each property.

(c) through (f). Amortization of (c) certified pollution control facilities, (d) railroad rolling stock, (e) on-the-job training facilities, and (f) child care facilities.—In items (c), (d), (e), and (f), enter the amount by which the amortization allowable for the year is more than the depreciation deduction otherwise allowable.

If you use the Class Life Asset Depreciation Range (CLADR) System, note the following:

• The asset guideline period provided is considered the same as straight-line useful life for lines 1(a) and 1(b).

• Any variance in useful life allowable under section 167(m)(1) is also considered the same as straight-line useful life for purposes of figuring tax preference item (a) but not (b).

• For lines 1(c) through 1(f), the asset guideline period provided (including any variance in useful life) is considered the useful life of the property in figuring the depreciation deduction otherwise allowable.

(g) Reserves for losses on bad debts of financial institutions.—Enter your share of the excess of the addition to the reserve for bad debts over the reasonable addition to the reserve for bad debts that would have been allowable if you had maintained the bad debt reserve for all tax years

based on actual experience. See section 57(a)(7) and regulation section 1.57–1(g).

(h) Stock options.—If you received stock by the exercise of a qualified stock option (as defined in section 422(b)) or a restricted stock option (as defined in section 424 (b)), enter the amount by which the fair market value of the shares at the time of exercise was more than the option price.

(i) Depletion.—Enter the amount you get (never less than zero) in the following way: From the deduction for depletion allowable under section 611, subtract the adjusted basis of the property at the end of the year. Include percentage depletion for geothermal deposits. Figure the adjusted basis without regard to the depletion deduction for the tax year, and figure the excess separately for each property.

(j) Intangible drilling costs.—Excess intangible drilling costs are a tax preference item only to the extent that they are more than your net income from oil, gas, and geothermal properties.

Figure excess intangible drilling costs in the following way: From the allowable intangible drilling and development costs (other than costs in drilling a nonproductive well), subtract the amount that would have been allowable if these costs had been capitalized and then (unless you make an election under section 57(d)(2)) amortized over a 120-month period beginning with the month production first began.

The net income from oil, gas, and geothermal properties is the gross income from these properties minus the deductions allocable to them, except for excess intangible drilling costs and nonproductive well costs.

Figure this tax preference item separately for oil and gas properties which are not geothermal deposits and for all properties which are geothermal deposits.

Limitations on Amounts Treated as Tax Preference Items in Certain Cases.—For limitations when the tax preference item did not result in a tax benefit, see section 58(h). If limitations apply, attach a schedule showing computation.

Partners, Beneficiaries of Estates and Trusts, etc.—If you are a partner, you must take into account separately your distributive share of items of income and deductions when figuring tax preference items. If you are a partner and have elected the optional adjustment to basis (see section 743), adjust the tax preference items that apply to reflect the election.

If you are a:

• beneficiary of an estate or trust, see section 58(c);

• shareholder of an electing small business corporation, see section 58(d);

• participant in a common trust fund, see section 58(e);

• shareholder or holder of beneficial interest in a regulated investment company or a real estate investment trust, see section 58(f).

If you have tax preferences attributable to foreign sources, see section 58(g).

Line 7. Adjustment in exclusion.—If this is a short-period return use the formula in section 443(d)(2) to determine the adjustment in exclusion for figuring the minimum tax on tax preference items.

Note: *If line 2 is more than either the adjusted exclusion or $10,000 ($5,000 if you are married and filing separately), file this form even though you owe no minimum tax.*

Line 10. 1980 net operating loss carryover to 1981.—Under some conditions, you may defer part or all of the amount on line 9 to a later year. See section 56(b).

Line 14. Minimum tax deferred from earlier year(s).—If a net operating loss carryover from an earlier year(s) reduces taxable income for 1980, and the net operating loss giving rise to the carryover resulted in the deferral of minimum tax in that earlier year(s), all or part of the deferred minimum tax may be includible on line 14 as tax liability for 1980. Figure the deferred minimum tax at the rate in effect for the year of the loss (15% for 1976 and later years; 10% for 1975). See section 56(b).

Line 16. Excess tax credits.—If Form 1040, line 47, is zero, you may be able to claim any unused part of certain credits against your minimum tax. Apply the credits in the order listed on this form. For example, if the amount on Form 1040, line 47 is zero after applying the credit for the elderly and a part of the credit for political contributions, apply the balance of the credit for political contributions, credit for child care expenses, and residential energy credits to the extent of the minimum tax on Form 4625, line 15. On lines 16(a) through 16(d), enter only that part of the credit or credits not used to reduce the tax on Form 1040, line 37.

For more information about minimum tax, see **Publication 525**, Taxable and Nontaxable Income.

ship has been formed, then indeed their cost may be deductible. Check this with your professional consultants, and with the General Partner when you investigate a particular real estate shelter investment.

HOW TO REPORT LIMITED PARTNERSHIPS ON YOUR PERSONAL INCOME-TAX RETURN

Many tax-shelter investors already have professional assistance in preparing their tax returns, and thus never become personally involved in the reporting of their partnership losses and gains. However, for those who prepare their own returns, the addition of partnership information does not add any great additional demands.

To illustrate all the procedures and understanding required, we will start with an actual Schedule K-1 from a hypothetical partnership, and then track through the use of each piece of information by a typical individual taxpayer. The K-1 is the investor's copy of the partnership informational form that the General Partner files each year with the IRS. It gives each partner the information required to include the partnership results in the individual tax return.

You will receive a separate K-1 for each partnership investment you have. Notice the partnership's name and identification number at the top of the form. This is one of the items you will transfer onto Part III of Schedule E of your 1040 tax filing.

Items from A through L give the IRS information about your percentage ownership and details your status as a partner. For your information we will describe why some of the these items appear on the form. The date on Line A(i) is important, since losses incurred prior to this date cannot generally be allocated to the new partner. Line A(ii) relates to the effective date of rules that apply after 1976, such as those governing nonrecourse loans. The questions in Item F are to alert the IRS that you may potentially have a taxable gain. Item J is very important. This is where the IRS checks to be sure the investor is claiming shelter only up to the amount of money "at risk." Only in real estate investment do they allow nonrecourse loans described here to be included in your tax basis. You can deduct an amount greater than the capital you invest because of these nonrecourse loans.

Item M provides the detail of your investment capital account at the end of the year. In the case of the example, this is a new investment made last year, so you started the year with no capital. The remaining boxes in Item M detail the following: You invested $20,000; you received a tax loss of $32,000 and, for the purpose of this example, a cash distribution of $500, although in reality this would be unusual in a heavier shelter investment such as this one.

The tax loss and the cash distribution are deducted from your capital account, creating a capital account of negative $12,500 at the end of the year.

None of the items from A through M have to be transferred to your 1040. However, the details listed under "distributive share items" should be transferred to your 1040 whenever an amount is typed in. If no amount is typed in, ignore the item. The IRS has been very helpful in that there is an instruction included following each piece of information indicating where it is to be shown in your 1040 filing.

To continue with our example, Sam Taxpayer would show the ordinary loss from Line 1b, Section M, $32,000, in Schedule E, Part III. This is illustrated in the sample of his Schedule E. The next item filled in is line 18, which reflects $1,283 of tax preference from accelerated depreciation on the property. This item is transferred onto Form 4625, line 1a(2), as indicated on the K-1 and shown on the accompanying sample form.

Interestingly, the $500 of cash flow Mr. Taxpayer received in that year is not required to be transferred onto Form 1040. This is because an individual reports his share of the partnership's taxable income or loss, but cash distributions to the partners have no effect on this result.

As you can see, there is really very little difficulty in filing the partnership tax information with your regular tax return. In general, the fears many people have relating to tax returns and audits are unfounded. Unless you are cheating don't be afraid of the IRS. Tax-shelter investments in real estate properties are after all intended by Congress to offer tax incentives.

How to Use Financial
Advisors Effectively

ADVISORS can be very important for many investors, because so many successful people simply cannot take the time away from their basic business or profession to become expert in the field of investment analysis and planning. Most of us do indeed need some assistance from qualified advisors.

Unfortunately, one of the most common and devastating errors made by many investors is to recognize their need for expert assistance and then put their trust in an advisor who is simply not qualified. Our culture tends to give excessive respect to professional people who we assume have special education and unique knowledge. We are hesitant about checking out their qualifications. We tend to listen without questioning or challenging. Even the strongest among us may accept a "guru-and-follower" relationship without realizing the danger.

THE IMPORTANCE OF USING ADVISORS
ONLY IN THEIR QUALIFIED AREAS

Nothing is quite as valuable as a truly qualified and effective advisor. Nothing is as dangerous as an advisor who is not qualified in the particular investment area under consideration.

The key to effective use of financial advisors is, of course, selection. To approach this task intelligently, you must accept the fact that all attorneys, accountants, and even "certified financial planners" are not automatically capable of serving as advisors in matters of tax planning and investment in real estate limited partnerships. These are specialized areas within broad professional territories, and it takes some effort to find the proper level of expertise.

Regrettably, the professions involved have done little to designate which practitioners are qualified in which areas. This makes your selection task all the more difficult. For example, in the medical field the various specialties are controlled by special boards or academies, which recognize those doctors who have achieved the required level of special knowledge and experience. If you have a heart condition, you are referred to a doctor who is certified by the American College of Cardiac Physicians. Even before the first contact, you know the doctor has the special training and experience to help you.

In the field of real estate investing there are very few specialists who can give you expert advice relating investment opportunities to your particular needs. We sometimes assume that any attorney or accountant can provide the guidance we need for investment success, and this simply is not true. While there are many professionals who will quickly tell you they are not the right individual for the job, there are others who will gladly accept your trust and proceed to prove their total incompetence—at your expense.

YOU OWE IT TO YOURSELF TO BECOME A "PROFESSIONAL" CLIENT

The bottom line of the relationship between client and advisor is that you either place yourself in the advisor's hands like a lump of putty, or you exercise your prerogative to make the relationship a joint effort. If you allow yourself to be psyched out by the mystique of the advisor, you may get some assistance if you are lucky, but you will never get as much as the client who accepts a joint responsibility for results.

To maximize your results, you need to become a "professional" client. You need to learn enough about the area to understand the advisor's thinking, to ask probing questions, and to participate in the final decisions after weighing and balancing the options presented by the advisor.

At first, an area such as limited-partnership investment may appear so foreign to your regular area of expertise, that it seems impossible to become a part of the advisory process. One of the purposes of this book is to help bring you, a potential investor, to the level of an adequate professional client. If you have read and understood the book to this point, you are well on your way to being able to get the most from your advisors.

As human beings, financial experts will automatically respond to the client who is better prepared, more responsive, more probing, and more caring. If you approach your advisors much the same way as you treat your business associates, you will achieve a great deal. Simply do a little preparation for your meetings, then participate and demonstrate that you want to be involved.

There is one key to developing a good relationship with an advisor. If you don't understand the reason for a position, ask. Probably the most valuable words you will ever use with an advisor are, "Why do you say that?"

What Professional Advice and Support Do You Need? There is no single, established way for an investor to use legal, accounting, and financial-planning assistance. Your needs and your best approach to this area will very much depend on your experience, the size of your income, the complexity of your tax return, and the size and diversity of your investment program.

An individual with modest income about to make an initial investment in a public limited partnership through a major broker does not really need any advice or counsel from an independent professional. You can rely on the broker to have screened the General Partner and the syndicator, so there is virtually no chance of out-and-out fraud or lack of professional capability. You are not yet at the stage of having to make complex decisions concerning tax consequences or long-term investment options.

For those with more sizable investments and financial flow, especially if they plan to invest in private limited partnerships, it is frequently necessary, or at least intelligent, to set up an ongoing relationship with one or more advisors to assure the most effective decisions and to provide the necessary functions involved in accounting, tax reporting, legal protection, and financial planning.

Generally speaking, if you are paying taxes at the 50 percent level, you will almost certainly benefit from professional tax planning, and this should include estate planning as well. If you are seriously considering a major investment oriented to tax shelter, or a continuing portfolio of such investments, again you will benefit from professional guidance. Finally, if you are considering deep tax shelter—anything over 1.3 dollars of shelter for each dollar of investment—you should definitely have a qualified advisor examine the total tax consequences of the particular deal involved and how they fit your needs. This would probably involve the use of an accountant or attorney or both.

THE ROLE OF THE FINANCIAL COUNSELOR OR FINANCIAL-INVESTMENT ADVISOR

A truly qualified financial counselor can be a tremendous asset in combining long-term planning with specific current investment guidance. At its best, this service will provide a living financial plan, an estate plan, and integrated planning of investments, life insurance, and taxes.

The problem is that this is a relatively new profession, and locating the truly qualified practitioner can be hard. I have tried to determine if there is any national organization that designates such highly qualified professionals but have been unable to locate one. Certain practitioners call themselves "certified," but upon questioning it turns out that this designation refers to a certificate received on the completion of several months of a course of special training and is not, in fact, an official designation. A group that is a reputable industry source is the International Financial Planners.

In many states, investment advisors must register with the state, but in fact there are no qualifications required for acceptance. A form consisting of background information is filed and the individual may then say he is a "registered advisor." He is indeed registered, but that fact means nothing as to qualification. If you are seeking an investment advisor, it would be wise to check with your state securities bureau for registration requirements.

Many financial-investment advisors have come out of the insurance business or the stock-brokerage business. As a result, they tend to concentrate on those areas and may know little about tax-shelter investments. A recent survey of registered investment advisors found that fewer than 25 percent felt that tax-advantaged investment fell into the realm of their advice to clients. All too often we have found advisors recommending against such investment because they did not want to admit their lack of understanding of tax-sheltered real estate.

On the other hand, many advisors are broadly competent and make a point of keeping abreast of many areas of financial relevance to their clients.

Compensation of Financial-Investment Advisors. Compensation of attorneys and accountants is a fairly straightforward fee, either determined in advance or to be based on an hourly rate. This gets a bit more complicated in the case of financial-investment advisors, because many of them receive compensation from brokers, insurance companies, or limited-partnership syndicators in connection with the investments made by their clients.

It could be argued that the advisor should be paid a fee by the client and not receive any commissions from investment sources in order to be completely unbiased. That would be ideal, but it might not be realistic. A good advisor is worth a lot of money, and many investors do not want to pay substantial fees simply for "advice." One of the biggest problems all advisors have is collecting money for advising a client not to enter into an investment, as clients resist paying a substantial fee for what they perceive to be no result. But this is short-sighted perception. Clearly, advice properly given to avoid an investment could save you a lot of money. I know of advisors who charge a retainer that will cover all of their service without any commission earnings. Then if commissions are received, they are fully disclosed to the client and credited against the retainer.

The obvious answer to potential problems is complete disclosure at the inception of the relationship. Be sure to understand exactly what charges will be made and what, if any, other income will accrue to the advisor as a result of his work for you. Ultimately, you must be comfortable about potential conflicts of interest, and this can be achieved only through discussion in advance.

THE ROLE OF THE ATTORNEY

Stated very simply, your attorney should be used in limited-partnership investing to protect you on all legal considerations. Primarily the attorney should review the legal documentation of the partnership to see if any potential liabilities or problems might occur due to the structure of the partnership or the paperwork. Good questions to ask your attorney would include "Is this syndication paperwork properly drafted?" and "Is my legal liability definitely limited to the amount of my investment?"

In the last few weeks alone, I've heard two stories of investors who thought their liability was limited, only to find out that they were General Partners with full liability. In one case, the General Partner did not file the appropriate limited-partnership certificate and subsequently filed tax returns as a general partnership. The supposed General Partner did such a bad job of managing the partnership that the investors had to become active in its affairs to protect their interests. All of this led to the confirmation of their being General Partners with liability.

In the second situation, the deal was actually syndicated with all investors (mostly doctors) being General Partners and a real estate man being the "head" General Partner. As these investors came to realize the implications, they were furious. But it was too late.

In both of these situations there was no legal advice, and sponsors were not knowledgeable professionals. Almost always, you should obtain legal advice to review your liability position. And again, make sure you are dealing with a competent professional person.

If your lawyer is a tax attorney and handles your tax matters, he would also review the tax areas of the partnership agreement. Do the projected tax losses appear reasonable? Will the loss be appropriate to your needs currently and in future years? Will the loss shelter income in appropriate tax brackets? Are there any risk factors you should be particularly concerned about? How do the tax-prefer-ence items fit into your overall tax planning?

Whether you wish to go beyond these technical matters with your attorney and include advice on the basic wisdom of the investment at hand is a matter of your overall relationship with the lawyer. Some attorneys can be very valuable as counselors in various busi-ness matters, including investment. Others can be disastrous in this role. This is a case where you must be the judge. Never assume your attorney is qualified to assist you in areas beyond legal issues, but do try to find out if he does have that capability.

From my own experience, I believe most successful lawyers are skilled technicians who exercise logical thinking beneficially. How-ever, some are also skilled actors who intimidate clients with a show of superior knowledge far beyond matters of law. This builds fees while producing no additional value. And finally, there are those few attorneys who are both skilled at their profession and blessed with the creativity to see a broad scope of business decisions well beyond the legal aspects. As a professional client you must try to make sure you are getting the best legal advice for your money.

THE ROLE OF YOUR ACCOUNTANT

While some individuals use tax attorneys to prepare their tax re-turns, most use a certified public accountant. This quite clearly de-fines the accountant's role as the furnishing of information and advice concerning all but the legal aspects of tax planning and tax investment. If your accountant prepares your tax returns, he be-comes the logical one to review a tax-shelter investment to see if it fits into your overall needs. In addition, your accountant can be of great assistance in preparing the cash-flow and taxable-income schedule suggested in Chapter 13. These are important and valu-able planning aids.

Accountants are so deeply immersed in taxation that they tend to have been students of tax-sheltered investment for many years. As always, you cannot assume this for any particular individual, but you will probably find that your accountant can render good counsel in this special investment area.

THE POTENTIAL ROLE OF YOUR SECURITIES BROKER

As I have mentioned earlier, many private real estate limited partnerships are sold through licensed securities brokers. While these
individuals are not full-service financial advisors, many of them are
expert in the area of tax-oriented investment, and they can play an
important role in providing you with facts and perspective as to the
right kinds of investment for your particular need. Obviously the individual who is selling you an investment is to be viewed in terms of
at least a potential conflict of interest. This does not mean that the
broker's advice won't be highly professional and in your best interest. It is up to you to determine the level of trust to have in this individual.

One of the affiliated group of companies I own that is involved in
limited-partnership syndication is our licensed securities broker,
Hall Securities Corporation. Our securities representatives are extremely successful professionals who are interested only in long-
term client relationships. For that reason it is normal for them to
advise a prospective investor *not* to invest in one of our partnerships, if they consider it unsuitable for the client. Being skilled in financial planning, they spend less time selling *per se* than in such an
advisory capacity, and since they are affiliated with the General
Partner, follow-through operations of the partnership and the property become long-term responsibilities. Happy investors, we realize,
will always be our best sales promotion.

I am sure many other brokers work on the same high professional
level, and you would do well to create a close relationship with one
of these knowledgeable people.

Part Three

SELECTING YOUR GENERAL PARTNER

Why the General Partner Is the Key to Your Success

No SINGLE factor in real estate limited-partnership investing is more important than the selection of a General Partner. The people who stand behind any investment are, of course, always a vital consideration, but even more than in most big corporations, the success of the enterprise in limited partnerships tends to reflect the drive and abilities of a few individuals. For this reason, I strongly recommend that you pay special attention to the suggestions made in this part of the book.

PERSONAL CONTROL

We normally think of a partnership as a business in which management is shared by two or more partners. As you no doubt realize by now, this is definitely not the case in a limited partnership. From the point of view of the limited partners, it is a passive investment, and all decision-making powers are delegated to the General Partner (or Partners). Your position of limited partner is somewhat similar to that of a shareholder in a public corporation.

This delegation is not bad in itself, since you also delegate all the headaches and operational problems of running a business. Perhaps most important of all, your position legally relieves you of responsibility for any liabilities beyond your personal investment. As a matter of fact, if you were to exercise much control as a limited partner, you could legally be treated as a General Partner and thus lose your limited-liability position. This is why, in your own best interest, limited-partnership agreements are specifically written to limit your control.

While all of this is understandable, and should be acceptable, it must lead to the conclusion that your General Partner is in fact the key to the success of your investment. For better or worse, when you join a limited partnership you are putting the fate of your investment funds in the hands of that General Partner. It is not a decision to be made lightly.

THE LEGAL POSITION OF YOUR GENERAL PARTNER

Legally, the General Partner is a fiduciary. By definition this implies a position of trust or confidence in a relationship wherein one person is entrusted to hold or manage property or money for another. Among the obligations that a fiduciary owes to his principal (the investor in this case) are loyalty, full disclosure, accounting for all monies, and the duty to use skill, care, and diligence. The fiduciary must at all times act in a responsible manner as regards the best interests of the principal.

These concepts apply in both a moral and legal sense, and they do provide some measure of protection for an investor. If fiduciary duties are breached, the principal can usually bring civil action for money damages and/or compel the fiduciary to forfeit compensation.

THE OPERATIONAL POSITION
OF YOUR GENERAL PARTNER

The General Partner acts in the capacity of the board of directors, chief executive officer, and chief operating officer of the limited-partnership venture. Depending on the organization involved, this awesome responsibility may be vested in one individual or in several, or even in a corporation acting as General Partner. Under most arrangements, the General Partner must make all decisions relative to the acquisition, financing and potential refinancing, and sale of the property.

In certain states you will encounter "democratic rights" under which you will receive the opportunity to vote on some specified critical decisions. For example, the North American Securities Administrators Association has in its guidelines a provision that there be a majority approval vote by limited partners on matters of sale or termination of the partnership.

All day-to-day operational decisions are under the control of the General Partner. This authority includes, but certainly is not limited to, the selection of a management company to run the property, regular review of its results, establishment of rental rates, policies regarding lease terms, decisions on maintenance expenditures, nature and amount of insurance to be purchased, and whether or not to appeal local tax assessments.

While many of the operational responsibilities of a General Partner may seem routine, they all require expertise and they all have a bearing on the success or failure of the investment.

Few investments succeed on their own momentum. Investments must be guided and nurtured by decisions made as a result of professional evaluation of frequently changing needs and conditions. This ongoing decision-making is a major responsibility of your General Partner.

ESSENTIAL QUALITIES OF
A SUCCESSFUL GENERAL PARTNER

Based on this brief description of a General Partner's position and responsibilities, it is obvious you will want a superior individual or group to occupy the position on your behalf. As a guide to your selection, I believe you can boil the criteria down to three all-encompassing qualities. These are very broad-based, and I suppose it could be argued that they smack of "Mom, the Flag, and Applie Pie." Still, if I were investing my money, these are the areas in which I would want my General Partner to shine:

- *Honesty and Integrity*—It is absolutely essential that your General Partner have a proven record of trustworthiness. Despite the legal safeguards that are inherent in the limited-partnership structure, lawsuits rarely settle anything satisfactorily. It is best never to need the assistance of the law. Your only real protection lies in the honesty and integrity of your General Partner.

· *Experience and Competence*—The knowledge needed to make the multitude of decisions required for sound acquisition, operation, and sale is too complex to be learned on the job as a General Partner. A solid foundation of actual experience in real estate and specifically in limited-partnership operation is required. General business experience may prove helpful, but it definitely is not enough to assure success.

While it may be laudable to give someone new a chance, make it a rule, in your own best interest, to let other investors be the pioneers. Stick to General Partners who have experience and a track record.

· *Dedication*—All too often, the difference between a so-so investment result and a super success can be measured by the determination, intensity, and plain hard work of the General Partner. The requirements of successful real estate partnership management are too demanding to be met by a partial effort.

In the next chapter there is a checklist of specific elements to look for in prospective General Partners as a yardstick to rating their suitability in each essential area. An old Wall Street slogan says, "Investigate, then invest." All too often, otherwise intelligent people ignore this sound advice and make major investment decisions on emotional reactions supported only by minimum knowledge. When the results prove less than desirable, these investors rarely understand that their lack of selectivity was the root of their bad experience.

Conversely, most consistently successful investors accept the responsibility to investigate potential General Partners. They ask intelligent questions, they dig for facts on which they can make a businesslike decision, and they check with references to get a good feel for the credibility of the people involved. Successful investors generally continue to work as intelligently at their investments as they did to make their money in the first place.

To elaborate on our consideration of the General Partner's importance to your investment success, we will now look into some of the critical areas controlled by General Partners that affect your interest as a limited partner.

Conflicts of Interest. One of the elements to consider when reviewing the structure of a limited partnership is potential conflict of interest.

A number of conflicts of interest may occur routinely because of the nature of a General Partner's broad responsibilities and activities. For example, it is often more economical and more effective to have affiliated companies that are owned by a General Partner provide services to properties, rather than to buy services from independent companies. The difficulty, of course, comes in that this creates a conflict of interest for the General Partner. How much does he charge? What is a fair price? Will he properly control the quality of the services rendered? Should he make a profit? How much?

Decisions that have the potential for conflict of interest may in fact benefit investors if they provide needed services of high quality and at a cost equal to or below market costs. The reason this frequently works well for the investor is that underlying the potential conflict there is a much more important desire on the part of the General Partner to contribute to the success of the investment.

The important consideration is that every conflict of interest be thoroughly disclosed in the offering document, or if it comes into existence later that it be communicated to the investors promptly. Even if a conflict of interest is not as obvious as the example cited, it is the absolute responsibility of the General Partner to communicate all such potential problems to investors, clearly and in advance.

The investor in turn owes it to himself to review all documentation and correspondence carefully, and to raise questions concerning conflicts about which he does not feel comfortable. A worthy General Partner makes enough money doing an honest and credible job of representing his investors so that the last thing he would want is to jeopardize the trust and respect necessary to maintain his position.

In the final analysis, the answer is one of trust, and that is a decision only you, the investor, can make.

Reporting and Communication. One of the most important services a General Partner should render is to maintain thorough reporting to the investors. While this is not done universally, it is a mark of professionalism, and is owed to those who invest their money.

Limited partners should receive a number of reports each year presented in a brief, readable format designed to keep them up to date on all matters of finances, operations, and property condition. Both good news and bad should be included and, in general, the investors should be kept right up to the moment about plans and expectations. Key elements you should expect in a good investor communication program include the following.

Quarterly Reports—Quarterly reports should have an unaudited operating statement that presents the financial aspects of the project. Additionally, a letter should provide the relevant facts of the operation during that quarter. Information covers such areas as occupancy, changes in promotional programs, physical improvements undertaken, competitive activities, changes in the marketplace, economic changes in the area, financial position of the partnership, and plans formulated for future activity.

We consider the quarterly report to be the cornerstone of our communication program. It is received by investors approximately thirty days after the end of each calendar quarter.

Special Reports—Between quarters, a special report should be sent whenever warranted, containing news of special significance. Such reports frequently deal with unexpected events, such as fires, damage by tornadoes, hurricanes, etc. We have even sent out reports stating that while our property was located in an area reported to have received heavy tornado damage, we were spared and the investors need not worry. Investors do react to news reports, and if their property might be involved, they will be concerned.

A recent major fire in one of our projects illustrates how seriously we take our responsibility to communicate with investors. Late on the day of the fire we mailed a long letter to all investors providing them with the facts, including the happy news that no one was seriously injured. We told them of some of the heroic measures taken by on-site personnel to assure the safety of our residents, and reviewed our insurance position, which would not only replace the building but cover the lost revenues as well.

That evening and the next day, the local newspapers, radio, and TV gave the fire considerable publicity, including some that was not altogether accurate. This resulted in a second letter, which directly responded to the publicity and provided a complete factual review. A few days later, to wrap up the communication, we sent investors a copy of the letter hand-delivered to all residents in the project providing details on the fire marshal's report, and our efforts to help the burned-out residents over their personal problems. This final communication also brought investors up to date about the effect of the fire on occupancy, rental traffic, the status of the insurance claim, and so on. Certainly such comprehensive reporting entails a lot of effort, but we feel it is an absolute responsibility of the General Partner to keep investors aware of all developments, good or bad.

Annual Financial Statement—Shortly after the end of each year an annual financial statement is provided to each investor. If this statement is a certified audit it may take as long as 90 to 120 days after year end before it is completed.

Tax Information—It is important that investors receive their tax information in time. As explained in Chapter 7, the K-1 provides all information you require to complete the partnership section of your personal income-tax return. For the first year of a new partnership, preparation will require extra time. In general, however, it is fair to expect your K-1 form within seventy-five days of the end of the year, or by March 15 at the latest. After the first year, we strive to have the forms out by February 15.

Partnership Meetings—Large public limited partnerships do not normally hold partnership meetings because their investors are too widely spread across the country. For private partnerships, however, an annual meeting provides an excellent opportunity for investors and the General Partner to meet informally in order to maintain personal contact and enhance communication. We do this as a matter of routine, with the first meeting shortly after the partnership is formed. Additional meetings are held annually for most of our partnerships, or more frequently if important issues arise. Many of our investors attend, and they seem to appreciate the opportunity for two-way communication.

Be Sure to Consider Backup Talent and Plans for Business Continuity. One of the inherent disadvantages of the smaller local individual General Partner is backup. What are the chances that things will be thrown into a big mess if the key person dies or becomes disabled? When you start investing substantial amounts of money, it is important to know that you're investing in more than just one individual. There must be a backup organization.

By itself, the involvement of highly qualified personnel in an organization does not assure continuity of the business. Unless legal arrangements for continuity are provided in the partnership agreement, the General Partner's death or incapacity can force the termination or dissolution of the partnership. Partnership assets may have to be sold at a bad time, and negative financial consequences can result for the limited partners.

Even if the matter of legal continuity is covered, and qualified backup people are involved, chaos can result unless a structure is established in advance to pass on power, responsibility, and financial reward to the people who will take over. At the Hall Real Estate Group, a great deal of effort has gone into establishing a plan that gives our key people the motivation and reward of ownership rather than encouraging a corporate-employee point of view. We believe we have achieved a unique form of entrepreneurial organization, both for today and to continue in the future, through a complex estate plan. While I hope everyone would miss me, I am confident the investors would be in good hands.

Many General Partners recognize the importance of continuity to their investors, and they take appropriate steps. Unfortunately, others simply ignore this potential problem. Certainly it is a fair question for you as a prospective investor to raise, and it should have some bearing on your investment decision. It is not necessarily a black-and-white issue, but it may well be considered a caution flag in terms of the size of investment you might be willing to make, even if everything else is extremely favorable.

GENERAL PARTNERS COME IN DIFFERENT SHAPES AND SIZES

Many General Partners must be classified as nonprofessionals. They are General Partners in one or more projects, but this is a secondary adjunct to their primary business. They may in fact really be builders or developers of new properties using the limited partnership to raise money. Or, the General Partner may be a real estate broker who creates a limited-partnership syndicate in order to create a buyer for a property he feels is a good opportunity.

There is nothing inherently wrong with a promoter acting as a General Partner or as an adjunct to another buisness. However, I would seriously question whether an individual can do justice to the demands of the General Partner's position while being immersed in another full-time business. My observation has been that nonprofessional General Partners frequently lack the seriousness and dedication necessary to do a superior job.

New General Partners with Narrow Experience Must Be Viewed with Caution. Another category of General Partner to consider with caution is the type I call "the grass-is-greener General Partner." While it is not categorically true of all attorneys, accountants, and securities salesmen who are affiliated with real estate syndication, as specialists required to put a package together, many of them do eventually decide to handle the whole thing themselves. The decision may be based on greed or on the fact that the job looks easy. One way or another, to those who are involved in special areas, the grass frequently looks greener on the General Partner's side. So instead of continuing to accept a fee for services rendered, the specialist makes a decision to take on the total job, and a new General Partner comes into being.

Some of these individuals are capable of being very proficient and responsible General Partners, but until they prove themselves they should be viewed as high-risk candidates. The problem usually is that while they have excellent experience in one aspect of limited-partnership operation, they are completely unprepared in others. They are not ready to do the full job, and are unwilling to learn through taking on junior-level responsibilities in order to get experience.

Many times I have been at meetings where people have asked, "Why wouldn't it be better for us to be General Partners ourselves and avoid the fees we pay to the General Partner?" Most of those same people realize how much expertise is required and involved in putting together the property acquisition and in properly evaluating the whole transaction. Nevertheless, they ask this kind of question in a half-serious manner.

At one such group meeting where this question was asked, one of the other prospective investors answered the question before I had a chance to. He said something like "You've got to be kidding." He went on to talk about his knowledge of how difficult it is for a General Partner and how much harassment and what a pain in the neck it is to own and operate property. He went on and on about understanding why it is wise to invest with a General Partner.

The same gentleman later asked me, "Why do you give up part of the upside to investors instead of putting all the money in and taking the deals yourself?" In a funny kind of a way that was an extremely perceptive question. A lot of real estate entrepreneurs do not want the hassle of limited partnerships. When they achieve a certain amount of success, they stop syndicating with limited partners. In my own case and that of a number of professional General Partners, we find the partnership arrangement a more favorable way to diversify and to own a piece of more properties. Personally, I find it better than to have my money in just a few deals at a time, even though I may reflect back on the sale of any one property and realize that it would have been more profitable to have owned the whole thing.

Experienced, professional General Partners usually have dedicated their business careers to sponsoring, organizing, and operating limited partnerships. Ideally their background includes a variety of experiences in real estate, and in lower-level work within limited-partnership organizations.

Professional General Partners include a broad spectrum from the very small, individual operator to the large corporate organization sponsoring public real estate funds.

The locally oriented, small but stable General Partner is usually a good selection for an investor. Because he is located in your area, you will have more access to information directly from the source. Because his reputation is the lifeblood of his business, he will give you a very fair shake. This type of General Partner is not geared to the development of large numbers of new investors. He usually relies on repeat investors and on referrals for his growth, so he knows he will live or die on the success or failure of his programs. This, of course, provides excellent motivation.

Corporate General Partners May Be Ideal for Smaller Investors. The corporate General Partner is often a big organization established to sponsor and administer large public funds. Generally, but not always, each partnership will have individual General Partners in addition to the corporate General Partner. These are usually officers of the corporation. It is an arrangement designed to satisfy what are called "safe harbor" rules, which establish that a General Partner must have a substantial net worth relative to the assets of the partnership in order to be able to meet partnership obligations. Individuals are usually required in this regard since their liability would not be limited in the same way as the liability of the corporation.

These corporate-related General Partners are almost always dedicated professionals who provide good real estate analysis and management services. In terms of relationship with investors, however, there is rarely a direct link. Public partnerships are usually sold through brokers, often Wall Street firms that sell stocks and other investments nationally. Therefore, it is most unusual for the investor actually to know or talk to the individual General Partners.

While everything is handled professionally and thoroughly, there is a lack of personal contact with the people who are making it all happen. For the individual investing $5,000 or $10,000, the relationship can be viewed as that with a mutual fund, and personal contact is not necessary. For the investor dealing with significant sums of money, however, a more personal relationship with the General Partner may be more desirable.

DON'T SHORT-CHANGE YOUR SELECTION EFFORT

This chapter has been designed to introduce the important subject of selecting your General Partner. In the next chapter we will get into more details of how to do it, complete with a checklist to help organize your considerations.

Remember, it's your money. You worked hard to earn it. You owe it to yourself to work just as hard to assure the success of the investments that will protect your capital against the ravages of taxation and inflation. It is both your right and your responsibility to exercise discrimination in selecting the people you count on for the success of those important investments.

How to Find and Evaluate Potential General Partners

As YOU start to seek out limited-partnership opportunities, you may be referred to sponsors, issuers, syndicators, promoters, underwriters, brokers, and securities salesmen, as well as to General Partners. This can become a little confusing, so let's sort out the cast.

Real estate limited-partnership interests are legally considered investments in real estate securities. Therefore, their sale is technically treated very much like the sale of stocks and bonds. Underwriters, brokers, and securities salesmen are people or entities licensed to engage in the sale of securities, and they are involved in the sale of all limited-partnership securities except the very smallest, which may be sold directly by the issuer.

The issuer is the legal entity technically responsible for making the offering—i.e., the partnership itself. The sponsor or promoter is the person or organization that put the deal together for offering to investors. The syndicator is the person or entity that actually handles the marketing of the investment, either directly or through a securities broker. The General Partner, of course, is the individual or organization that will be responsible for all of the decisions and activities of the partnership.

LOCATING PUBLIC LIMITED PARTNERSHIPS

With the growing popularity of real estate limited-partnership investing, most brokerage firms, both national and local, now offer limited-partnership investment units. Most of the public offerings are sold through the national brokerage firms. These firms also represent some private offerings.

While each brokerage firm does not offer all public partnerships that may be on the market at a given time, they do try to have available a range of investment opportunities in terms of different objectives, different types of properties, and suitability for investors in different income brackets. Thus, learning about the availability of public real estate limited partnerships is essentially as easy as talking to one or two brokerage companies in your own community.

Appendix 3 of this book will help you locate both public and private limited-partnership sponsors. The largest public operators are listed with background information and home-office addresses. A letter asking for references and a nearby contact will put you in touch with the sources you need for full consideration and action. The Appendix also indicates which public and private partnerships are represented by each of the major brokerage houses. This will give you some indication of the degree of involvement in real estate by the firms you may previously have considered interested only in stocks and bonds. Since these major brokerage firms have offices throughout the country, including many small towns, this list should help you establish convenient sources of direct information.

Track Record Is the Most Important Point to Consider in Public Limited Partnerships. In Chapter 3, we pointed out that one of the major differences between public and private limited partnerships is that most public offerings do not involve a particular piece of real estate specified in advance of the investor's involvement. This means you cannot analyze an individual deal as the basis for your investment decision. The overall previous results achieved by the same organization must become your primary consideration. Furthermore, since public partnerships are generally sold through a brokerage firm, you will not have much opportunity to appraise the individuals who will be guiding your investment activity. Their track record becomes extremely important in making your appraisal.

All prospectuses for public limited partnerships must be accompanied by a total and detailed history of all of the investment programs operated by that organization. This provides investors with an excellent basis for consideration and comparison.

Because both public limited partnership sponsors and brokerage companies realize that many new investors are being attracted to real estate opportunities, both are doing an outstanding job of making information and guidance available at the local level. Local brokers are being trained to be completely knowledgeable about real estate, and some have become quite expert in assisting investors in their selection. Moreover, the sponsoring organizations frequently have regional managers throughout the country who hold scheduled educational seminars, and who may be available for personal consultation with prospective investors.

As always, it is up to the investor to take advantage of the information and aid that is available. Do not just assume that all brokers are equally knowledgeable about real estate limited partnerships. Many top-notch stockbrokers simply do not know much about tax shelter and real estate. If, instead of taking the first available broker, you check with the manager of the office and specifically ask for a specialist in this investment field, you will be well served.

WHY PRIVATE LIMITED PARTNERSHIPS
ARE A WELL-KEPT "SECRET"

One of the strangest things about the limited-partnership business is that unless you are an active participant, you may be entirely unaware of the people and organizations involved in private placements in your own locality. This is surprising when you consider that *Tax Shelter Digest* estimates that about 90 percent of all tax-advantaged investments are made through private limited partnerships! That translates into more than $9 billion invested through private placement in 1980. You may well wonder why the industry has such a low profile.

The answer is simple. The securities laws that allow private limited partnerships to be exempt from SEC registration preclude advertising and seriously restrict solicitation. Before a General Partner can even discuss a limited partnership with a prospective investor, he must be sure the individual meets the requirements for financial suitability or has specific expertise to evaluate the offering in terms of its risks as well as its merits. Thus, reputable General Partners generally eschew promotion. They select their limited partners with considerable care.

How Private Limited Partnerships Are Offered for Sale. Until recently, major brokers rarely offered private limited partnerships. This is changing rapidly. Brokerage houses today are developing an aggressive interest in this area, and some firms have become quite active in it. Statistics are not yet available, but the private partnerships sold on a widespread or national basis are still probably a very small percentage of the total.

One interesting development in this area is the activity of large syndicators that specialize in putting together private real estate partnerships for sale nationwide through brokers. They act as skilled middlemen between the developers and the ultimate investors. The developer usually stays on as the General Partner, while the syndicator handles the horrendous work involved in preparing the offering.

But the bulk of private limited partnerships is not sold that way. Most General Partners choose to sell either through their own organization, or through local or regional brokers. With the growing need for tax-oriented investments, as more and more people move into higher tax brackets, experienced General Partners have greater difficulty finding good investments than they do finding suitable investors.

Of course, aggressive, growth-oriented General Partners do want to meet and work with prospective new investors, but your own chances will probably depend on your making the first move.

LOCATING PRIVATE LIMITED-PARTNERSHIP SOURCES IN YOUR COMMUNITY

One of the best places to start looking for private limited-partnership sponsors or dealers is in the Yellow Pages of your telephone directory. Exactly what listing to check will depend somewhat on the size of your community.

In large cities or their business-oriented suburbs, you will probably find local General Partner organizations listed under "Investment Securities," "Real Estate" (other than home sales), or "Property Management." Call the sales manager of any of the organizations listed for information about their operations and to arrange a meeting.

In both large and small communities you can find local and regional securities brokers who sell private real estate partnerships as well as the more usual bonds and mutual funds. Simply check the Yellow Pages under "Stock and Bond Brokers." This listing will include the familiar names of the leading national firms, along with many others less familiar. It is this latter group of firms, particularly those *not* listed as New York Stock Exchange members, who are most likely to represent the local and regional General Partners you are seeking. Make a few telephone calls and simply ask if the firm deals in private real estate limited partnerships. You will soon be in touch with an active source that will be happy to meet with you and provide information.

Incidentally, buying through a local or national broker is no more costly than buying directly from a sponsor. The commission is built into the established unit investment price, and if a broker is involved, that commission is paid by the General Partner.

How to Get Information about General Partners in Your Area.
Operating "blindly" in locating a source of private limited partnerships, as suggested in the previous section, may be a good way to start, but the more serious you get, the more you will need a basis of evaluation. My grandmother had a great saying—"If you want to learn, just ask." That certainly applies here. The question, of course, is who to ask. I know that many of our new investors come to our organization through each of the sources discussed below, so I recommend them, and assure you they can prove helpful.

Personal Friends and Business Associates. If you are in an income bracket that will benefit importantly from tax-sheltered investment, it is likely many of your social and business friends are in the same

economic position. Start asking if any of them are involved in limited partnerships. You will probably be amazed at how much activity
you uncover. Discuss it with one of the investors whose judgment
you particularly trust, and learn more about his experience. If it
sounds encouraging, arrange an introduction to the General Partner
or representative and pursue the lead.

Attorneys and Accountants. More and more attorneys and accountants are making it their business to learn of tax-shelter investment sources, and to develop the ability to analyze programs so
they can make recommendations to their clients. Clients expect
their accountants to stay on top of the tax-advantaged investment
situations as an extra dimension of their overall service. In most
cases, if all you need is a list of good partnership sponsors, the accountant or tax attorney is happy to provide this without charge. Of
course, if your need is for tax and investment planning as well, you
can expect to be charged a professional fee. Don't be afraid to spend
money for professional advice. Good counsel in these areas from attorneys and accountants is well worth the fee.

Financial Advisors. If you are in the upper income brackets, you
may already have a financial advisor working with you on estate
matters and possibly on investments as well. Historically, these advisors are most knowledgeable in the fields of insurance and stock
market investment, and only a relatively small percentage have
studied real estate limited-partnership investing in any depth. If
your financial advisor is knowledgeable about limited partnerships,
he will be able to guide you to sources that will best fill your overall
needs. However, before relying on a financial consultant for this assistance, make sure there is personal expertise involved. There is always the danger that such a specialist's lack of limited-partnership
knowledge may be covered up defensively, usually by adopting a
negative position.

The Securities Bureau of Your State. Most states have a securities
bureau charged with regulating a broad spectrum of securities activity, including real estate syndication. The degree to which real
estate securities must be filed or registered will vary from state to

state, so the amount of information will also vary. While these bureaus are not primarily organized to help the public locate General Partners, I have found them willing to help whenever possible. They may well be able to provide a list of people active in organizing real estate syndications, and they may also offer helpful advice and guidance. In addition, all matters of complaint, investigation, or other information on file at the Securities Bureaus are legally a matter of public information. Procedures are established to allow individual access to these records.

Real Estate Securities and Syndication Institute. This is a national organization of partnership sponsors, and its main office is listed in Appendix 1. RESSI will provide you with a list of members in your area upon request.

Management of Attractive Investment Properties. Since the end result of your interest in a General Partner is to invest in real estate, why not look at some real estate? In your day-to-day local travel, you have undoubtedly been impressed by a few large residential or commercial projects that appear to be particularly attractive and well run—just the kind in which you would like to invest.

Stop in and find out from the on-site manager who owns the property and who manages it. The owner may well be a private limited partnership. If not, the management company may be involved with other properties owned by the kind of sponsor you are seeking. Tracking down a General Partner's example of quality work can be a promising way to start a worthwhile investment relationship.

A PROVEN PLAN TO EVALUATE
PRIVATE-PLACEMENT GENERAL PARTNERS

The following five-step program virtually assures you of selecting an honest, dependable, and successful General Partner. Nothing can absolutely guarantee investment success, but this cautious approach will put you a lot closer. Unfortunately, it is not the way most new investors select a General Partner, but it is definitely the way I would approach this most important decision.

I have tested this evaluation program on a cross-section of General Partners, and it is surprisingly effective in accurately assessing their desirability as judged by peers who know their operations intimately.

Carrying out the five steps detailed below entails a significant effort, so if you have a number of candidates, it would make sense first to screen all of them with obvious, commonsense observations that might eliminate some prospects immediately. Then apply full consideration only to the most likely candidates. The securities salesman or broker with whom you will probably be working can and should be of great assistance in making your evaluation. Hopefully you will have good rapport and a lot of basic trust in this representative, and if so, you can rely on him for much of the information you will want.

To finalize your five-step evaluation, I will provide a simple scorecard that will help you assign an overall "Desirability Rating" to each General Partner under serious consideration. The purpose is to take as much guesswork and emotion out of the decision-making process as possible.

Here are the five steps to evaluation of local private limited-partnership organizations.

1. Meet Key People in the General Partner's Organization. Early in your assessment you will certainly want to meet several of the key people involved in the operation. This is probably the best opportunity for your first screening.

As to specific questions and areas of interest, simply prepare yourself from the subjects covered in the Desirability Rating later in this chapter. A great deal of important information can be picked up through casual conversation.

Even more important, this first meeting will allow you to react to the style and attitudes of the people involved. While this kind of subjective reaction may not be very scientific, I do think it is valuable. No matter how positive the background and accomplishments of a General Partner, I would not want to invest my money unless a gut-level feeling of trust, security, and comfort also existed. Obviously, my final decision would be made on facts, but I would reserve the right to screen out individuals about whom I did not feel good.

2. Review Materials Presented. I assume you will be talking to each General Partner–Syndicator about a specific, currently available limited partnership, for which a prospectus will be made available to you. If you should want to check out a General Partner who has no immediate product for sale, simply ask to borrow a prospectus for a partnership previously offered so you can judge this important aspect of the business.

Read all materials carefully and completely, and rate their adequacy based on the criteria below. If necessary, get assistance from a qualified advisor. Much more detailed information concerning documentation is provided in Chapter 12.

- Is the presentation clearly written and professionally presented? This is a good indication of the overall business approach and attitude likely to be followed by the General Partner throughout your investment relationship.
- Is the offering registered or exempted with the state securities bureau as required by the laws of your state? (Check your securities bureau as to its requirements.)
- If it's a "specified asset" offering, do the materials clearly and specifically describe the property involved? If it's a "blind pool" (unspecified offering), are the objectives of the partnership clearly identified?
- Are the purchase conditions and the price spelled out and is the use of the money to be raised from investors explained in detail?
- Are economic risks to investors explained? In particular, are explanations given for areas of financial assumptions that could be wrong?
- Are conflicts of interest presented?
- Are the General Partner's fees described in precise terms?

3. Talk to Existing Investors. If you don't know any of the General Partner's investors, ask for the names of a few who live in your area, or who work in your field, or otherwise might be accessible to you. Of course, the names of investors is private information, and a proper General Partner will not give any to you until he has the permission of the individuals. But that permission can be secured, and often will be by the General Partner as a matter of pride.

Contact these investors and discuss their feelings about the General Partner. Ask how previous investments have worked out. Find out if they plan to do business with this syndicator again.

Investors are probably your single best source of information. They will tend to be frank with you and, if anything, will lean toward the negative if there is anything they have been at all unhappy about. After all, investors get nothing out of promoting their General Partner, and they will emotionally relate with a fellow investor. If the General Partner under consideration can stand the test of current investors, you have reason to feel a high degree of comfort.

4. Visit Existing Properties. Another important step in evaluating the real ability and experience of General Partners is to visit some of the properties they currently own and operate (if you have not already done this as a means to locating a General Partner). In a sense, what happens at the properties is the real bottom line of limited-partnership operation, and you have to see it and feel it to pass judgment. Frankly, you don't have to be an expert to form a valid opinion. Just look at the operation from the point of view of a prospective tenant and you'll form some important judgments.

Consider these points:

· Does the property appear neat and well cared for?
· What is the exterior physical condition? Check for cracked paint, broken windows, downspouts askew, broken sidewalks, etc.
· Step into a hallway if possible. Are carpets threadbare or are they in good condition? Are halls clean? Is interior paint in good condition?
· Talk to at least one employee—management, rental, or maintenance. Ask some questions that will allow you to judge morale and attitude.

The obvious impression will quickly tell you a lot about an organization. Remember that the real value of a property is often made or broken at the property, not at the home office.

5. Check with the State Securities Bureau. Your state securities bureau may not know all of the good guys in the business, but they certainly will be able to tell you if you're dealing with a rotten apple. Specifically check with your securities bureau to determine if the General Partner has had any major violations, legal problems, or investor complaints.

It is important to understand that most General Partners who have been active in syndications for a length of time will have had an occasional technical infraction. These can probably be forgiven if they were rectified. The key to look for is have the General Partners violated any security regulation in a manner that was unfair or injurious to their investors.

THE DESIRABILITY RATING FOR
PROSPECTIVE GENERAL PARTNERS

On the next pages you will find a form that will assist you in establishing a Desirability Rating for each General Partner you may consider. It is designed to integrate the facts you gather with your subjective judgments, and to weigh the various elements to arrive at a realistic balance of the qualities required for General Partner success.

To help you use this rating form, I have given guidelines below, defining the nature of the areas being evaluated and suggesting some techniques you may find helpful in gathering the required information.

Guidelines for Using the Desirability-Rating Form.

Honesty and Integrity. This is the one area in which you cannot afford to be partially satisfied. If there is any reason to doubt the honesty of the individual or organization you are considering, I strongly suggest you look elsewhere.

The best way I know to evaluate honesty and integrity is through reputation. Look for positive reputation as well as the absence of negative reputation. The previously discussed five-step evaluation should provide ample information for a judgment as to honesty and integrity.

General Partner Type and Time Allocation. These criteria were fully discussed in Chapter 9, and at this point our purpose is merely to include them in the overall evaluation with proper weight.

Obviously, the success of any one real estate limited partnership will not need the undivided attention or the knowledge gained by many years of experience, day after day. The important point is that there may well be times during an investment project when only a great deal of experience and limitless energy can stop a problem from turning into a disaster. This is the reason the rating system is heavily biased in favor of a professional, experienced, constantly available General Partner.

It may seem unfair to give no points at all in the rating chart for "other" business experience, unrelated to real estate. Certainly it is true that challenging management experience of any kind should have some carryover value. However, my observations indicate that the real estate limited-partnership business benefits very little from general experience, and truly requires on-the-job experience. In some cases you may be justified in awarding points for outstanding experience and results in other fields, but I would limit this to one half point per year, with an absolute maximum of three points.

The information you need for this area of evaluation can be elicited through conversation with the prospective General Partner or his associates.

Knowledge of Limited Partnerships and Real Estate; Dedication to Success of Limited Partnership. Of necessity you will have to make somewhat subjective judgments in these areas. Of course, the years of experience of the General Partner, and the results achieved, will give some indications. The best way to develop accurate feelings will be to indulge in conversation, ask broad questions that invite anecdotal answers, and listen very carefully. Again, get opinions from active investors who have lived through some deals with the General Partners in question.

Investment Results. Only past performance can really be meaningful in evaluating a General Partner's track record. Current projections are interesting, but they cannot be depended upon. Evaluation of past performance is an art in itself, for there are sever-

General Partner Desirability Rating

DATE: _____

NAME OF SPONSOR ORGANIZATION: _____

NAME OF MANAGING GENERAL PARTNER: _____

Areas of Evaluation	Scoring Guide		Points Awarded
Honesty and integrity	• Superior reputation • Nothing negative • Any indication of dishonesty	15 points 5 points no points	DO NOT PROCEED IF LESS THAN 5 POINTS AWARDED
General Partner type and time allocation	• Professional General Partner devoting full time to one or more limited partnerships and directly affiliated business • Professional General Partner with major concentration on limited partnerships, but some time devoted to nonaffiliated businesses • Nonprofessional part-time General Partner with limited partner-ship activity definitely secondary to other business	10 points 5 to 8 points no points	
Knowledge of limited partner-ships and real estate	Subjective evaluation	1 to 10 points	
Dedication to success of limited partnership	Subjective evaluation	1 to 10 points	

Areas of Evaluation	Scoring Guide	Points Awarded
Years of experience	For each year of experience as: · General Partner of real estate limited partnerships 2 points · Partner experience in real estate limited-partnership operation 1 point · Real estate experience in other than limited-partnership operation ½ point · For other business experience no points	(MAXIMUM 15 POINTS MAY BE AWARDED)
Investment results	After-tax return on investment per year, calculated for investor in 50% tax bracket · 25% or more 20 points · 20% to 24% 18 points · 18% to 19% 15 points · 15% to 17% 12 points · 12% to 14% 6 points · 10% to 11% 2 points · Less than 10% no points · No record established no points (This item may require estimation)	
Accuracy of projected investment result to actual achievement	· Within 10% 10 points · Within 15% 6 points · Within 20% 2 points · Less than 20% no points (This item may require estimation)	
General Partner action in troubled projects	· Has loaned money to partnerships or guaranteed loans 10 points · Has become personally involved in nonfinancial action to solve problems 5 points · Has resigned as GP or turned problem over to limited partners. Score depends on your analysis of circumstances 0 to −20 points	

Areas of Evaluation	Scoring Guide	Points Awarded
Plans for business continuity	Complete and highly protective <div align="right">10 points</div> · Arrangements in force but not fully assuring to investor 1 to 8 points · No arrangements no points	
Investor communication program	· Regular reporting quarterly plus special occasion—clear and complete 10 points · Regular reporting, but less than desirable quality 1 to 8 points · Fewer than four reports a year no points	

TOTAL

GUIDE TO DESIRABILITY RATINGS

Over 100	Outstanding. Highly desirable
90 to 99	Excellent. Above average
75 to 89	Satisfactory, if specific deal is particularly attractive
65 to 74	Marginal. Might try small investment if attitudes are exceptional
Under 65	Keep looking elsewhere

al factors that interrelate to provide the overall economic benefit received by the investors. If you are considering a sizable investment and are not an expert at analyzing financial reports, seek assistance from your accountant or some other financial professional.

Probably the single most revealing figure after a property has been purchased, operated, and resold is the annual after-tax return on investment. Since there are several methods that may be used to compute this important figure, it is essential that you have some understanding of this area before attempting an evaluation. This is provided for you in Chapter 11.

Private limited partnerships have a peculiar situation in terms of offering this kind of information to prospective investors. Under Guide 60 of SEC regulations, if they offer to supply past results as part of a sales prospectus, they must supply them for all partnerships the company has been involved in since its inception. Moreover, they must continue to supply this information to all prospects for all future partnerships, and it must be done in a special format that is difficult and expensive to keep up. While this regulation has understandable aims, it can also create an inordinate cost for a General Partner. As a result, most choose not to show results as a part of their sales presentation.

Properly approached, nearly all General Partners will be happy to comply with reasonable requests to discuss past performance, consistent with the limitations of Guide 60. I would suggest that the most meaningful information will have to do with properties resold in the last several years. You might ask to see the communications regarding partnerships of this vintage, and thus see the results in which you are interested. Another approach is to ask if you can contact some of the investors involved in recently concluded partnerships.

To be sure you get the bad news with the good, you should specifically ask if any properties have become bankrupt or have been sold for less than their purchase price. If so, ask about the circumstances and the financial effect on the investors.

The question of how a General Partner handles major problems is extremely important. If you show me a General Partner who says he has never had bad times during the ownership of a property, I'll show you a novice or an individual with a very bad memory. Real estate is a business made up of problems, and the key to living with them successfully is the General Partner. The best ones are perfectly willing to discuss what they do during times of high vacancy or unexpected maintenance expense, because in fact they know what to do and how to do it. That is one reason I suggest you award extra points on the desirability rating for General Partners who have in the past loaned money to troubled partnerships or personally guaranteed loans to them. This can be an essential and extremely valuable service from time to time. In our own case, we have done it whenever it was necessary, and in several situations it has saved the investors from potentially serious loss.

As an example, I can recall the problems we originally had with Sunset Manor, an apartment property that we bought in 1977 for $14,837,000. The property was a "turnaround" investment. Occupancy had been in the area of 80 percent at its high point and was about 79 percent when we took over. The physical condition of the project was extremely bad. We bought the property from the second-mortgage lender and structured a deal that gave us extremely favorable terms. On the other hand, the difficulties of the project were such that one local banker told me that he would eat his hat if it succeeded. Others involved in the various complexities of the financing of this development told me that we had finally met our Waterloo. I must admit that I personally was a little scared, but we persevered and acquired the property.

Since the project was in bad physical repair, one of the major things we were going to do to improve its value was fix it up. That's simple enough and makes logical sense, but it's easier said than done. In managing the turnaround of a project that needs physical rehabilitation as much as Sunset Manor did, one must estimate the cost of various items that are extremely hard to determine. It is always easier to determine the cost of new construction than of the rehabilitation of an existing project. That was the position we were in at Sunset Manor, so we had to take our best shot. Frankly, we blew it.

We estimated everything we could see and provided for a large contingency reserve. We proved way off on our calculations. When we raised the limited-partner investment money, we based our numbers on construction estimates we believed to be accurate. Unfortunately, the budget, which originally was $725,000, turned out to be more like $1,200,000. Items that contributed to the overruns, for example, were the entire roof structure of the indoor pool, which we found was rotting and needed repair of structural items that were far more extensive than we originally anticipated. We also found many structural problems with the steps leading up to a number of the buildings. All in all, we began to realize that we had two choices: either cut short the work that we had in hand and not really finish everything to A-1 condition, or somehow find other funds to finish the work. This is the kind of tension and pressure that General Partners go through from time to time. It also represents the contingency that drives many General Partners to write a long letter to the limited partners stating "Dear Investor: We need more money."

Having a lot of pride, and being of the belief that the limited partners' original investment should be their only investment, we determined the extra money we needed and loaned it in to the project ourselves. Part of it was loaned directly and part of it was obtained from our lines of credit at the corporation's banks with my personal guarantees.

We are not the only sponsor to have done this. There are a number of General Partners in the business who put their reputation and image above all else in business dealings. Fortunately, in our case and again in the case of a number of highly qualified professionals, because of the relative profitability of the business, we are able to back up our deals and go beyond what the legal agreements state.

In the case of Sunset Manor, the investors received 19 percent greater tax loss during the period that the money was spent for various deferred-maintenance items. The overruns did end up deferring cash flow from the originally scheduled time period in order to pay back the loan, but ironically, in this particular deal, the extra amount of investment through our loaning the money into the project resulted in the investors' getting in excess of a $2 writeoff for every $1 they invested. In other words, any individual in the 50 percent tax bracket or higher actually had no money in the deal during the term of the investment. Furthermore, the money that we had put in greatly enhanced the project and turned it around economically. We were careful to explain to the investors in detail, both at partnership meetings and in written correspondence, what the problems were and how we decided to deal with them. It is that kind of communication and explanation, as well as that kind of commitment, that has helped us in being able to develop and maintain good long-term relations with a number of investors, from that partnership and others.

Again, as I have previously stated, I think there are a number of good General Partners who, if you look into their past history, have done similar things which were totally above and beyond the call of the legal agreements of the investment. To a great extent what you are investing in is people. If you check into past performance by talking to other investors, you will get to know the people in whom you are investing.

Arrangements for Business Continuity. I have previously mentioned the importance of planned continuity in the event of a General Partner's death or incapacity. Let me reinforce this by pointing out that unless proper safeguards are taken, the disability of the General Partner can force the termination or dissolution of the partnership. Partnership assets may be forced to be sold in spite of bad timing and negative consequences for the limited partners.

When judging the ability of a general partnership to survive the death of a key individual, I suggest that you review the points made in Chapter 9.

Investor-Communications Program. This area was also discussed in some detail in Chapter 9, which again provides ample criteria for your consideration.

It has always been surprising to me that some General Partners do not provide investors with even minimum ongoing information and communication other than Schedule K-1, the tax-information return. It seems grossly improper to take investors' money and then simply ignore them, yet this does happen. Investor communication varies broadly, so it is well worth your effort to check it out through discussion and inspection of examples of what a General Partner has actually sent out. Not only will this affect your comfort with the investment, but I suggest it as good indication of the General Partner's dedication and basic attitude toward investors.

CONTINUING YOUR VIGILANCE AFTER
YOU ENTER A LIMITED PARTNERSHIP

If you do a good job of selecting a General Partner, chances are your investment will be properly handled. Certainly there may be problems as in any business, but with the right General Partner you will know about them, and you will find that appropriate efforts will be taken in your behalf.

This does not mean you can simply ignore what is going on. An intelligent investor will carefully read and analyze all communications from the General Partner and be alert to any important deviations from the projected progress of the investment. If things are not working out as anticipated, it is perfectly in order for the investor to contact the General Partner or a representative and ask questions about problems and any efforts being made to resolve them. If you are satisfied with the response, express your support and keep in touch.

There are some danger signs that should get more aggressive attention from investors. These include:

· Difficulty in contacting the General Partner
· Complete lack of responsiveness to questions
· Sudden lack of financial statements and other established communications
· Announcement from the General Partner that you must invest further funds to protect the project, even though such additional investment is not required by the partnership agreement.

These are indications that you may not have selected your General Partner wisely, and your investment may be in jeopardy. It is time for prompt action to determine the facts and then act to protect yourself.

WHAT TO DO IF YOU FEEL THE GENERAL
PARTNER IS NOT SERVING YOU PROPERLY

The first thing to do is to contact your state's securities bureau, and, if it's a nationally registered partnership, the SEC. Find out if there have been other queries or complaints, and get advice. Secondly, contact your attorney for advice and guidance.

If it becomes evident that the General Partner is failing to carry out his fiduciary responsibilities, be prepared to band together with other limited partners in order to exercise your legal and, where they apply, "democratic" rights. "Democratic" rights are provisions in the partnership agreement that establish limited partner votes of approval on certain of the General Partner's decisions such as selling the project. Depending on the circumstances, it may be possible to remove and replace the General Partner.

While this would be a rare situation, I mention it here to underscore, again, the importance of proper selection in the first place, and to point out that if a mistake is made it should be faced and resolved as soon as it becomes apparent.

Part Four

SELECTING SPECIFIC INVESTMENTS

CHAPTER 11

Evaluating the Deal

THERE comes a time when an absolute decision must be made. You are done with conceptual or philosophical thinking, and now it is time to decide, "Will I put my hard-earned cash into this particular deal?"

In evaluating a specific deal, there are four primary considerations: the risks involved, the kind of property, the anticipated return on investment, and the fees to be paid to the General Partner. This chapter will provide criteria for each of these considerations, while the next chapter deals with how to examine the legal documentation to be sure the terms of the deal give you the rights, conditions, and protection you anticipate.

To go back to a familiar theme for just a moment, before you examine any deal be sure you first examine the General Partner–Syndicator. The specific deal can only be as good as the organization behind it. Therefore, if you are considering a public limited partnership, check the organization's track record and experience. If you are considering a private limited partnership, study the General Partner organization as detailed in Chapter 10 and assure yourself that the people involved are experienced, honest, and capable in all respects. If you are truly comfortable with the operational side of the partnership, your selection of a specific deal will be much easier.

CONSIDERATION OF RISKS

Specific risks relating to the property itself and all other risks of the transaction should be included in the "Risk Factors" section of the offering document, usually near its beginning. Start by reviewing and evaluating this material.

The following is a guide to consideration of specific risk elements connected with any particular investment. Your purpose in reviewing these items should not be to expect absolute perfection, but rather to compare and eliminate those deals that seem to fly in the face of risks that are absent or moderated in other offers.

Staying Power and Reserves. Being properly capitalized with reserves for contingencies beyond original plans is a key to staying power. As a minimum, 5 percent of the amount of the syndication should be set aside for unforeseen problems. If the property has potential physical problems or if it is in an area of rent volatility, the reserve should be larger. The investor should be convinced that the financial structure and the strength of the General Partner will provide more than enough staying power to cover all potential needs.

Physical Problems of the Property. The need for major repairs and replacements creates a risk only if it is not anticipated through reserves or in maintenance budgets established in the offering document. When used property is involved, be sure a detailed physical inspection has been made by qualified people, and that the findings are reflected in the financial structure.

Local Economic Conditions. Changing local economic conditions can add to the investment's risk or reward. If an area is suffering specific problems—such as Seattle did when Boeing was in trouble, or Michigan during the automobile sales crunch—an investment in those areas must be viable with *less than* normal occupancy. If the operation costs and debt service are in tune with the anticipated economic problems of the area, there is probably no special risk. If the projects are out of tune with reality, risk can be excessive. Buying in an economy that is suffering can produce very favorable investment bargains.

Location Desirability. Is the location stable, is it becoming more desirable, or is it slipping? The nature of the location can add to the value or create serious risk. This is a particularly important factor in considering inner-city property, which may have seemingly attractive prices but can be extremely risky because of a possible downward trend in the desirability of the location.

Additional Competition. This possibility is usually covered in the prospectus by pointing out the availability of suitably zoned vacant land nearby. It is most important when the investment involves new construction and there is a consideration of how much property can be supported in the area. If, on the other hand, the investment is an existing property, the risk is less because any new construction will have inflated costs and, therefore, will require higher rents for similar accommodations.

Litigation. If any litigation is pending against either the property or the partnership, it should be disclosed in the prospectus. If none is noted, ask your securities representative or the General Partner just to be sure. If litigation is pending, get as much detail as you can to make an assessment of that potential risk to your investment. Consider the effect on the investment if the matter is decided against your interest, and act accordingly.

Some economic and tax elements should be reviewed as part of the risk evaluation of every potential investment. These include the following.

Tax Law Changes and Tax Audit. Tax law changes have generally not been retroactive and, therefore, should be a relatively minor risk. Any pending legislation that might affect the investment should be spelled out in the prospectus and should be carefully reviewed with your tax advisor, for both future and possibly retroactive consequences.

There is always some risk of having tax losses reversed through IRS audit, and this should be reviewed by your accountant or tax attorney. If the tax-loss projections are based on normal practices broadly accepted by the IRS, there is little risk. If the projected tax loss is unusually large or is based on an exotic or unique idea, the risk should be considered with great caution.

Most audits that dramatically reverse tax losses deal with exotic ideas dreamed up by overambitious sponsors. It is amazing how often these deals simply ignore clear-cut tax regulations. A review by a qualified tax advisor will almost always steer the investor away from these bad risks.

Economic Depression. In evaluating risks, it is important to keep in mind that a major *deflationary* depression such as that of the 1930s would be extremely negative for real estate investment. This is a remote possibility, but nevertheless it should be considered. If you become convinced that a deflationary depression is going to occur, you should not invest in real estate.

On the other hand, periodic recessions or an *inflationary* depression may have temporary adverse effects on real estate but in the longer run will result in increases in value. In the final analysis the inflation that causes the temporary economic problems will eventually force the value of the property higher, and the investor will profit.

Government Intervention. There are three forms of potential government interference with free-market action in real estate investment: rent controls, prohibition of condominium conversion, and increased public-housing programs. At the moment none of these is a major risk on a national level, but the degree of any such potential problem should be constantly reviewed.

Rent control risks are discussed in detail in Chapter 15.

Prohibition of condominium conversion is a new and current threat. If it indeed materializes, it will curtail a large market for highly profitable sales of residential investment properties. Right now there is pressure and a lot of public discussion concerning condominium-conversion legislation. I do not anticipate any effective legislated prohibition being enacted, but the risk should be reviewed if this type of investment is being considered.

Public-housing programs were very active in the early seventies, and created some difficulty for investors because low-interest government loans were made for directly competitive housing in middle- and even high-rent developments. The trend now is to encourage housing development through private investment, and during the Reagan administration, public housing should not be an important risk factor.

The potential downside of the investment, with any or all of these risk factors considered, should be more important to you than the potential upside. Worry about how safe a deal is rather than let greed carry you into high-risk situations. Good, sound investing is usually rewarded with solid profits, whereas speculation has far more losers than winners. Study and understand the risks. If they seem minimal to reasonable, go forward.

Should You Visit the Property? In analyzing the risk factors you may wonder how important it is to inspect the property personally. If you have satisfied yourself about the reliability and expertise of the General Partner, I would say it is perfectly reasonable to trust his presentation of the facts of the property. Your risk review can then concentrate on questions of reserves and projections established by the General Partner on the basis of those facts.

The reason I say this is that the proper physical analysis of a property and its location requires considerable skill and experience. If the General Partner has achieved a record of success and honesty, I consider that to be a good demonstration that the skill and knowledge required of property evaluation have been exercised. Obviously you should raise questions and expect completely satisfying explanations, but a personal inspection is generally not necessary. If you do not feel comfortable about the General Partner's knowledge concerning the property, I would suggest a review of your decision to do business with that General Partner.

Still, despite such reasoning, you may on occasion want to inspect the property personally. The best approach is to put yourself in the position of a prospective tenant. Go through the normal process of telephoning for information, then visiting the rental office and taking whatever tour or showing is offered.

Judge the viability of the property by what you see as well as by what you are told. Assuming you are in the market serviced by the property, do you find it attractive? Are you pleased by the presentation? Are your questions or doubts well answered? This commonsense approach will allow you to make a valid analysis, one that may raise questions worthy of further discussion with a representative of the General Partner. And there is a special circumstance: if the property is to be a "turnaround" investment, one for which major improvements are planned, you will be looking at the "before" version, and the General Partner should then provide information about the final product. As a service to the reader who is interested in a detailed understanding of the kind of property analysis that should be made by the General Partner, Appendix 5 is a basic checklist that will aid you in this kind of investigation.

TYPES OF REAL ESTATE

Up to this point, we have not differentiated among the various kinds of properties available for investment. Most of our examples have dealt with apartment projects, simply because those are the type with which I am most familiar and they represent an extremely large segment of the market. The general strengths and liabilities of limited-partnership investment can apply to all kinds of real estate, but of course there are inherent differences among different types of property, and these should be considered.

I will present here an overview of the pluses and minuses as they exist today. It is important to understand, however, that the factors regarding each kind of property will vary over time with changing market conditions and economic factors. It is not wise to invest solely and invariably in one kind of real estate. Review your position from time to time, particularly in terms of the implications of tax law and the economics of the marketplace.

Commercial Real Estate. Commercial properties include shopping centers and other retail storefronts. The location may be downtown, in a neighborhood, or at the edge of town. In size, a commercial property may range from a small free-standing store to a strip center to a large mall.

Commercial property offers many advantages. First of all, there is little likelihood of adverse political actions. Rent control, condominium-conversion control, and similar actions are much less likely to affect commercial property than residential.

Another major plus for commercial property is that it requires relatively low management effort. There is less turnover than in residential, therefore less repeat rental effort. There are far fewer tenants, therefore far less contact, and fewer complaints and requests to handle.

In an economically strong area where retailers are doing well and commercial space is in good demand, commercial leases often have added value in that the landlord may be able to negotiate percentage rents. In addition to a base rental rate, there will be an additional rent or "kicker" due if the tenant exceeds certain levels of expectation in the operation of the business. These levels are often tied to gross income; therefore, as inflation moves retail prices up, the landlord will receive additional income.

A good friend of mine who is a commercial owner takes the position that being a commercial landlord is like being a partner in many different retail businesses, without the headaches. The best part of the arrangement is that he gets his share of the partnership off the top, while the retailer works long hours to produce a bottom line that will leave some profit dollars for himself. This is an interesting viewpoint in favor of commercial real estate investment.

On the negative side, commercial real estate has a tendency to be a feast-or-famine proposition. If vacancies occur when the market is soft, it is far more difficult to find commercial tenants than to compete in the more broadly based residential market. Even one or two vacancies in a commercial property may represent a significant percentage of the total income. They can quickly throw the project into a negative cash-flow situation.

While I painted a happy financial picture when discussing percentage leases, it is important to realize that all leases are not of this type. Many properties have long-term leases locked into the low rental rates that prevailed some years ago, and there is no way they can be changed. This can create a very difficult situation when trying to buy an existing shopping center. Physically, that center may be worth much more money than can be warranted by income based on the length of leases established at rental rates below the current market.

The value of tenant leaseholds can be substantial. The difference between the current market value and what the tenant is paying is, in a sense, value owned by the tenant rather than the landlord. While percentage kicker leases do try to anticipate inflation, they are not always sufficient. When long-term leases get out of balance with the economy, inflation becomes the enemy of commercial-property value, instead of the factor that adds value.

When buying a commercial property, value must be determined based on existing leases. These must be anlayzed in great detail and with the utmost caution. The investor in existing commercial property is, of course, bound by the existing leases, so these are as much a part of the purchase as property bricks and mortar.

Another, more subtle potential problem is the question of what happens when your tenants cannot pay their rent. When the economy goes sour as a result of both inflation and recession, many retailers are squeezed tremendously. If your tenant cannot afford to pay you, it does not matter how good your lease is—you have problems.

If we were to analyze the bottom-line profits of many retailers today, we would find that a high percentage of their profit is derived from paying rents below current market value. What happens, then, when the lease held by this type of tenant expires and the landlord wants to raise the rents? The retailer, particularly one who has a marginal operation, may simply be unable to pay the higher rate and, in a slow economy, the landlord may be faced with a very unhappy choice: continue to accept insufficient rent, or create a vacancy.

As with all real estate, the value of commercial property is heavily affected by location. In some locations, commercial property value will be held down because retail operations cannot afford the true physical value of the property. In other areas, retail business will be strong and demand for stores high, so merchants will pay much higher rates than the innate property value would suggest.

The major disadvantage to buying existing commercial property in a prime location at this time is that the entire investment community assumes it is going to have ever-increasing rental rates with corresponding increases in property value. Like a good growth stock, good commercial real estate has had a lot of its future value discounted out by high current value. In short, good commercial real estate is very difficult to buy at this time.

Markets, after all, are made by buyers and sellers. At this time, institutional and foreign investors are bidding up the commercial real estate market because they feel it offers dependable growth with extremely little management. They would rather overpay for a piece of commercial real estate than buy another kind of property requiring more management and, in their view, carrying more risk.

As a result, commercial properties are generally purchased today for eventual economic return rather than tax shelter, and they offer very low current returns. Investors will accept 4 to 7 percent cash on cash returns on decent commercial property because their profit objectives are focused on major future value increases. They are making purchases with extremely large amounts of cash down and fairly limited amounts of leverage. These factors add to the difficulty of buying commercial real estate. It is currently an extremely competitive segment of the market.

To sum up, it is impossible to say that commercial real estate is generally either a desirable or undesirable investment. Because it is heavily discounted as to future value by large, cash-rich investors, it must be selected with great prudence. Properly acquired commercial real estate in good locations should have a very strong future; in marginal locations it can be fraught with problems, even though it may appear sound and promising at the time of purchase.

Office Space. There are many advantages to investing in office space, and generally they parallel the advantages of commercial property. There is, for example, little likelihood of adverse legislation. While the management requirements are somewhat more intensive than in commercial property, they are far less so than in residential. Office tenants are usually sound financially and pay promptly.

A strong market for office space offers good price elasticity. Generally speaking, office space has always been cheap, and even today it represents a relatively small part of most company budgets. Since companies pride themselves on the appearance, comfort, and convenience of their physical location, more and more we are finding corporations willing to pay well for first-class office space.

On the minus side, an investment in office space can be a disaster in a weak market. Rental rates are usually established on the premise that the tenant will pay all or at least a substantial portion of the cost of redecoration. In markets that become weak or marginal, the landlord frequently ends up having to pay for redecoration to entice tenants, and the costs can be astronomical. When a tenant moves out after expiration of a three- to five-year lease, the cost of moving walls and of painting and recarpeting for a new tenant can eat up all the cash-flow profit from the previous lease, and then some.

Again, as in commercial property, good office locations have had a lot of their future value discounted by high current prices. Still, if properly acquired, office space can be a very advantageous investment. The key is to be extremely cautious in selecting the market and location and to buy the right space on the right terms.

Industrial Properties. Real estate built for use in manufacturing, warehousing, or other industrial use tends to offer a very high return compared to the cost of construction. Such investments often provide a generous and dependable income stream, since the tenants are usually strong financially, and they are willing to pay high rent for the right property because they will use it to produce income. Another major advantage is that industrial property probably takes the least management of any kind of real estate.

While the rent usually starts out as a handsome return on the construction cost, it is fixed and usually extends over an extremely long lease period. Traditionally, industrial leases have relieved the landlord of all variable costs such as taxes and maintenance. But then the rental rate rarely has any inflationary kicker. Thus, with continued inflation, the economic value of the building can be reduced by the decreasing value of the fixed income.

Since most industrial real estate is leased to a single tenant, there is always the overhanging possibility of the loss of the tenant through bankruptcy. This does not happen often with a properly selected tenant, but when it does it can be extremely costly, since it usually takes a long time to find a suitable replacement—and meanwhile the debt service and other costs continue. Above all else, industrial real estate is a highly specialized type of investment. Leasing should be approached only with General Partners who have knowledge and experience in this area. It is a true feast-or-famine business.

To sum up, the advisability of investing in industrial property depends, to a large degree, on the objectives of the investor. It has low management requirements and, generally, low risk, assuming the proper tenant has been selected and a strong lease negotiated. Industrial real estate lacks some of the immediate inflation hedge of other types, but this may well be balanced by a much stronger current return on investment.

Apartment Complexes. As a part of our total housing system, apartments are a basic necessity. The present economics of housing indicate that in the foreseeable future demand for apartments will be strong, and the value of existing properties should increase markedly.

In comparison to other types of investment real estate, the apartment market is the broadest and most competitive. This is an advantage during periods of difficulty, as there will still be residents to be found. So there is always the opportunity to compete and to win. This may not be true in the more limited types of real estate, which tend to produce either feast or famine for owners.

Another positive factor for apartment investment is the fact that most "big money" is not interested in apartment investment because of the need for intense management. Foreign and institutional investors who tend to pay very high prices for real estate and, thus, discount future values, simply do not want the management involvement of apartments. Because they tend to stay out of this market, groups of smaller investors are provided a competitive edge they do not have in the commercial or office-space fields.

In theory, the fact that age demographics show our population in the next five years moving away from traditional apartment dwellers and becoming heavier among the traditional home-ownership group should be a negative influence. However, as I detail in Chapter 15, I believe the economics of home ownership will effectively change the marketplace and force hundreds of thousands of would-be homeowners to continue to be apartment renters, at least throughout the 1980s. Unless some unforeseen new economic developments occur, this may become a permanent aspect of our housing situation.

The fact that many residents will be at an age when they would rather own than rent will fuel a continued strong demand for condominiums. This will result in an extremely favorable market for the sale of apartment properties to condominium converters at prices higher than their value as rental real estate.

There are, of course, some realistic negatives to the selection of apartments as an investment vehicle. The fact that apartments are the most management-intensive of all types of real estate cannot be dismissed lightly. Most investors must rely on a management organization, which may or may not measure up to the complexities of the task. This adds a serious need to select limited-partnership sponsors who have proven management organizations.

Land. Land investments vary significantly in terms of risks and rewards. Land, of course, cannot be depreciated, and it possesses few other tax advantages. Most land is leased for temporary purposes—e.g., as a farming field or as a parking lot—and will make only enough money to defray some of the holding costs. Land usually has a significant negative cash flow. You are paying taxes, insurance, and payments on debt, or if the land is free and clear, you have tied up money that could be used elsewhere. And with rapid changes in interest rates and with construction prices at such high levels, development of unimproved property by builders has lately been slow. In other words, you could end up sitting on a negative cash flow with only minor tax benefits for a lot longer than you might have expected. Even then the value has to increase in excess of 20 percent per year on the average for you to come out with true profit, considering your costs of carrying the property.

On the positive side, some land increases in value quite substantially over short periods of time. Investing in unique pieces of property that are being bought a year or two prior to major development in their area can be very profitable. In Chapter 4, for example, we talked about a partnership put together to buy land on an island off the west coast of Florida. The land was sold for a sizable profit in a little over a year. It was a situation of buying when development was slow, but when things picked up the land proved one of the few choice sites available. To be a successful investment, land must be a unique site in an area of few alternatives—e.g., land by the interchange of a new expressway, prime downtown land, and so on. The key is to buy first before everyone else wants it for development.

I view land as a potentially profitable but highly risky situation. The key ingredients to finding the right site occur only every so often. Accordingly, be very cautious about investing in land.

Special-Purpose Buildings. As a final category of real estate investment there are numerous kinds of special-purpose buildings, including those for athletic and recreational facilities, restaurants, and other uses. These are usually leased net to qualified tenants and, because the buildings are unique, they will frequently earn premium rents. The cash flow can be extremely attractive and will often include percentage rent arrangements to protect the landlord against inflation.

On the negative side, these kinds of property are a classic feast-or-famine proposition. As long as the tenant is financially healthy everything is fine, but the landlord often does not realize he is literally gambling on that health. If the tenant falls into financial trouble, the landlord probably will sustain a massive loss while trying to find a tenant with the same specialized needs.

Since the tenants of specialized buildings are frequently independent entrepreneurs, their financial health is not guaranteed by the assets of a huge corporation, as is often the case with industrial properties. By its nature, I consider this kind of real estate suitable only for investors who are willing to take major speculative risks. However, if the company on the lease is financially strong, the investment can be viewed less speculatively.

HOW IMPORTANT IS IT TO SELECT
THE RIGHT KIND OF PROPERTY?

There are no absolutes in terms of selecting the right type of real estate for investment. You cannot say that one kind is good, and another necessarily bad. As a matter of fact, there is some logic to including several types of real estate in a portfolio of investments. Based on the brief guidelines provided in the preceding discussion, as well as personal inclinations, you may decide to lean toward one or another type of property. That makes sense, but I do not suggest a position that limits you to just one kind of real estate.

Much more important than the type of real estate *per se* is the nature of the acquisition and the suitability of the sponsor involved. As I have pointed out before, the most important element in assuring success is your General Partner, and that applies for passive investment in any type of real estate. If the General Partner has the ability to acquire property under favorable terms, and the experience to know when to buy and when to hold off, almost any kind of property is potentially a successful investment.

WHAT RETURN ON INVESTMENT IS REASONABLE TO EXPECT FROM A REAL ESTATE LIMITED PARTNERSHIP?

This is the question we are asked most often. Certainly it is an appropriate question. Return on investment is the real reason for anyone to invest in anything, so you should want to know what to anticipate.

Most people expect me to respond to their questions about return with a specific, exciting, high percentage which they can hang on to as a magic number that assures them they are wise to make this kind of investment. Unfortunately, it is not quite that easy. Later in this chapter I will provide a minimum percentage return to anticipate, but in fairness we first have to come to grips with just what "return on investment" means in real estate, and we need to consider as well how to put projected returns into perspective so they can be compared with others.

FACTORS TO CONSIDER IN COMPARING RETURNS ON INVESTMENT

Your objective in any real estate investment should be to receive your money back and a return or profit on your money. Further, your objective should include a high degree of safety or security while your money is at risk. Potential return cannot be considered in a vacuum. You have to view it as one of a combination of factors. How good does the return look over time? How fast will your investment dollars be returned? How realistic are the assumptions involved in projecting the return? How serious are the inherent risk factors?

It is important to recognize that the financial objectives of real estate investment are usually achieved through a combination of tax savings, cash distributions, and proceeds from the sale of the property. Considering all of these economic benefits, you can calculate a single return-on-investment figure, but it is much more complicated than understanding something like the interest you get on money in a bank account.

For real estate return on investment to be meaningful, it must be analyzed in terms of *after-tax* results. After all, just as tax consequences are especially valuable to real estate investors, they also play an important but usually negative role in any investor's ultimate results. If a stock-market investor were to say, "I made a 30 percent return on that stock investment in only eight months," how valid would it be if he failed to mention that he had to pay half of his gain to Uncle Sam as income tax? In these days of high tax brackets, the only meaningful measure for any investment is in terms of *after-tax* dollars.

As I have stated several times throughout this book, the higher your tax bracket, the more beneficial real estate investment will be to you. It is my view that even in public real estate limited partnerships, which are usually less oriented to tax shelter, investors should at the very minimum be in the 30 percent tax bracket. Therefore, all of our discussion of return on investment will be in after-tax dollars, and for easy comparison we will assume the investor is dealing in income subject to 50 percent income tax.

In Chapter 4 I showed a comparison of economic benefits on a particular deal between a 50 percent taxpayer and a lower bracket taxpayer. Of course, that comparison would not necessarily be accurate for another deal, but it does provide some basis for comparison. To understand the true potential benefits of a particular deal for your particular income situation, you are well advised to get assistance from your regular tax preparer.

In considering the potential return on a real estate investment, you have to work with assumptions about the nature of the ultimate sale, as well as simply the amount of money for which the property may be sold. Later in this chapter I will discuss how to analyze these assumptions and determine whether they are reasonable.

In any event, when you or your accountant are comparing one investment against another, be sure that all of the comparisons use after-tax figures. The projections included in the offering materials for any real estate investment should be on this basis as well. If not, ask the General Partner why.

THE IMPORTANCE OF UNDERSTANDING
RETURN-ON-INVESTMENT CALCULATION METHODS

If a prospectus presents a projected return on investment, you may well regard this as a very important part of your consideration in determining your interest in the investment. Warning—there is more than one legitimate way to calculate percentage returns on investment. It can be an illusory game, and comparison from one deal to another may become more an art than a science. This is not to say that someone will intentionally try to deceive you, but you may very well find yourself comparing an orange to an apple without realizing it.

To protect yourself, you should understand a bit about each of the commonly used methods, and you should always identify which method was used to prepare each return-on-investment percentage you see in different offering prospectuses. If this is not clearly described, be sure to ask. Once again, this is an area in which a professional accountant can be of considerable assistance. For your general guidance, I will introduce below the most important methods used.

Accounting Rate of Return. Perhaps the simplest and therefore most commonly used method of calculating investment return is the "accounting rate of return." This method takes all investment returns (including tax savings, which will vary by investor) and all distributions of cash from operations and after-tax sale proceeds, and compares them to the amount of investment on an annual basis. If the investment was made in installments, then the average annual investment must be calculated in order to account more accurately for the amount of money invested and the time it was actually committed to the investment.

For example, if an investor makes the investment shown in Table 7 and receives the returns there, the accounting rate of return would be calculated as described.

TABLE 7
Accounting Rate of Return

Year	Investment	Tax savings	Cash distribution
1	$ 5,000	$ 4,000	$ 0
2	10,000	7,500	300
3	8,000	5,000	500
4	5,000	3,000	600
5	0	(1,000)	5,000
6	0	(1,500)	6,000
7	0	(2,000)	10,000
	$28,000	$15,000	$22,400

To determine the top half of our investment-return fraction, add up all of the after-tax cash benefits and divide by the number of years in the investment.

Tax savings (net of tax payments)	$15,000
Cash distributions	22,400
	$37,400
Divide by 7 years	÷7
Average annual after-tax return	$5,343

Now, calculate the average annual investment by multiplying the payments by the length of time the money was invested and divide that product by the total time the money was invested:

5,000 × 7 years =	$ 35,000
10,000 × 6 years =	60,000
8,000 × 5 years =	40,000
5,000 × 4 years =	20,000
	$155,000
Divide by total years of investments	÷7
Average annual investment	$ 22,143

To calculate the accounting rate of return, simply divide the average annual after-tax return by the average annual investment:

$$\$5,343 \div \$22,143 = 24.13\%$$

More Sophisticated Methods. Although the accounting rate of return is relatively easy to calculate and is commonly used in the industry, its weakness is that it does not "weight" the various payments and returns according to their timing. In financial jargon, it ignores the "time value of money" and implicitly assumes that a dollar received today is worth the same as one received seven years from today. This is simply not accurate, especially in today's inflationary economy.

There are several methods that take the time value of money into account. The main one is the "discounted rate of return," which is also known as the "internal rate of return."

Rather than go through the involved mechanics of exactly how to calculate this manually, I will tell you that the discounted rate of return for the example used above is 25.88 percent. This can be calculated with an inexpensive hand calculator that features financial programs. The formula itself is provided later in this chapter.

Comparison of Methods. There is very little consistent correlation between the results of the accounting rate of return and the discounted rate of return. In the above example they were relatively close. In other examples the accounting rate of return can give considerably higher or lower percentage numbers than the discounted rate of return depending on the timing of investment payments and returns. If an investment features heavy returns in the early years, such as in a deep tax shelter, the accounting rate of return will understate the percentage return. If an investment features heavy returns in later years, such as in property with light tax shelter and a profitable sale, the accounting rate of return will tend to overstate the value of the dollars received in later years and, therefore, overstate the percentage return.

Refinements of the internal rate of return are available whereby the cost of capital and reinvestment rates can be set at rates other than the discounted rate of return. This means that you can assume the money invested is being taken from an account that bears interest at some rate and in which the returns are being reinvested at that same or some other rate. This kind of method is often called the "financial management rate of return."

Although this type of analysis may be still more realistic than the discounted rate of return, its calculation is far too complex for the average investor, and one can again have the problem of comparing apples with oranges if one does not know what assumptions were used for the "cost of capital" and "reinvestment rate" for two different investments. With the discounted rate of return, you know that these two rates are equal to your final percentage answer.

At the Hall Real Estate Group we use the discounted rate of return as the yardstick by which to measure percentage investment return. It accounts for the time value of money, is reasonably easy to understand and calculate (with a little electronic assistance), and gives the investor the most assurance of a consistent measure of percentage return.

Technical Mathematical Aspects. The following short explanation is included for readers with an above-average interest in technical financial math:

$$NPV = \sum_{t=1}^{N} \frac{R_t}{(1+k)^t} - C = \sum_{t=1}^{n} \frac{R_t}{(1+r)^t} - C = 0$$

By adjusting the rate of return so the "net present value" equals zero, you will have determined the discounted rate of return for the investment. This rate of return will be identical to the internal rate of return. This is a point many sophisticated analysts do not realize: The rate used to calculate NPV is equal to the internal rate of return when NPV equals zero.

Where C is the investment, R is the stream of cash flows, k is the cost of capital, t is the period, N and n are the total number of periods, and r is the internal rate of return.

SPECIFIC RETURNS TO ANTICIPATE
FROM REAL ESTATE LIMITED PARTNERSHIPS

With this considerable background, we can now get back to the essential question of what return on investment a real estate limited partner can expect. My belief is that when the partnership has been completed and all assets distributed, the after-tax annual return should exceed 20 percent of the original amount invested. This assumes a taxpayer in the 50 percent bracket.

Remember, each deal must stand on its own. It is possible for a particular investment to develop problems and show a far lower return, no return, or a loss. On the other hand, you have seen details throughout this book of specific programs in which I was involved that resulted in annual after-tax returns on investment of 23.42, 31.9, and 38.04 percent. So 20 percent is by no means the maximum reasonable potential for good private limited-partnership investment. And remember, this is *after-tax*. Accordingly, the same 50 percent bracket investor would have to make over *40 percent per year* on an interest-bearing investment to achieve a comparable return.

It is difficult to provide a comparison for public offerings, because they tend to have a long investment life, and only a very few have actually gone through the total cycle from investment to completed sales. Based on published analysis of a number of public partnerships initiated in the early seventies, the annual after-tax rate averaged about 17 percent by the accounting rate-of-return method (assuming, just to keep the comparison even, a 50 percent bracket investor). Converted to the discount rate of return used for the private limited-partnership information above, this would indicate an average of about 19 percent for these early public limited partnerships. While this is a slightly lower rate than I suggest should be expected for private limited partnerships, it is still an extremely favorable *after-tax* return compared to most other investments. My personal belief is that increased inflation will provide current public limited partnerships with even more attractive returns in the future.

These figures reinforce some interesting differences between the private and public investment opportunity. Because private deals tend to provide greater tax shelter, the investor gets his money back faster and the time-use-of-money return is usually higher. This is particularly beneficial to high-bracket investors. The disadvantage of private limited-partnership investment is its general requirement for larger sums of capital from each investor, and less opportunity to see track records and have real assurance in advance of the competency of the General Partner.

When comparing these various returns to any pretax-type investment, one can easily see the significant value of the tax shelter and capital-gain aspects inherent in most real estate investments. These are major factors in providing the high after-tax benefits enjoyed by real estate investors.

TIMING AND RETURN OF MONEY

One of the important elements to consider in evaluating any real estate deal is how fast you will get your invested capital back. Money received from whatever source at least limits your risk, and it gives you the use of the capital for reinvestment.

The question of how fast the investment will pay back your original capital is determined by a "payback" analysis. Most real estate investments should be designed to pay back your capital within the first four to seven years. If they can do this, you are well on your way to a successful investment experience. This, of course, will vary by type of property and other conditions, and it should not in itself be a determining factor. It is, however, one of the things that should be considered.

Faster payback is one reason my organization tends to favor tax-sheltered investments. A real estate investment designed for tax shelter usually has a shorter payback period and is more dependable in terms of delivering the economic benefits promised to the investor. The trouble with cash flow as a projected benefit for investors is that the determining assumptions are too highly variable to be depended upon. A slight downturn in occupancy, possibly coupled with an upturn in expense, can completely wipe out cash flow for a year. For this reason you can be much more confident of those projections from a real estate investment in which the predominant current cash benefit is the value of tax savings.

HOW TO REVIEW ASSUMPTIONS

Since various assumptions made by the sponsor of a real estate investment opportunity underlie virtually all of the economic projections, it is essential that you concern yourself with the assumptions before any other comparison or analysis. Remember, most public offerings are blind pools in which the actual property to be purchased is not known or identified. Therefore, they will not include specific projections of anticipated results, and you will in fact have to rely primarily on track records. On the other hand, private offerings, dealing as they do with a specific property, will present detailed projections of what is anticipated in terms of operation and ultimate sale of the property.

Whenever you are considering a real estate investment in which economic projections are presented, the following areas of the transaction should be identified and considered simply as matters of common sense and "reasonableness."

Income—This is based on assumptions about occupancy, rental rates, and rental increases over time. If these are not spelled out in the prospectus, find out what assumptions were used to project income. Determine whether you think they are reasonable in terms of the property's past history, the status of the market area, and the nature of any competition. If necessary, seek the advice of local experts.

Expenses—What is the percentage of expense compared to gross income? How does it compare with other similar properties? How do the anticipated expenses compare to the historical expenses of the property? Ask the General Partner or your securities representative to explain these comparisons.

Refinancing—If the partnership projection assumes refinancing at a future date, will they be able to obtain such refinancing? Are the assumed rates reasonable?

Current Financing—If the current financing for the project is on a variable rate, are the assumed rates in future years reasonable?

Capital Expenditure—The capital being raised by the partnership may well include funds to rehabilitate or refurbish some elements of the property. Other capital expenditures beyond the original purchase may also be budgeted in the pro forma statements. To determine the reasonableness of these numbers, feel free to ask how they were developed. Are they based on an analysis of the cost of accomplishing specific refurbishing, or are they just a generalized set of figures, with the money to be spent as needs are determined?

Market Statistics—Of necessity, the projected operating results and future value of any real estate must be based on certain beliefs regarding the property's market and location. The General Partner should be able to provide marketing statistics or other satisfactory evidence to support underlying assumptions regarding the market.

There are no right or wrong answers to these questions, but it is absolutely essential that you as an investor be comfortable with the common sense and reasonableness of the thinking that lies behind the assumptions. More than guesses and hunches should motivate your decision. You can, of course, hire a professional to help you with this analysis, but the advice you receive will still be based on the General Partner's information.

Since you are ultimately going to put your full faith and confidence in the General Partner anyway, perhaps the best approach is to discuss these matters with the General Partner's representatives and trust your impression as to their competency in answering your questions. Don't sell yourself short as a judge of what is good common sense and what is reasonable. With just a little fact-gathering, you can become amazingly competent in making judgments about the assumptions in a real estate investment.

Ask about some of the areas listed above so you can decide whether or not the sponsor of the investment knows what he is doing. Your source of information may be your securities representative or the General Partner himself, as appropriate for a particular organization. Certainly anyone involved in selling the investment to you should be completely willing and able to discuss your logical questions about the assumptions underlying economic projections.

DON'T LET OVEROPTIMISM RUB OFF

Newer sponsors may tend to be overly optimistic about their projections. This is usually not in an effort to take advantage of investors but rather as a reflection of the individual's enthusiasm and lack of experience. Beware of the infectious nature of such enthusiasm. Take nothing at face value. Ask questions and be painfully realistic in your own evaluation. There is no profit in being either an optimist or a pessimist at this stage.

Remember, as much as judging the projections themselves, your goals should be to judge the quality of logical thinking, and the underlying experience and competence of the people you will be relying on if you decide to make the investment.

EVALUATING THE FEES INVOLVED
IN LIMITED-PARTNERSHIP INVESTING

I'm sure you have assumed there is some cost involved to pay for the work of a General Partner. That seems logical enough, but the problem is that fees are just one side of a coin. The other side consists of services and results. Until you understand that second side, it can be hard to make sense of the fee side.

To this point in the book I have chosen to concentrate on the activities and potential achievement of real estate limited partnerships and have simply ignored the question of fees. Now that you are reasonably aware of the efforts of the General Partner's organization and of the economic benefits that can be created for the limited partners, it is time to discuss the matter of compensation fully.

Let's start by understanding that this compensation usually consists of fees and a portion of ownership in the property. Both come from the capital invested by the limited partners or, in some cases, from the operation or sale of the property. In no event do they involve any additional payment by the investors beyond the amount of their investment. The fees actually come from the *partnership*, and only indirectly from the limited partners.

Specific fees will vary, but generally there is a front-end or syndication fee, which covers the overall work of the sponsor in putting the deal together and guiding its operation through its lifetime. In addition, various fees for specific services may be paid to the General Partner or affiliates as they are performed. These may include a fee for management of the property and normal real estate commissions if an affiliated brokerage firm is involved in buying or selling the property. The areas covered by these specific service fees vary widely from deal to deal. They should be clearly disclosed in the prospectus of each partnership so prospective investors can consider if they're reasonable.

The ownership interest of the General Partner is frequently subordinated to the return of the limited partners' capital, or to the return of capital plus a specified percentage return on the investment.

Fees and Ownership Interest. Fees as a percentage of capital vary greatly, but this is because the types of deals and the nature of the services rendered cover such a wide spectrum. In general, competition works wonders in keeping compensation within reasonable limits. The syndicator who arbitrarily tries to establish unreasonably high fees will soon have a poor reputation and have trouble finding investors.

Considering a broad range of private limited partnerships, the General Partner's fees plus those of its affiliates tend to range from 10 to 50 percent of the capital invested, and the General Partner's ownership interest might range from 1 to 50 percent, with various combinations of subordination to the limited partners' return on investment. The fees include the broker's fee and all other fees.

Public limited-partnership fees and ownership interest tend to lie in a somewhat narrower range. This is understandable, because the nature of these investments creates fewer cases of special risk or effort on the part of the General Partner. Furthermore, since these investments usually have less leverage than private tax-shelter-oriented deals, the capital raised is proportionately larger—thus a smaller percentage will provide ample compensation. In general, public limited partnerships will involve fees ranging from 20 to 40 percent and ownership interest from 10 to 15 percent with various subordinations to investors' return. Again, the range quoted includes all fees. The securities broker's fee itself usually runs from 8 to 12 percent of the money raised.

Obviously this is too complex an area in which to say simply that any given compensation package is right or wrong. The broad percentage ranges are a result of great variation in services and equally important differences in the amount of capital raised relative to the size and complexity of the investment. Thus, evaluation should focus less on the percentage of compensation than on the value received by the investor in terms of services and investment expertise.

Why Percentage Evaluation of Fees Can Be Misleading. Percentage evaluation can be tricky, since it all depends on the amount of capital required rather than the overall value of the property purchased. Usually, investors are better off with lower down payments and higher leverage. However, the very achievement of this objective makes the General Partner's fee look larger!

Consider the case of a $10 million property. Depending on the negotiating skill of the General Partner in terms of keeping the down payment low, the partnership capital may require either $2 million or $1.5 million. Assume that in each case the General Partner charges a $450,000 fee. In the first situation the General Partner receives a 22.5 percent fee; in the second case it is a 30 percent fee.

Of course the General Partner receives the same amount of money in each case, but the investors would be much better off with the lower down payment, higher leverage, and higher fee percentage. Nevertheless, the perception probably would be that the fee was too high in the case of the deal requiring less cash investment and offering greater opportunities for profit. It doesn't make much sense, but that is what can happen when too much attention is paid to percentages when evaluating fees.

This illustration also explains why you will find that fees for deals oriented to tax shelter will generally seem higher than for other real estate investments. It is a simple matter of the way tax shelters are structured. To receive the maximum tax advantage, it is important to have the highest prudent leverage. This means that capital investment will be kept low and borrowed money will be a high proportion of the total. This has the effect of making the General Partner's fee high as a percentage of capital.

To get a better perspective, you may find it interesting to compare fees as a percentage of the total *price* of the real estate purchased, rather than as a percentage of capital raised.

However you analyze it, the fact remains that substantial fees are necessary to support the cost of initiating and managing successful real estate investments. Knowledgeable investors look at fees in their proper context as a contributing part of the investment, not as a dilution or giveaway. They focus their evaluation on services, on competitive cost for similar deals, and on potential return on investment.

The Myth of "Dilution." There is a mental trap that can make it difficult for an investor to evaluate fees in a rational manner. It is commonly referred to as "dilution" and simply means that the investor feels only some portion of his capital is going into the actual investment while the balance is presumably lining the pockets of the sponsor.

This is understandable, since the most conventional method of evaluating fees is to consider them as a percentage of the total capital raised, leading to the assumption that the investor's capital contribution is diluted by that percentage. The fallacy in this point of view is that only one side of the coin is being considered. The other side is, of course, the services and expertise necessary to make the investment viable. Without the General Partner's involvement there would be no investment. With it, there can be highly desirable economic benefits.

Frequently, I have had prospective investors ask me, "Exactly how much of my money will really go into the investment?" My answer is, "All of it." Obviously, all of the capital will not go into the property itself, but all of it will go toward the achievement of the objectives of the partnership and the realization of the projected return on investment.

The Relationship between Services, Fees, and Return on Investment. It is most important to realize that when higher fees are required to support special services, there is usually a higher potential profit on the deal. In essence, the fees should more than pay for themselves in results.

As an example, some syndicators merely put together deals that are brought to them by developers. They raise the money and turn the property over to a management company. Other syndicators put together "turnaround deals," in which an underproductive and perhaps seriously troubled property is purchased for the specific purpose of turning it into a highly productive and profitable property. This happens to be an area in which Hall Real Estate has specialized and for which we have developed specific techniques over the last fourteen years. I can assure you that the organization and the concentrated effort required to create a turnaround do cost a lot more than the first more typical real estate venture described. Turnarounds also provide a great deal more potential for partnership profit.

You may recall the Crestwood Commons case history presented in Chapter 4. That was a typical turnaround. In describing it earlier, I merely explained how we turned a costly clubhouse operation into a separate business and used it both as a new source of income and a bonus attraction to build occupancy. That sounds simple enough, but in fact it would never have happened if our organization had not had the ability to conceive the idea, carry out market research and complex financial analysis, and finally, create and operate a consumer business, a task that is distinctly different from managing real estate. Certainly the fees had to be somewhat higher than for a more passive real estate deal, but so were the returns on the investment.

Differences in Acquisition Methods That Justify Higher Fees. Another area of important service difference is the manner in which syndicators acquire property for their limited partnerships. Some act as principals and actually buy the property themselves at the lowest possible price, then raise money from investors after the fact. Our company works in this way. It creates personal risk for us and it certainly ties up a lot of very expensive money. On the other hand, it provides a great benefit to our limited partners, in that it allows us to negotiate extremely good purchase prices and terms.

Most syndicators merely tie up a piece of property through a low-cost option while they attempt to syndicate the partnership. Since the seller in these situations is unsure of the sale, he usually demands and gets a higher price or better terms for himself.

A General Partner, with the financial strength to buy instead of option, and with acquisition specialists who know how to negotiate, will often buy apartments for $2,000 to $3,000 per unit less than a new sponsor just learning the business. The difference in a three-hundred-unit apartment complex could easily be $600,000, and that extra value in the investment could well be more than the entire fee the General Partner charges for the syndication.

As I was describing our technique of buying property in advance of syndication, you may have thought, "Aha! I bet he marks it up and makes a nice profit when he sells it to the partnership." Some syndicators do that, and they may or may not disclose it. Even if they disclose it, the profit certainly constitutes an additional fee. In the case of Hall Real Estate and many other syndicators, we transfer the property to the limited-partnership investors at exactly the same cost basis as our purchase. There are, of course, costs to us involved, but we consider these part of our cost of doing business. The best possible acquisition is a service the General Partner owes investors.

Whenever new construction is involved in a limited partnership, the investor should pay particular attention to the cost of acquisition. In many cases, the new building will be developed by the sponsor or an affiliated company and when completed it will be sold to the partnership at a fixed price not arrived at through arm's-length negotiation.

This is perfectly legitimate if it is disclosed in the prospectus in the "Acquisition" section. It is also reasonable and proper for the agreed price to include a profit for the entity handling the development, since that entity has accepted responsibility for the work and is taking a financial risk in providing the finished product at a fixed price.

The question that should concern the investor is whether the acquisition price is reasonable in comparison to similar properties being developed in the same area at the same time. Since the price was not established in the open market, there is always the chance of it being excessive. Indication of this should be questioned, and the sponsor should be able to substantiate the reasonableness of the acquisition cost through comparisons.

The Importance of Having a Profitable General Partner. In addition to requiring compensation for specific services and organizational capabilities, the General Partner requires a profit, as does any other business. Investors sometimes have mixed emotions about contributing to the financial success of their General Partner and may feel a twinge of jealousy over the General Partner's personal financial success. In fact, the same thing applies here as in any other business dealing. You are always better off doing business with someone who is financially secure rather than someone who is struggling to stay afloat.

One extremely important benefit of such security was mentioned in Chapter 10: the possibility that the General Partner may provide the partnership with substantial loans in times of financial distress. There is no legal requirement for a General Partner to do this, but when he has an established and successful organization he will want to protect his reputation as a sponsor of successful ventures. Real estate success involves staying power. That's why most deals are structured as long-term investments and why they have reserves in their structure. Still, conditions can and on occasion do require extraordinary staying power and, at that point, a financially strong General Partner may be the total difference between a good long-term investment and one that never has the chance to see the long term.

Obviously, a General Partner who undercharges for his services cannot be expected to help in a crunch. He simply won't have the financial strength. Even worse, many General Partners who undercharge end up as failed businesses. A General Partner who is in financial trouble is a very bad manager for your property and an even worse General Partner for your partnership.

EVALUATING FEES AS PART OF A
TOTAL BUSINESS RELATIONSHIP

Motivation and incentive are needed to assure long-term interest and commitment to the property and the partnership. This is best achieved through a substantial General Partner ownership interest that is subordinated to some specified return to the limited partners.

Hall Real Estate receives very little from each partnership until the investors have gotten all of their money back, at a minimum. The formula varies with the type of investment, the amount of capital, the time required to return the investment, the degree of risk, and the special involvement of the General Partner organization. The important point is that the limited partners are put in front of the General Partner in terms of return and payback. While we charge fees sufficient to maintain our organization in a profitable manner, the bulk of our return comes at the end of a deal, and only after investors have made money. I believe this is logical and fair.

In a successful venture, most of the General Partner's profit should come from his ownership position and not from his front-end fees. If the investors make a good profit, the General Partner is also entitled to a good profit. If the deal does not work out well, the limited partners should get the priority return. Since it is the General Partner's expertise and effort that affects success or failure, it is proper that he be rewarded only after success has been achieved.

Once again, I return to the fundamental position that the most important decision you will make as a limited-partnership investor is the selection of your General Partner. As in all other things, you are likely to get what you pay for, so don't look for bargains. Look beyond the fee itself until you find the highest level of quality service available. In the long run, quality is invariably your best buy.

TIMING REAL ESTATE INVESTMENTS

In general, timing is less critical in making real estate investments than in buying and selling something like stock. Real estate is not subject to the daily fluctuations of the stock market, so the question of timing relates to longer-term factors. Unless you foresee a deflationary depression, timing should not be a particularly important consideration if a specific deal is favorable.

Nevertheless, most investors automatically respond to short-term timing indicators, and frequently they will pass up excellent investment opportunities during periods of temporary recession. In fact, such periods are frequently the best times to invest!

The Effect of Recessions. Real estate is affected in a number of significant ways by recessions. If you are an investor, you may view recession as a negative, which can create serious operational problems and reduced cash flow. Recessions tend to have the effect of temporarily lowering real estate values or, at the very least, interrupting long-term upward pressures. From my personal point of view, I believe recessions should be viewed as buying opportunities.

Imagine for a moment what it would be like if real estate were traded like stock on a huge national exchange, complete with a quote ticker and constantly changing prices. Real estate would, like stocks, have trends over long and short periods of time, but within these trends it would have daily ups and downs as the market reacted to a thousand variables.

One of the unique things about real estate is that we do not get daily quotations, so we really don't see price fluctuation on any kind of regular basis. We only know what our property is really worth when we try to sell it and thereby find out what the market will offer. If we did have my mythical daily-quotation system, we would quickly see that as a recession sets in, prices retreat.

There are a number of solid reasons for soft real estate prices during a recession. Big owners and developers are frequently caught in a cash squeeze as well as an emotional squeeze during these periods, and they respond by selling at bargain rates. A builder who has several projects underway, with interest rates floating far above anything he anticipated and sales slower than anticipated, usually must unload some properties in order to salvage others.

People who are cash short can easily get emotionally down about the longer-term future on top of their immediate problems. Strangely, other investors with no immediate recession-oriented problem also start to worry—it seems to be a communicable disease. They start to wonder if the recession is just the tip of the iceberg. They get the idea that maybe the recession will turn into a depression. Without any real rationale, investors may well let their emotions get the best of their logic and decide to bail out.

In the real estate field, profitable operation does become a big challenge during recessions as occupancy tends to drop. This is especially true of apartment projects, but also has a bearing on commercial and office properties.

In the case of apartments, there is a tremendous impact from doubling-up as families in economic trouble move in with others, and the total number of households temporarily shrinks. During the 1980–81 recession, Michigan was hard hit by unemployment, and the resultant doubling-up, plus moves out of state, cut rental occupancy by 10 to 15 percent, depending on location. This created a substantial reduction in operating income. On a national basis, one respected market-research company reported that over 200,000 households were lost through doubling-up in May and June of 1980. In addition, rent increases were significantly outpaced by expense increases during the same time period.

The effect of recession on commercial and office properties tends to come a bit more slowly and is felt later in the recession period or even after the recession is over. While the effect is spreading out, the number of bankruptcies does increase as a result of recession. Many of the commercial and office tenants who remain will become slow in paying their rent, and thus add to the problem.

Real estate owners who have financial strength can usually weather a recessionary period, if they want to *emotionally*. Unfortunately, many become emotionally weary so they decide to sell despite depressed prices. This is generally a costly error. Obviously an owner must evaluate if a recession is indeed going to be temporary, or if it is the tip of a depression iceberg. The real point, however, is that often instead of making these decisions as a result of rational evaluation, people tend to let their emotions take over. Emotions, unfortunately, usually go too far in any direction, and wrong decisions are the result.

Buying against the Trend. As I have said before, it seems like the most obvious and logical common sense to say, "Buy low, sell high." Ironically, when recessions depress the market or slow the upward price spiral, most people think about selling instead of buying. I suppose it is human nature to want to get out when things get tough, and to lose faith in the long haul just because there is a bad bump. Still, I think the negative reaction to downturns is a major mistake in real estate investment philosophy.

At Hall Real Estate we have chosen to buy during recessions and sell during prosperous periods. This strategy has served our investors well through several cycles, and continues to bolster profitabil-ity. We have no intention of changing this fundamental strategy.

Our investors sometimes find it difficult to understand our posi-tion, because it is so contrary to their own emotional bias. Still, it does make sense if you can ignore the emotion of the moment and concentrate on the long-term probabilities. Through the 1980–1982 recession, we hope to buy between $200 and $250 million of real es-tate. While this recession has been shallow thus far, we nevertheless believe the prices we are paying will turn out to be far less than the values that will be established when prosperity returns.

It is not always realistic for an investor to wait for a recession to start to build a desired position. As long as the investment value is satisfactory, there is no reason to hold out for a recession in order to squeeze the last possible dime out of a purchase price. However, when a recession does offer exceptional value, my advice is to take advantage of the opportunity.

12

Evaluating the Documentation

THE legal documentation for a real estate limited partnership consists of three items:

- The offering memorandum or prospectus
- The partnership agreement
- Subscription documents

All of the relationships and financial arrangements so far discussed generally in this book are set out specifically for individual investments in these documents. Obviously, they are important as sources of information to guide your consideration of investment opportunities, and they are vital in establishing your rights and position once you enter a partnership.

Unless you are dealing with a sponsor with whom you have placed previous investments, and unless the prospectus and partnership agreements are identical to those of your past experience, I would urge you to have these materials reviewed by your legal counsel. You should also seek the advice of your accountant regarding the financial aspects of the transaction and, particularly, the appropriateness of the investment for your tax situation. If you normally work with a financial-investment advisor, you will also want that individual to consider the suitability of the investment.

Beyond seeking competent professional counsel, you should make a point of understanding at least the basic elements of your own investments. No matter how much you trust your advisors, such minimal involvement can be both financially and personally rewarding. I think most advisors would agree that the investor's own understanding adds a healthy dimension to decision-making.

While it is boring to go through every line of the documentation checking for legal details, it can be exciting to track the major elements and reveal the art as well as the science involved in structuring a truly worthwhile investment. This chapter will introduce you to the content, style, and key sections of these documents.

THE OFFERING MEMORANDUM

The purpose of the offering memorandum or prospectus is to provide an investor with all the information required, including knowledge of risks, to make an informed evaluation of a particular investment opportunity.

Its contents and much of its language are shaped by the requirements of state and federal securities law and by a large bureaucracy attempting to protect investors. The unfortunate result is that the form of these documents tends to be extremely long and full of legalistic "boilerplate" statements that have little or no meaning to most investors. The general impression many readers may have is that the offering memorandum consists of a thousand and one reasons not to become involved in the investment.

Legal limitations make it difficult to provide certain information that could be valuable to investors, including much about the essential background and ability of the people involved. In most private offerings, there is no indication of a track record. This is not because such information is disallowed, but because the rigorous requirements of how it must be presented and kept up from that point forward (Securities Guide 60 requirements) make it virtually unworkable for most private syndicators.

But despite this and other limitations, the prospectus does provide extremely valuable structured information you will want to use as a basis for initial evaluation and as a reference during the life of the investment.

If you are presented with an opportunity for investing in a real estate limited partnership, but are not shown a prospectus or offering document, ask why. In most, but not all, states this documentation is required. Even if you happen to be in a state where it is legal to offer an investment without this documentation, I would personally have serious questions about pursuing the matter if a prospectus were not available.

From state to state, there will be some variation in the semantics of titles of sections covered in offering memoranda, and some subjects may be covered in certain states but not in others. What follows briefly describes the information generally covered under most state requirements.

Introduction. This rather comprehensive section is worthwhile, since its purpose is to present an overview of the total offering. It includes a general description of the offering, its purpose, the partnership objectives, description of the investment units offered, how much capital will be required from the limited partners, and in general terms, how that capital will be used. The introduction also tells who the General Partner is, who the underwriter is, who the professional consultants are, and it defines the terms used in the memorandum. It then goes on to explain how the benefits of the partnership will be allocated, describes the liability of limited partners and the liability and risk of the General Partner, and tells how much compensation the General Partner will receive. The reader is referred to the balance of the prospectus for more detail in all the areas covered in the introduction.

Risk Factors. This section gives a brief description of all the risks involved in the transaction. In fact, most of this material is "boiler-plate" listing of risks that are inherent in any investment, and it is generally the same in every prospectus. The section actually protects the General Partner more than the investors, since it discloses all of the horrible things that could happen and all of the ways money could be lost, no matter how remote the possibilities, so that an investor cannot later come back to the General Partner and say

"You didn't tell me that could happen." Nevertheless, this full disclosure is beneficial in that it encourages the limited partner to think about all such risks. In certain situations, special risks are added about the nature of the specific projects, and these are usually very helpful.

Description of the Development. In a specified offering—that is to say, one involving a particular property or group of properties that have already been acquired—this section will provide a complete but nontechnical description of the property and its operation. For a typical apartment complex, the information would include such facts as the number of rental units, their size, construction, and special features, current rents, utilities arrangements, resident profile, area competition, market and marketing information, current occupancy and financial-operating status, and a description of the local area and its economy. Many offerings include photographs of the property as well as maps of the area. If the property is viewed as a turnaround investment, this section will also contain a description of the planned operating philosophy and some of the turnaround plans and objectives. If the property is commercial, the section may include copies of important leases that affect the property's value.

In the case of a blind-pool offering that does not have specific property purchased or selected, this section would be replaced by one in which the intentions of the partnership in terms of types of property would be described.

Potential Conflicts of Interest. This section discloses and discusses the planned working relationship between the partnership and any companies that are owned or controlled by the General Partner or individuals involved with the General Partner or with the promotion of the offering. The purpose, of course, is to make completely public any situation that might later be considered as a conflict of interest. In addition, this section points out the other business activities of the General Partner and his affiliates that could conceivably create a conflict in terms of assignment of required expertise, personnel, and availability of facilities.

The indication is usually made that the principals feel sufficient capacity is available to avoid any of the potential conflicts, and that the anticipated financial arrangements will be fair and equitable despite the lack of arm's-length negotiation.

This section should be carefully reviewed, and each item should be considered on its merits. The prudent investor may well seek additional detail about how certain of the potential conflicts will be handled in order to assure fair and effective operations.

Acquisition of Development. This section is involved only in offerings with specified properties. It explains in considerable detail the background and financial arrangements of the acquisition. It will include the date of purchase, the total purchase price, nature of the mortgage, the financer to whom money is owed, the interest rate, payment schedule, prepayment penalty, maturity date, and other similar data. In addition, the seller will be specifically identified, and the organization of the transaction will be presented.

Source and Use of Funds. This is generally a one-page financial statement organized to show a general outline of cash flow through the partnership over a period of years. It clearly indicates when capital from the partners will come in, and what the anticipated funds will be spent for each year of operating the property. If any short-term borrowings are planned, these will also be shown as a source of funds, as will the proceeds of planned refinancing. The use of funds will list all of the capital requirements of the property as well as planned operating expenses, reserves, and other expenses of the partnership.

Partnership's Balance Sheet. This is usually a very simple section covering the initial balance sheet of the partnership in accordance with the generally accepted accounting principles.

Underwriter. The underwriter is, of course, the organization responsible for the sale of the investment units of the partnership. This section describes who the underwriter is and what, if any, relationship exists directly to the General Partner. The fee the underwriter will receive is specified, as well as the timing of payments.

Also specified is whether the underwriting is being done on a firm (guaranteed) basis or on a best-efforts understanding.

Services of Affiliates of the General Partner. Depending on the format of various types of offerings, there will be one or more sections describing the affiliates of the General Partner and detailing the services he will (or may) provide to the partnership. The fees to be paid for such services will also be discussed in general terms, and there may be a reference to specific contracts covering these arrangements.

These sections offer additional information concerning potential conflicts of interest and should be given careful consideration. In general, I believe it is to the investor's benefit to have affiliates of the General Partner involved in the operation of the partnership's property. Still, the investor should feel comfortable that the affiliate organizations are competent and the fees involved are competitive.

General Partner. The purpose of this section is to provide the background and related experience of the General Partner, and it should be considered one of your key points of evaluation as a prospective investor. Its material should be weighed carefully and reviewed with your professional advisors to satisfy yourself as to the competence and capability of the individual(s) who will direct the operation of the investment.

The Offering. This section describes the pertinent federal and state securities acts under which this particular investment is being offered to potential investors. It will either be offered pursuant to a "claim of exemption" or pursuant to a "registration" (both of which I will detail shortly).

The section then goes on to explain the plan of distribution; that is to say, how the particular partnership interests will be sold, what happens if they are not all sold by a specified date, what happens if a subscriber is not accepted by the partnership, and other similar contingencies. Particularly if this is your first limited-partnership investment, pay special attention to the material in this section that deals with restrictions on resale of the investment units. While the language in the prospectus may be legalistic boilerplate, it does make an important distinction in showing resale as an area in which limited-partnership interests are quite different from those for listed stocks and bonds. The General Partner or your securities representative should be asked about the realities of resale in each particular offering, and your attorney should also be consulted as to exactly what your options will be should you ever want to sell your interest.

Suitability Standards for Investors. This section describes the minimum income and/or net worth an investor must have to be qualified for this investment. It may also specify a minimum taxable income bracket for qualification. Review this section carefully and make sure that you do qualify. Later, as part of your subscription to the investment, you will be required to complete a questionnaire in which you must swear to the fact that you do meet the suitability standards.

Summary of Provisions of the Partnership Agreement. This section describes each of the major elements of the partnership agreement and summarizes the important concepts. It is an excellent section for the prospective investor to read for general understanding and from which to prepare questions for later discussion with professional advisors, but absorbing it should not be regarded as a substitute for a complete review of the entire partnership agreement.

Description of Blue-Sky Laws. "Blue-sky laws" is the term popularly used to refer to state securities laws. Since virtually all syndications of real estate are structured as limited partnerships, this brief section simply describes the "limited partnership act" of the particular state, as it applies to the particular investment.

Federal Income-Tax Consequences. This section describes current federal income-tax laws as they relate to the proposed investment. It generally includes a discussion of the tax aspects of being classified as a partnership, taxation of limited partners, the tax basis

and nonrecourse indebtedness, a description of depreciation and recapture, prepaid interest, and other expenses, treatment of gain or
loss when the property is sold or disposed of on foreclosure, and provisions relating to liquidation or termination of the partnership. Additionally, the section will cover investment interest, capital gains or
losses, minimum-tax and tax-preference items, maximum tax on
personal-service income, retroactive allocations, allocation of profits
and losses, deductions for real property taxes, and any particular tax
aspects that may be unique to the state in which the transaction is
being made.

Most of these tax aspects are commonly put in all offering memoranda in order to point out the current status of the law and the
risks created by tax law. They are important for overall technical
consideration, but are likely to be less than meaningful to the lay-
man. Some people may want to read this section out of intellectual
interest, but for most I would recommend a brief explanation from
your accountant or financial advisor.

While this section is usually cut-and-dried for standard real estate
investments, that is not necessarily the case when it describes one of
the more exotic, deep-sheltered limited partnerships. In these cases,
it may include highly questionable interpretations of tax law—and
in fact the entire investment value may hinge on a point of tax law
that has not yet been proved by either IRS action or court cases.
When considering this type of investment, the tax-consequences
section should be thoroughly reviewed by your professional advisors, who should then explain in detail the risks you are taking in
terms of potential negative decisions by the IRS or courts.

Financial Projections. This section does not apply in the case of a
blind pool, as it is concerned with a statement of projected or anticipated operating results. In the case of a specified property, projections are based on assumptions, showing cash flow, if any, and
projected taxable loss or income.

The assumptions are detailed in footnotes elaborating on the projections. Careful reading and consideration of these assumptions
and all other footnotes is as important as studying the projections
themselves. Usually the numbers will be presented on a per-invest-

ment-unit basis as well as for the entire partnership. This will help you see how much cash flow and how much tax loss are anticipated for whatever interest you may purchase.

There is no established format for these projections, and their presentation and content will vary from one prospectus to another. In some cases there will be a projection or a series of projections showing the effect of sale at different times or under different conditions. This allows a projection of your tax consequences right to the conclusion of the investment.

As I have indicated throughout this book, the only time you really know how well any investment has worked out is when it is concluded. Since the capital-gains aspect is so critical to success in real estate investment, it is particularly important to see the influence of a sale. In our projections at Hall Real Estate, we always show five different potential sale circumstances. This gives an investor the facts to anticipate over a wide range of possibilities, from a very poor situation to a spectacular success. Interestingly, investors may learn that based on tax consequences they can come out ahead even if no money is made on the economic aspects of the investment.

THE PARTNERSHIP AGREEMENT

The partnership agreement is the legal document that governs all of the relationships and activity of the partnership. It is not nearly as awesome or complicated as it may seem at first glance. The key to understanding it is to take it slow and easy and to read each section. Make notes about anything you don't fully understand, and be sure to get answers to every question from your securities representative or your attorney.

For the most part, much of the partnership agreement is, like the prospectus, necessary legal boilerplate. If this is your first investment with a particular General Partner, or if you feel at all unsure, have an attorney review both the partnership agreement and the prospectus.

The partnership agreement generally will cover in more detail all of the items discussed in the summary of the partnership agreement contained in the main body of the offering memorandum or prospectus. Among other provisions, the partnership agreement should cover the following.

Capital. The partnership agreement will discuss who puts in how much money both in terms of the general and the limited partners. In the case of capital installments, it will specify when the money is due and what happens if it is not paid on schedule. It will also discuss advances and loans to the partnership and the use of the funds.

General Housekeeping Items. This section will cover things like the name of the partnership, location of its headquarters, and the purpose of the partnership.

Participation in Partnership Property. There will generally be a section stating that all partners own an undivided share and none can claim what is called "partitioning" and divide up the property. This is for the protection and benefit of all partners.

Management. This section will describe the powers of the General Partner and outline how decisions are to be made for the partnership.

Allocation of Profits and Losses and Distribution of Cash. As the title implies, this section will specify the division between general and limited partners of profit, loss, and cash under all foreseeable circumstances. It should include cash flow from operations, refinancing proceeds, and sale proceeds. Generally, it should be a very precise and detailed section to avoid any possibility of questions or misinterpretation in the future.

Accounting. This establishes the nature of the books and records to be maintained, what fiscal year will be used, and how tax returns will be reported. In addition, it should indicate that records and reports will be available for the inspection of the partners at any reasonable time.

Terms and Dissolution. This section establishes an ending date for the partnership and what happens when the partnership is concluded or "dissolved." It describes who gets what and the whole process of liquidation. Events that can cause the termination of a partnership before the natural term are also discussed.

It is absolutely essential that this material be included, because partnerships, unlike corporations, are not legally considered perpetual. It is also important for tax considerations. If partnerships do not meet certain tests of limited term and limited transferability, they can be treated as associations, which are taxed as corporations. This, of course, would create double taxation and lose one of the major tax advantages enjoyed by partnerships.

Assignments. This is another element included to meet the legal provisions of limited-partnership law. The section describes the binding effect of the agreement and the restriction on transferring partnership interests. It also describes certain circumstances under which a General Partner may be removed.

General Provisions. This is a catch-all section for such items as how the certificate will be legally filed, the fact that the agreement does not have to be signed by all partners at the same time, how amendments may be put into the agreement, how notices are to be initiated and distributed, and other similar routine matters.

Liability. The liability section of the limited-partnership agreement should fully describe the liabilities of the two classes of partners. Make sure there are no liabilities established for limited partners beyond those which you understand and accept, based on your discussions of the investment.

In general, a limited partner is liable for the original amount of capital invested as stated in the partnership certificate, still another document that will be filed and become a matter of public record. That amount of capital may include both actual cash contributed and notes or other property. Any deferred-installment notes that you have signed, payable to the partnership, will be included in your overall liability.

Nevertheless, it is possible for a limited partner to have further liabilities if they are established in this section of the partnership agreement. Limited partners are normally entitled to the benefit of specifically limited downside risk in each investment, and this should be safeguarded. For further recommendations in this vital area, see the last section of this chapter.

Calls for Additional Capital. Some partnership agreements have provisions allowing the General Partner to "call" additional capital if the partnership needs more funds. This would usually be exercised at a time when the partnership has what are hoped to be temporary financial difficulties. The provisions vary widely and are not necessarily unfair or dangerous, though they should be carefully reviewed, since they can commit the investor to additional investment.

Some call provisions involve a mandatory percentage of your investment. In other words, if you have a ten percent mandatory provision, any time you are asked to contribute up to that amount, you have to comply or you will be financially penalized in a prescribed fashion.

Other limited-partnership agreements have a more complicated arrangement that gives limited partners an opportunity, but not the requirement, to meet calls. In these cases, if the General Partner feels it is appropriate and necessary, there is a method established for a restructuring of the partnership capital to allow additional money to be brought in. Each limited partner has the right to participate in ratio to his original share, though such participation is not mandatory.

As you can see, the partnership agreement provides a kind of working constitution for the venture. Much of the detail is determined by the partnership laws of the state, but there are key areas open to discretion in the writing of the agreement.

As previously stated, if you have any questions, or if this is your first investment with a particular General Partner, the document should be reviewed by your lawyer. Be aware, however, that partnership agreements are generally standardized and cannot be changed to meet the desires of any one partner. A technical issue that may be unsatisfactory to a particularly picky attorney should be considered by you on the basis of business judgment. It is unlikely you will be able to have the wording changed.

While technical review of these documents is prudent for your safety, you should also remember that the bottom line will still be the experience and the reputation of your General Partner. There can be few problems of mutuality of intent and interest when you have a General Partner who has a valuable reputation to protect.

SUBSCRIPTION DOCUMENTS

The subscription documents are the papers required from the investor in order actually to join the partnership. Generally they include a subscription agreement or application form and a suitability questionnaire. They may also include an investment letter and a promissory note.

The investor questionnaire requires financial information to ascertain that you meet the suitability standards established for the particular investment. And, if the investment can be sold only to residents of certain states, the questionnaire will include items to establish residency. All of the information requested is for the exclusive and mutual benefit of the investor, the sponsor, and the broker, and it is treated confidentially.

The subscription agreement or application form establishes what interest you are buying, in what partnership, for how much money, and so on. It broadly describes the nature of the investment and then grants the General Partner a limited power of attorney to execute the partnership agreement and certain other documents on your behalf.

Although subscription documents differ in detail, these are the general matters covered. When signed by you, the agreement is an offer to buy an interest in the limited partnership. When the agreement is countersigned by the General Partner, that offer is accepted and you become a limited partner. The agreement is returned to you, generally after having been notarized. It is your official record of being a limited partner and it should be kept with other important documents. A promissory note to the partnership should be signed only if the investment has deferred capital contributions. If so, the note will describe the amounts, due dates, and default provisions of the required payments.

The investment letter is designed to preserve the General Partner's exemption from registration if that is involved. It is executed by the investor for the partnership's records and will usually specify that you are buying the investment for your own purposes and will include representations as to your suitability for the investment.

SECURITIES-BUREAU INVOLVEMENT

While the securities bureaus of the various states do not pass judgment on or endorse any investments, you can take a certain amount of comfort in and place more reliance on the documentation if you know that these agencies have reviewed the offering. Securities bureaus in some states do issue an exemption letter or order for private offerings. If this has been received, it will be referred to in the "Offering" section of the prospectus.

In essence, in an exemption order, the securities bureau is saying that while it doesn't want to be liable for judging the investment as a good thing, it has reviewed the papers and finds that legally they meet its standards.

Standards vary considerably from state to state. In some states the review is concerned only with full disclosure. In many others, consideration is applied under the "fair, just, and equitable doctrine." This requires not only that everything be disclosed, but that all elements of the deal be proper from the investor's point of view.

While I would be one of the last to say that a bureaucracy can properly understand and evaluate risks, I must admit that this kind of governmental involvement does at least give some degree of protection and has value. There is no question that unscrupulous, unfair, or unreasonable deals that are submitted to securities bureaus will not be given an exemption order. If the bureau in a state following the "fair, just, and equitable doctrine" has reviewed a document, you know that at the very least the deal is reasonable. Even in those states concerned only with full disclosure, the investor will be getting better documentation if the offering memorandum has been reviewed and found to comply with state laws.

At the federal level, most private offerings are exempt and do not go through registration. Public limited partnerships, because they are sold to large numbers of people across state lines, are registered with the Securities and Exchange Commission. Again, a certain degree of reliance about reasonableness can be put on the review involved in such registration.

HOW TO DECREASE YOUR LIABILITY
DURING THE LIFE OF YOUR INVESTMENT

After you have become a limited partner, there is one more important thing that can be done to increase the safety of your position. Sophisticated General Partners know that limited-partnership certificates can be amended to lower the capital shown on the certificate as cash distributions are made to limited partners. We do this at Hall Real Estate as a matter of standard procedure. In effect we are lowering the liability that each investor might otherwise be subject to.

As you know, the basic theory of limited-partnership liability is that the General Partner is fully liable for all partnership debts and that the limited partner is liable only to the extent of capital contributed. This capital is shown on the limited-partnership certificate, which is filed as a public record. However, even if part of your capital is returned through cash flow, you are, if that certificate stands unchanged, still liable for the full amount of the capital amount shown on its face! If, on the other hand, the certificate is amended from time to time to reflect your reduced capital account, your liability for claims arising after the amended filing will be reduced accordingly.

If the certificate is not amended, you could experience a substantial cash flow over a period of years and then be forced to put all of that money back into the deal if a lawsuit against the partnership were to prevail. Assume, for instance, that you received a 10 percent cash flow for each of six years. That's great, but then some unforeseen event occurs and a legal judgment for a large amount of money is placed against the partnership. Instead of your liability being limited to the remaining 40 percent of your original investment, you would be liable for the entire invested amount and, in addition, be responsible to return the 60 percent you had withdrawn.

In this example, most investors would consider the 10 percent annual cash flow as profit or return *on* investment, not as return *of* investment. But, in fact, according to partnership law, that cash flow is a partial return of capital. If the partnership certificate is not amended to show a reduction in capital invested, the limited partners continue to be liable for the entire investment amount shown on public record. It should be pointed out that the actual likelihood of such a situation occurring is remote at best, but why not protect yourself as much as possible?

Part Five

FINANCIAL PLANNING FOR REAL ESTATE INVESTMENT

The Happy Road to Long-Range Security

As I stated at the beginning of this book, you cannot depend on the investment methods of the 1960s for security in today's turbulent times of inflation and steadily higher tax brackets. Putting money in so-called safe investments such as bonds, bank accounts, or even blue-chip stocks is simply not the way to move your buying power ahead. Shakespeare's theory of "neither a borrower nor a lender be" was probably great in his time, but in the 1980s it is a sure way to get yourself into bad financial shape.

As many people are finally realizing, one of the worst things you can do right now is pay off an existing mortgage that locks in the lower interest rate of a few years ago. It once was an intelligent move to pay off a little extra on the mortgage whenever you were a few dollars ahead. Today, those rates of 6, 7, or 8 percent—even 9 percent—seem like a gift to be held on to as long as possible. In fact, it pays to be heavily in debt today, if the debt gives you control of solid, tangible assets.

Throughout this book, my purpose has been to show how intelligent investment in real estate will help you reduce income tax and increase your purchasing power. I hope you now understand the financial power of real estate investment and know how to go about finding and evaluating suitable real estate investment opportunities.

PLANNING IS ESSENTIAL FOR SUCCESS

Understanding the basic premise of tax-advantaged investment and the special values of real estate is a good beginning. To put this knowledge to work requires one more step: planning how much money to invest and how often to make additional investments.

An occasional tax-sheltered investment made when you get the urge or when a securities salesperson informs you of an attractive investment is not the best approach. For maximum value on your investments, you should invest on a planned basis, scaled to your income and to the personal profit you can gain from tax shelter. By far the best approach is to establish a long-range investment plan, one that will reflect growth in your earnings and allow for reinvestment of the profit of earlier investments as they are sold. The result can be an absolute lid on your income-tax bracket and a dramatic build-up of your net worth over time. It takes some effort and financial discipline, but as you will see later in this chapter, it can produce amazing results.

HOW TO DECIDE ON THE SIZE OF YOUR FIRST TAX-SHELTERED REAL ESTATE INVESTMENT

There are three points to consider as you ponder your first real estate limited-partnership investment:

1. Do you have sufficient financial security to invest?
2. How much tax shelter can you use effectively?
3. How much cash do you have available for investment?

As a guide to readers who want to plan initial investments for themselves, we will briefly discuss the aspects of each of these questions and provide some suggestions for personal planning. Even those readers who are already limited-partnership investors may find this material interesting as different planning concepts are covered. Later in this chapter, specific planning ideas for established investors will be presented.

Do You Have Enough Financial Security to Afford to Invest?
This question is designed to make you come to grips with the fact that real estate limited-partnership investments must be recognized as long-term commitments. You have to assume that this money will not be available if you unexpectedly need cash. Unless you have a relatively assured income sufficient to cover your living costs and reasonable reserves to take care of unforeseen needs, you are not financially ready for this kind of investment.

The amount of reserve you need relates to the nature of your income. If you are an entrepreneur, or if a major portion of your income depends on commissions or bonuses, I suggest you would do well to have a cash reserve equal to about a year's basic living expense. If you receive a salary from an extremely secure job, you might decide to have a reserve equal to only three or four months' cost of living. The actual span of time you should cover in your reserve is a rather personal decision. It is really a question of what makes you comfortable, though I suggest you lean to the conservative side and put away a bit more than you think you will ever need.

When I suggest that this reserve should cover your living expenses, I do not mean it should be equal to your normal income for the period in question. First, since this will be money on which you have already paid income tax, you certainly do not need that portion of your income. Secondly, if you ever get into an emergency and need to live on this money, you will be able to temporarily eliminate some large items such as savings for major new purchases, vacations, and so on. Simply calculate what you would need to maintain a reasonably similar standard of living for a period of emergency and tuck that amount of money into an immediately available interest-bearing account. It probably will not keep up with inflation, but that is the price you pay for this important security and peace of mind.

Next, be sure you have enough life insurance to protect dependents in the event of your death, and major-medical insurance to cover the costs of a catastrophic illness.

If you have provided these fundamental security funds and have enough current income to cover your standard of living, you are indeed in a position to plan a program of inflation-and-tax-fighting investments.

How Much Tax Shelter Can You Use Effectively? As you know, our income-tax structure is progressive. That is, the more you earn, the higher the tax percentage. This works in steps, with each level of your earnings being taxed at a progressively higher percentage. It is important to understand that when we say someone is in the 49 percent tax bracket, we do not mean he or she pays 49 percent income tax on all money earned. The bracket percentage applies only to the amount of income included on the top step the taxpayer has reached. The other side of this coin is that as you shelter your income down to lower steps, you will be reducing the applicable tax percentages and will get proportionately less cash saving from the tax shelter.

As an example, let us say that in 1980 you were a married taxpayer filing jointly with your spouse. Your combined taxable income (after itemized deductions and personal exemptions) was $55,000. The top $9,200 of this total was taxed at 49 percent. The next layer down, from $35,200 to $45,800, was taxed at 43 percent. On the amount below that, down to $29,900, you paid Uncle Sam 37 percent. Each lower bracket carried a lighter tax bite, until the final $3,400, which was not taxed at all!

This kind of tax-bracket analysis for your own situation is quite easy to calculate. Just ask your accountant or the local IRS office for the appropriate charts.

Now, you may ask why you should pay any income tax. Why not shelter all the way down and save the whole thing? This is legal, but quite apart from any ethical question of supporting your government, it is generally not good economics. Since a good portion of the return on your real estate limited-partnership investment will come through tax savings, you are cutting this return way down if you are protecting lower-bracket taxation. Assume you have invested $20,000 and you will receive about $25,000 worth of tax deductions over the life of the investment. If those deductions shelter income on which you would otherwise have been taxed at 49 percent, the immediate cash savings will be about $12,250. If the shelter affects income taxed at 40 percent, the immediate savings will be $10,000. But, if you had too much shelter and this investment covered only income which would have been taxed at 20 percent, your savings would only amount to $5,000.

In Chapter 5, where the basics of tax shelter were explained, I pointed out that shelter is not a gift, but really a very valuable deferral. Tax savings provide much of the current income from real estate investment in that they give you cash savings to work with during the investment period. When the property is sold, under the best circumstances the previously deducted shelter will be taxed as capital gain. Of course, this means only 40 percent of the amount will be taxed, whatever your bracket is at the time. Assuming that when your limited-partnership property is sold your tax bracket will be the same as or lower than it was when you made the investment, you will have a real tax saving.

On the other hand, if you originally sheltered income in a low tax bracket, it is entirely possible you will have to pay your capital-gains tax in a much higher bracket. Even though only 40 percent of the capital gain is taxed, it is possible to lose money on the deal if your original shelter was at too low a rate. If recapture taxation is involved when your property is sold, your chance of losing on the total tax transaction is even greater if you sheltered too deeply.

So I certainly do not recommend shelter to the extent that all your income tax be eliminated. Many people will tell you that it is not wise to shelter below 49 percent, but I do not agree with this either. That figure was often appropriate prior to the Tax Reform Act of 1976, when deep shelters were popular and many of the investments were not designed for ultimate profit. Today, there are not many legitimate shelter investments that really require that high a tax bracket to be economically advantageous.

Under present laws and conditions, assuming an investment offers shelter of not more than 1.5 or 1.8 times the invested amount and is oriented to ultimate profit, I feel it is quite reasonable to shelter income at least as low as 37 percent. Not every investment opportunity is necessarily suitable for shelter at that level, but many are. Just remember, the higher the tax bracket being sheltered, the more valuable the shelter will be to your investment.

How to Calculate Your Personal Tax-Shelter Opportunity. To suggest an approach to this planning function that will work for you, let us review a specific case. Marge and Stan Harrison are in their early forties, both employed as public-school teachers with over twenty years of seniority. Stan is currently paid $25,800, while Marge's salary is $27,000 because she serves as a department head in addition to teaching. Apart from salary, they have a fairly good retirement plan and excellent insurance benefits.

The Harrisons have no children. They own a satisfactory home with an 8 percent mortgage, one car that is paid for and another with twenty-six payments yet to go. Stan inherited two hundred shares of stock with a market value of about $20,000 and annual dividends of $1,500. In addition, the Harrisons have a bank savings account that fluctuates between $2,000 and $3,000 and a money-market certificate for $20,000, which is currently paying 11.55 percent interest.

The Harrisons' union-negotiated contract has assured them of a raise in pay each year, but because they are near the top of the scale for their profession, this has only averaged a bit over 6 percent annually over recent years. Because of their double income, they are doing all right financially, but they feel they are falling behind because of inflation and high taxes. They have decided to look into a real estate investment.

The first planning the Harrisons did was to get out last year's income-tax return to find out what tax shelter might do for them. With total income from all sources of $56,747, they calculated a taxable income of $52,150 and a federal tax of $15,831. In the great American tradition, they had risen to the 49 percent income-tax bracket!

At this point they went to work with the appropriate IRS tax-rate schedules to see just what tax shelter could accomplish for them. After setting up a number of hypothetical situations, they decided that the best result for them would be to shelter about $17,000 of income. This would defer the tax on all of their 40 and 49 percent tax-bracket income, and would give them an immediate cash savings of about $7,700. If they sheltered another $5,000 they would save only an additional $1,850. They felt that would be stretching their investment capital too far.

Based on the idea of an investment that would provide about 1.2 dollars of shelter for each dollar of investment, the Harrisons assumed they would need to invest about $14,000 to achieve their immediate goal, and this they could handle easily. They arranged next to meet with the very knowledgeable securities representative who had first introduced them to the idea of a real estate limited-partnership investment.

He quickly pointed out one error in their plan. Because real estate investments are long-term, it is not usually possible to invest in private limited partnerships for shelter in only one year. The total amount projected is usually spread over a number of years, generally on a declining schedule. Thus, their total investment would have to be larger to achieve the $17,000 they wanted this year—but it would also produce shelter in future years. As the representative pointed out, the Harrisons' need for shelter would continue, so they would be wise to plan for several years rather than just for one.

With this in mind, the Harrisons started to look at specific available programs producing shelter at the level they had decided upon. Their final choice involved a total investment of $37,500 over a four-year period. As indicated below, it saved them what they wanted in the first year and gave them a good start on shelter in each of the following three years. In addition, they liked the economic potential for profit and the location of the large and modern apartment complex involved. Table 8 shows the cost and shelter facts involved in the Harrisons' investment choice:

TABLE 8
Investment Cost and Shelter
(Marge and Stan Harrison)

Year	Investment	Cash distribution	Tax shelter deduction/ taxable income
1981	$13,000	$ 0	($18,133)
1982	10,500	0	(12,078)
1983	7,000	0	(7,062)
1984	7,000	0	(7,590)
Subtotal	$37,500	0	($44,863)
1985–1989	0	26,053	10,032
Total	$37,500	$26,053	($34,831)

As the final part of their plan, the Harrisons analyzed their ability to pay the investment installments involved without any strain.

They hope to be able to add additional investments to bring the amount of shelter each year up to $17,000, or whatever they may need to shelter all or most of their 40 and 49 percent bracket income.

Notice that after the four years of projected shelter, this investment projects a healthy cash-flow return. The amount indicated is projected as partly sheltered and partly taxable. The Harrisons have not planned this far ahead, but they hope to be able to reinvest this cash in additional limited-partnership interests.

How Much Cash Do You Have Available for Real Estate Investment? This, of course, is the other side of the question relating to how much investment you can profitably use. In order to achieve the desired shelter you must start with sufficient cash. The first-time real estate investor should not come up with an answer to the cash availability question too rapidly. Many people who are earning enough to use real estate investments profitably feel instinctively that they do not have the funds available. In fact, a careful analysis of their situation will frequently show them that they could shift out of less valuable investments or use some of their discretionary income to make real estate investing feasible.

The best approach is to list all of your present assets and calmly consider what each is doing for you and which might better be put to work in a real estate limited partnership. Always keep in mind the importance of maintaining both an emergency fund and sufficient cash flow for your established standard of living. As you come up with a suitable plan, be sure to put it in writing. This is essential to allow easy review from time to time and to give you the basis for financial discipline.

As an example of how this planning should be carried out, Table 9 shows the Harrisons' investment plan based on the financial information previously provided.

TABLE 9
Investment Cash Availability
(Marge and Stan Harrison)

Source	1981	1982	1983	1984
Tax savings from shelter in previous year	$ 0	$ 8,103	$ 9,000*	$10,000*
Sale of stock (net)	19,000	0	0	0
Regular savings	2,000	2,000	2,000	2,000
Money-market certificate	20,000	28,000	21,000	15,000
Savings account	2,500	2,500	2,500	2,500
Total capital available	$43,500	$40,603	34,500	$29,500
Capital contribution to investment #1	$13,000	$10,500	$ 7,000	$ 7,000
Additional investments	$ 0	$ 6,500*	$10,000*	$10,500*

*Estimated

Plan for 1981—Take $13,000 investment capital from sale of stock, add balance of stock money and regular savings to money-market certificate.

Plan for 1982—Make investments with tax savings plus $9,000 held out of money-market certificate when rolled over. Add regular savings to certificate.

Plan for 1983—With shelter somewhat larger because of annual income increase, pay for additional investments with last year's tax savings plus withdrawal from money-market certificate.

Plan for 1984—Same pattern as 1983.

You will notice that at no time in the next four years will the Harrisons' liquid cash reserves dip below $12,000. This is the minimum they decided they need. It is not a large amount, but they feel it is sufficient in view of their extremely stable employment.

This plan does an excellent job of using the tax-shelter benefits each year to create additional shelter for future years. Additional investment funds come from a shift of existing investments and from savings that the Harrisons were already accumulating each year. They do not plan to invest any of their annual salary increases, because they assume these dollars will be needed to keep up with inflated costs of living.

It may appear that the Harrisons' capital is declining each year (from $43,500 in 1980 to $29,500 in 1983). That, of course, is their available or uninvested capital. If you add back their total investment in real estate of $64,500, you will see that as of 1983 their total capital will have increased from $43,500 to $108,000. To a large degree, this is because they will have transformed potential tax payments into investment capital. As a matter of fact, by 1983 the properties in which they will have invested will probably have had a substantial increase in value due to inflation, so their actual net worth will probably be much higher.

While this planning has centered on tax shelter, the Harrisons are also looking for economic profit from their investments. They will not know how this works out until their first property is sold and the profit realized. However, they do know there is excellent potential. Based on the projections provided in the prospectus, if the property is sold at the end of the fifth year of the investment, and if a moderate 7 percent annual appreciation in value is realized, this is what their overall return on their first investment will look like. These figures assume that the Harrisons will shelter tax at approximately 45 percent bracket, but that the profit on sale will be taxed in a 49 percent bracket:

TABLE 10
Investment Return Projection
(Marge and Stan Harrison)

Tax savings	$20,278*
Cash distributions	4,026
Cash returned at sale	53,506
Tax on sale: ordinary	(1,185)
capital	(12,611)
After-tax proceeds	64,014
Less capital contributed	37,500*
Net after-tax return	26,514*
Annual *after-tax* discounted rate of return	21.22%

*Since the Harrisons will have used all tax savings for capital contributions during the life of the investment, the capital contributed actually consisted of only $17,222 of their previously earned income.

Again, the discounted rate of return includes the benefits of tax shelter, cash flow, and after-tax sale proceeds.

A PLANNING CONCEPT FOR HIGHER-INCOME PEOPLE THAT CAN TURN THEM INTO MILLIONAIRES

While people with incomes moderate by today's standards can achieve important benefits from real estate investment, those with higher incomes can benefit dramatically. It has always saddened me to see investors with earnings in the neighborhood of $100,000 per year invest in real estate only sporadically. They are missing so much of their opportunity by not creating a planned approach that will assure consistent tax benefits and steady growth in after-tax net worth every year.

The executive or professional or business owner in the high earning range tends to receive a steady growth in income each year due to the pressure of inflation. However, income tax will eat up most of these gains and most of the return from conventional investments. These people need real estate investments more than any other group, and they need them on a planned basis.

To dramatize this opportunity, I have developed the Step Investing Plan. It is really a very simple concept involving some basic planning and two annual reviews. It assumes that a person has determined what range of cash is required to maintain the desired family living standard and what level of tax he or she desires to pay. (As pointed out earlier in this chapter, the taxation level should be decided through careful analysis and probably with professional guidance.)

With these two basic financial benchmarks established, the Step Investing Plan focuses on how much tax-advantaged real estate investment to make each year to maintain the desired results. Assuming that the investor's income moves up as a result of inflation, additional investment steps are added in order to maintain roughly the same taxable percentage rate on an annual basis. And as tax shelter from past investments declines, additional steps must be added to maintain the amount of shelter required.

One result of an investment program guided by the Step Investing Plan is a gradual increase in the size and number of limited partnership investments, a kind of planned discipline lacking with hit-or-miss sporadic investment. There are two major impacts. First, taxable income is maintained at or near a predetermined level while the growing number of dollars that would have gone to pay taxes is diverted to increasing net worth. Second, and most important, the investor is building a solid fortune for future freedom and security.

The Step Investing Plan can make a millionaire out of any reasonably high-earning individual in ten to fifteen years! This is not pie in the sky. It is simply a matter of setting goals and then having the discipline to adhere to them. Economically viewed, it is a matter of using our tax laws and the horrendous forces of inflation to personal benefit.

An Example of How the Step Investing Plan Works. To quickly show the action of a Step Investing Plan, consider the case of John Parkhurst, M.D. John is a physician with income from fees, interest, and dividends of just under $100,000 in 1981. He anticipates a 5 to 10 percent increase each year in gross income, depending on the economy. Back in 1978 John started to hit the high-income range, and as his tax bite got bigger along with his style of living, his personal finances started to get out of control. He actually had to borrow money that year to pay bills. In a long and personal chat with his accountant, John was strongly advised to start an investment program that would get his taxes under control and start to build some net worth. The result was a plan based on our step investment concept, which went into action in 1979.

Chart 3 illustrates the actual investments and results of John's planning in 1979, 1980, and 1981, as well as his forecast of real estate limited-partnership investment for the following three years. The basic original premise was to get taxable income down to about $50,000 and to keep it there despite increased gross income. It was felt that John's cash living requirements would not allow enough investment to shelter below this level.

The chart is not a detailed planning tool, but simply a visualization of the plan. Details are recorded and reviewed on a Personalized Tax Analysis, which is illustrated and discussed in the next section of this chapter.

Several interesting things can be noted in Chart 3. First, during the initial year John was not able to achieve his tax-shelter goal because he did not have enough investment funds available. Nevertheless, he got started, and because he planned ahead, he was able to meet his objective in 1980. (The actual taxable-income level achieved in each year will vary somewhat from the objective, since investments are selected by a number of criteria and may or may not precisely fit the desired shelter amount.)

Notice that during the three years of actual operation John recognized a growing shelter need each year. This was the result of his increasing income, tied to the fact that shelter from previous investments commonly decreases year by year. The important fact to recognize is that this left a trail of investment dollars working for John as an inflation hedge. In the future, as each property is sold at a profit, John's net worth will take a quantum leap.

Notice that, in planning for 1984, John at the advice of his General Partner has anticipated the sale of his first investment for an increase in his taxable income. He will counter this by a suitable increase in shelter.

Through 1984 in his Step Investing Plan, John will have invested $173,000. By 1989, ten years after he started, he will have probably invested $475,000. About $400,000 of this will have been funded by tax-deferral dollars, $37,000 from tax-sheltered cash flow, and only $38,000 from after-tax money earned by John. The most important projection is that if we assume a moderate 7 percent annual appreciation in the properties involved, his net worth from these investments alone at the end of just ten years will be in excess of $690,000.

Annual Tax Planning Analysis to Detail Step-Investment Decisions. The Personalized Tax Analysis form has been developed by the Hall Real Estate Group to help our clients anticipate their shelter-investment needs on a timely basis. Many people put off tax considerations until the very end of the year, by which time it is simply too late to make intelligent investments that will provide the proper benefits.

CHART 3

Step Investing Plan
Prepared for John Parkhurst, M.D.

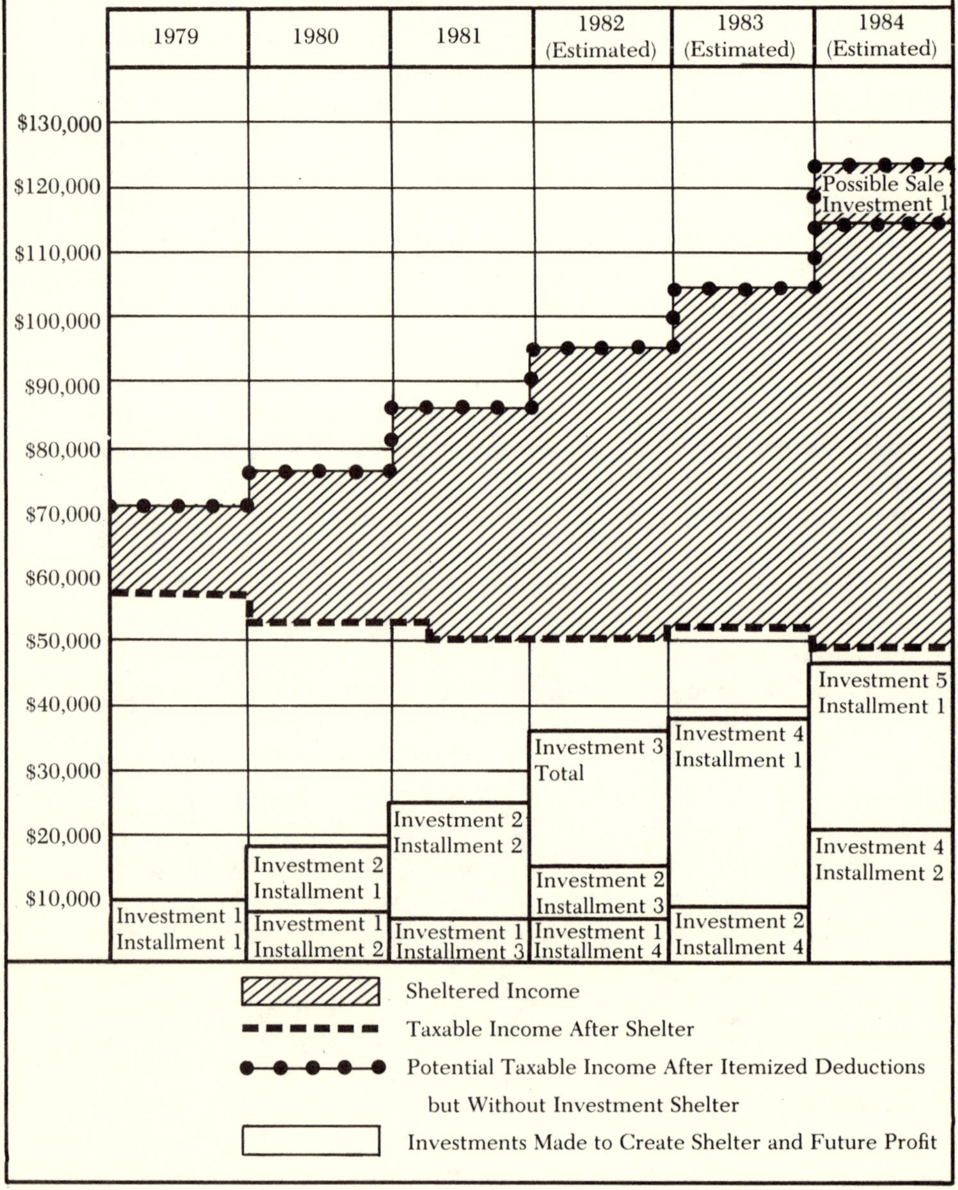

The objective of your tax planning should be to anticipate your personal income, less itemized deductions and other tax shelter, and arrive at your estimated taxable income for the year at hand. This will tell you if you are in a tax bracket in which additional tax-advantaged investment will be needed.

The ideal time to do this planning is at the end of each year as you look ahead to the new year. While you may not be able to be completely accurate in forecasting your total income for the coming year, you should get a fairly realistic feeling. If you are off by 10 percent or even a bit more, the error will not be costly. Total avoidance of any early planning, on the other hand, can be very costly.

With an early idea of your shelter needs, you will be able to keep your eyes open for opportunities from January on. If you find an outstanding investment, you will be ready to review your forecast and move without hesitation. In any event, review your tax-planning analysis in April. This is the time that most of us focus on tax, so it is particularly appropriate. Also, one quarter of the year will be history, so you should be able to forecast the full year of income with clearer accuracy.

The format of the Personalized Tax Analysis is quite straightforward, and once you have started to use it you will find it very easy to maintain. Let us go through it briefly to clarify each area.

Line 1 is computed by first adding up all income from various sources. This usually includes income covered on the W-2 form plus interest from bank accounts, profit or loss, and dividends from investments. Your accountant can brief you on the current exclusions allowed for various types of interest and dividends. Also, based on the previous year's returns, you should include your estimated itemized deductions and personal exemptions. Line 2 is your estimated tax on this amount.

Line 3 is the total of tax-loss deductions anticipated from previously purchased tax-shelter investments. These should be itemized and checked out specifically, since there is considerable change in the shelter from any investment from year to year. The investment prospectus probably provides a projection of shelter for each year; to be more precise, you can check with the investment source.

Deduct line 3 from line 1 to get line 4, your estimated taxable in-

Hall Real Estate Personalized Tax Analysis

Prepared for:
Date:

	1982		1983		1984		1985		Total
	*	Dollars	*	Dollars	*	Dollars	*	Dollars	
1 Estimated taxable income after standard deductions									
2 Estimated tax									
Estimated deductions from previously purchased tax shelters:									

3	Total								
4	Estimated taxable income after tax-sheltered deductions (1 minus 3)								
5	Tentative tax on line 4, taken from tax-rate schedules for last year								
6	Additional deductions from [ ] units of [ ]								
7	Adjusted taxable income (4 minus 6)								
8	Tax owed on line 7, taken from tax-rate schedules for last year								
9	Tax dollars saved by new investment (5 minus 8)								
10	Total tax dollars saved (2 minus 8)								

While this form may assist you in your tax planning, it is not intended as a substitute for professional tax planning. See your tax advisor about what investments are appropriate in your individual circumstances. These estimates are subject to change due to the variables in operation.

* = Tax bracket percentage

come. This figure should then be looked up on the appropriate IRS tax-rate chart from the most recent year to get your tentative tax (line 5). The IRS or your accountant will provide the necessary chart.

Line 6 is used to set up a pro forma look at the consequences of adding additional tax shelter. You may try this either with an arbitrary amount of additional shelter or with a particular investment possibility that will render a specific amount of shelter.

Lines 7, 8, and 9 show the result of the investment entered on line 6 in terms of reducing your taxable income and thus reducing your tax. Line 10 shows the total taxes saved by your entire shelter program, including proposed new investments.

Once you have used this analysis to help pinpoint your need, make your decision and take action. The Step Investing Plan will work only if you continue to apply the discipline necessary to achieve your objectives. Vacillation is a sure way to become a loser.

CASH-FLOW PLANNING

Along with planning your tax-shelter need, it is equally important to review and plan your cash flow. You must keep your investment activity in balance with your cash position and your personal living expenses. There is no sense in creating problems in your everyday living in an overzealous effort to cut taxes and build your net worth.

At the time you analyze your income in terms of tax planning, I suggest you also analyze and project your overall cash flow. This need not be done in great detail, as our spending habits tend to fall into a pattern that remains fairly stable from year to year. The important thing is to recognize special expenditures as they are planned and make provision to handle them with ease. Examples of this would include major home remodeling, refurnishing, or a major vacation trip. As tax-shelter investments are made, it is also important to put any commitment for later capital contributions into your cash-flow plan.

A simple form for an annual cash-flow analysis is provided as a guide to this element of planning.

BORROWING TO INVEST

While planning cash flow is of paramount importance, many high-earning investors are short of cash when investment opportunities come along. Prudent borrowing to invest can be a very sound and effective tool. Make sure, however, that the repayment plan for any such borrowing fits into your future cash-flow capabilities. If you are in the 49 percent or higher tax bracket and have a dependably high future source of income, by all means consider reasonable borrowing for investing. Your tax savings will pay back a great portion of the loan quite quickly. However, always make sure you don't over-extend yourself through borrowing.

HOW PLANNING CAN ELIMINATE THE TAX-PREFERENCE SHOCK SYNDROME

Back in Chapter 5, I pointed out that under certain conditions tax shelters can come back to create an inordinate tax payment. This has to do with the taxation of shelters achieved through so-called "tax-preference" items in recapture at the time of sale or foreclosure.

Tax preference applies to specific kinds of deductions involved in equipment leasing, oil and gas, real estate, and some other investments. In the case of real estate it is generally created by accelerated depreciation. Tax-preference legislation was approved in an effort on the part of the government to gain back some tax revenue where "excessive" shelter had been involved. As is so often the case, the legislation didn't necessarily work out as intended. The tax consequences are directly proportionate to the percentage of tax-preference losses to total tax losses. There is no direct relationship between this proportion and the overall tax-loss ratio. In other words, for any given amount of shelter, you may incur very little or very great potential tax liability in the event of a future foreclosure or unfavorable sale. It all depends on the proportion of tax-preference items involved in the shelter—the greater the tax preference, the more tax you'll have to pay.

Cash-Flow Analysis for Year of _____

Name _____
Date _____

Item	Jan	Feb	Mar	Apr	May	Jun	Jul	Aug	Sep	Oct	Nov	Dec	Total
1. Cash carry forward													
2. Regular earned income (net after withholding)													
3. Bonus or other special income (net)													
4. Investment income													
5. Total cash flow (Add lines 1 + 2 + 3 + 4)													
6. Regular living expenses (mortgage, household, car operations, charge accounts, average medical, clothing and entertainment)													

7. Infrequent expenses (insurance, taxes, vacations)				
8. Extraordinary planned expenses (remodeling, refurnishing, new car)				
9. Deferred capital contributions to limited partnerships				
10. Total expense				
11. Cash carry forward (Deduct line 10 from line 5 and put remainder in line 1 for next month)				

Tax-preference shock may occur when an investor in a deal with heavy tax-preference shelter experiences a profitable sale, an unprofitable sale, or a foreclosure. In the case of a profitable sale the surprise is that a great portion of the proceeds may now be taxed as ordinary income instead of capital gains. There will be money available to pay the tax, but the deal will still be less profitable than anticipated.

In the case of an unfavorable sale at or near the amount of the existing mortgage, the result can be extremely painful. In the case of a foreclosure, the transaction is treated for tax purposes as a sale at the mortgage balance. No cash proceeds are received, and yet very high taxes may be owed due to recapture of the tax-preference shelter as ordinary income. This can place many investors in the top bracket for that year.

What can you do to avoid tax-preference shock? First, carefully check each investment for the percentage of the total shelter that is created by tax-preference items. The securities representative or General Partner will be able to give you this information. If tax-preference shelter is less than 10 percent of the total, the effect will be negligible and you need not be concerned. If the percentage is above 10 percent, the advisability of that particular investment will depend on your income and tax situation, and these should be reviewed with a knowledgeable tax advisor.

As a general rule, the less tax preference involved, the better. However, an investor willing to assume the potential risks may find that other attractive elements of the investment make it desirable despite high tax-preference involvement. In these situations, I strongly suggest that an analysis be made to determine the degree of potential recapture. Depending on the extent of risk, you might be well advised to give consideration to the "set-aside" concept described below, which will assure cash being available to handle whatever tax consequences may occur on an unfavorable termination of the investment.

THE TAX-PREFERENCE SET-ASIDE CONCEPT

As a matter of intelligent planning, it is wise for the investor to know year by year what a tax consequence of a foreclosure or unprofitable sale would be. This can be developed by your accountant. As a guide, the amount of recapture and capital gain the investor will realize at the conclusion of the investment is equal to all of the tax-preference deductions he has received, times his tax bracket, plus all other deductions he has received, times 0.4 (the capital-gains adjustment), times the investor's tax bracket for all losses above the original investment. The investor's potential capital-gains liability will also be increased for every dollar of cash distribution he receives by the amount of cash distributions, times 0.4, times his tax bracket. Based on this information you can then determine what percentage of each year's cash savings achieved from the tax shelter should be set aside as a "rainy-day" fund to assure cash on hand. The percentage to be set aside will vary considerably, depending on the proportion of tax-preference items involved.

Our recommendation is to establish a set-aside fund only when the potential tax consequences would create a difficult tax bind for the investor in the event of an unfavorable investment result. Under these circumstances, the predetermined portion of each year's tax saving should go into an interest-bearing investment that is completely liquid. While this will remove some cash from your normal reinvestment stream, it creates great peace-of-mind protection.

Assuming the investment is carried to a successful conclusion, the set-aside fund can then be liquidated and the accumulated reserve added to your sale proceeds, free for any desired use.

DIVERSIFICATION FOR SAFETY AND PROFIT

If you follow the Step Investing Plan you will probably need enough shelter each year to give you an excellent chance to diversify within the broad real estate field. I strongly urge you to do this instead of putting your entire investment each year into just one limited partnership. Since no one can foresee or control all of the events that may affect a given investment, it just makes good sense to split up your involvement and thus lessen the effect of any one problem that may occur.

As your investment funds become large enough, just divide them up each year and select two or three different limited-partnership opportunities instead of just one. This will give you an opportunity to diversify in geographic markets and in types of real estate, as you desire.

If you make just two investments per year for ten years, you will have twenty different properties working for you. Of these, it is likely that one or two will turn into unexpectedly large winners. This will nicely offset any that surprise you by turning out to be losers (that too can happen). With this kind of diversification and consistent investment build-up, you will be well on your way to financial security beyond your fondest dreams.

THE VALUE OF OVERALL PLANNING

We have completed our consideration of planning as it applies to real estate limited-partnership investment, but I would like to add a few thoughts about broader planning in relation to your total financial position, your place in your career field, your place in society, and anything else that may be important to you.

It has always amazed me that many people devote time and serious effort to planning their estate and other matters connected with their deaths, but rarely give any consideration to a "living plan." I have found that most people can achieve just about anything they really want in this life, but it takes a sound plan and determination to make it work.

If this section on real estate investment planning makes sense to you, I urge you to broaden the idea and apply it to your total financial situation, and to all of the things you want to achieve in life. Planning is not any more complicated than clearly defining goals, analyzing the steps required to reach them, and putting the decisions you make in writing.

The ultimate difference between planning and just dreaming of greater glory is what you do with your plan after you have created it. If you make it a part of your life, with frequent reviews and with realistic fine-tuning, you have *something to make real*. It is this kind of planning that is the key to using real estate to beat inflation and taxes. It can also be the key to achieving anything else you want in life.

Evaluating the Total Investment Opportunity for You

TEN CRITICAL AREAS OF EVALUATION

OVER the years a number of highly competent accountants and tax attorneys have asked me for suggestions about analyzing offering documents of real estate limited partnerships for their clients. Obviously they need no guidance in examining the financial aspects of the investment opportunities, but they felt a need to go beyond that and have a basis for judging the total package.

This chapter is a response to that need. In some areas the material that follows will review and summarize previous sections of this book. Where appropriate I will refer to these sections for detail.

What follows is organized by areas of consideration that do not necessarily correspond to the way a prospectus is organized. It may require a certain amount of flipping back and forth through a mass of paper to sift out the meaningful data and eliminate the legal jargon. You will find that when the material is viewed in parts it is not nearly as complicated as it first seems, and when the exercise is completed you will have a good basis for decision-making.

Area 1: Overall Format and Disclosure. Your first consideration in this kind of overview should be to evaluate the format and the clarity of the document itself. Is the presentation intelligently structured? Is the format clear and easy to read? Is the quality of printing appropriate?

It may be unfair to equate form with substance, but sloppy form may very well be a clue to sloppy substance. Furthermore, the document is a representation of the sponsor, and to that extent its form may tell you a good bit about the self-image and working approach of the people behind the investment.

In addition to the class and quality of the presentation itself, carefully consider the tone and detail of all disclosure elements. Does it appear that the General Partner–Sponsor is fully disclosing negative aspects of the property as well as describing the favorable conditions? This should entail more than just brief mentions of existing or potential problems. Those problems should be documented and detailed just as heavily as the more positive aspects.

Carefully review the document to see how it stands up to these standards for tone, disclosure, and informational communication.

Area 2: General Partner–Sponsor. As I have stressed throughout this book, the General Partner is the key to the success of any real estate investment. Invest all the effort necessary to make a sound judgment in this area. Most of the information you should consider will be found in the prospectus. Some may require further questioning of either your securities representative or individuals in the General Partner's organization.

Read the section on the General Partner's background and experience with care. Pay special attention to the General Partner's related experience. Does he have a substantial track record in the area in which he proposes to lead this investment? Does his experience appear to be close enough to the needs of this investment so that he will not require an on-the-job education for which you will pay?

Next, consider the financial strength of the General Partner. Is his net worth substantial? Is it large enough to provide a short-term loan, if necessary to support the partnership?

Consider the depth of the General Partner and his sponsoring affiliates. Do they have sufficient personnel and experience and a program for continuity to assure that the inability of one or more key individuals will not throw the entire organization into disaster? What is the back-up strength within the organization?

Finally, you should be very concerned with the incentive of the General Partner. Does he have enough at stake, either in the form of cash invested or in established reputation, to assure every possible effort to achieve success for this venture? Obviously, dollars invested create excellent incentive, but don't underestimate the power of desiring to maintain an established reputation. A substantial General Partner with a well-established track record considers his reputation to be his most valuable asset. He knows that in the investment business you are only as good as your last deal, so he will generally go to great lengths to assure success.

Check out past actions of the General Partner in terms of special efforts when conditions require them. Every experienced General Partner has had problems. Your questions should be what they did about them. Did he support his problem projects either financially or with special management attention? Has he been successful in turning problems back into successes?

Area 3: Financial Projections. If you are convinced that the people involved in the investment look good, consider the potential benefits of the deal. How much do you need to invest? Is this in line with your available funds and your overall investment planning? Does the sponsor show a statement of source and use of funds? Review where the invested money goes to be sure you are satisfied that this is fair and reasonable.

How much return is indicated in each of the years during which you will be putting capital into the investment? How much will you make over the first five years? Ten years?

Consider how the projected earnings break down in terms of cash flow and tax shelter. Is the split appropriate to your personal needs and other projected income over those same years? What tax bracket do you expect to be in during each of the years involved, and what tax savings does that indicate you will receive? Do the projections include any sale of the property? If so, when? at what price? under what terms? While no one can predict the future, do you feel these projections are reasonable, based on history and your own future economic expectations? How will the sale projections translate into dollars of return for your interest in the partnership?

Area 4: Financial Assumptions. Before you get too excited about how good this investment is going to be and how much money you are going to make, take a hard look at the underlying assumptions on which these projections are based. Most of these are usually found in the footnotes to the financial projections, but some may also be found in sections on the description of the project, source and use of funds, acquisition, and development.

In considering these assumptions, it may be important to probe beyond the stated items and find out more about why certain positions were taken. Your securities representative should be able to provide such detail. It will also be revealing to find out who prepared the assumptions, the qualifications of the individual, and whether or not personal investigation in the market around the property was conducted.

Particularly consider the projections for occupancy and for expense factors. How do these items compare with past operations? If they are significantly different, why?

What are the tax assumptions leading to the projected tax loss? Is the depreciation schedule reasonable and in keeping with IRS regulations? Are any areas of assumption affecting taxes particularly aggressive and likely to be challenged on audit?

Finally, and I suggest most importantly, is the question of whether the reserves or "cushions" established in the projections are adequate for prudent protection of the partnership.

Area 5: The Project Itself. If you have decided that the financial aspects make sense and you feel comfortable about the people involved, move on to look at the property to see if that contributes to the opportunity. Where is the property located? Consider both the general location and the specific location. In general terms, is the area economically strong or expected to have an upturn in the future? As to a specific location within an area, is it desirable in terms of population trends, transportation, shopping, and other amenities?

What type of property is it? How does this meet current market demand? What is the current economic condition of the operation? What are the possibilities for capital appreciation? What is the current physical condition? How much competition exists or is likely to develop? For more details of property consideration, see Chapter 11 and Appendix 5.

Area 6: Risk Factors. Consider both the general risks appropriate to all real estate investments, and the specific risks that should be specified in the prospectus.

Do the risks appear to be fully disclosed? Are there any unusual risks that apply to this property? How serious or real are they toward possibly harming the value of the investment?

As detailed in Chapter 12, each of the following areas of risk should be reviewed:

- Staying power and reserves
- Physical problems of the property
- Local economic conditions
- Location desirability
- Additional competition
- Litigation
- Tax-law changes and tax audit
- Economic depression
- Government intervention

Area 7: Fees. What are the General Partner's fees in the transaction? What services are being provided for the fees? Are the fees too high for the value of the services to the investors? Are they too low, and might this indicate that the General Partner will not have the financial wherewithal or incentive to carry out the services required by the partnership?

Is the purchase price of the property being passed on to the limited partners at the General Partner's direct cost, or is it being sold at a profit? If the property is being sold at a profit, has that been fully and clearly disclosed, and does it seem fair to the investors?

If you are uncertain about any of these details, feel free to ask your securities representative or the General Partner himself for the information you need. Be sure you understand all fee considerations before you make your decision.

Area 8: Liabilities. Are there any call provisions in the partnership? A call provision gives the General Partner the right to ask limited partners for more money. Be sure you know whether there is such a right and, if so, that you understand and agree to it.

Has the General Partner described your limits on liability? Be sure the General Partner is planning to file a limited-partnership certificate and that it will specifically describe the extent of your liability.

Area 9: Conflicts of Interest. Most conflicts of interest reported in the prospectus will describe the worst-possible-case situations. Review each of these carefully and decide whether, in your opinion, the General Partner is likely to be in a position to abuse authority or take advantage of the conflict situation to your detriment. More important than his being in such a position is his inclination or incentive to take advantage of his investors.

Remember, a General Partner with an established reputation will make enough money legitimately to eliminate any need or desire to make a little more through unethical tactics. Very likely, if all matters of conflict of interest have been fully disclosed, you are dealing with the type of General Partner who will make future decisions openly and equitably.

As previously stated in this book, while employing affiliates of the General Partner to serve the needs of a partnership is technically a conflict of interest, it may in fact be beneficial to the investors. The quality and reputation of the General Partner should be the determining factor in consideration of this area.

Area 10: Suitability. We have assumed throughout this evaluation that you are qualified for the investment under consideration. That assumption, however, should be very specifically reviewed by your securities representative and yourself. Examine the suitability standards specified in the prospectus and make sure you do qualify. Don't stretch to qualify, no matter how enticing the assumptions, because likely as not it will still be an inappropriate investment for you.

Standards of income and/or net worth are established for each investment to assure that investors can shoulder the risk of the investment without undue hardship and, in the case of tax-advantaged investments, will be able to use those benefits effectively. If you do not qualify, you will still be able to find another real estate investment with lower suitability standards that will serve you well. More important than just suitability is to make sure that you can properly use the tax benefits from the investment. If you have doubts about this, consult your tax advisor.

THREE BASIC PRINCIPLES
THAT MAKE OR BREAK A DEAL

While the ten critical areas to examine give you a great understanding of a particular investment and ample information for an investment decision, I suggest an even more basic way to summarize your consideration.

An attorney friend of mine who for years was involved in securities regulation—first with the SEC and later as the securities commissioner for the state of Michigan, also as president of the National Securities Administrators of North America—stated that there are three basic principles to be considered in evaluating a real estate investment:

1. People
2. Project
3. Proceeds

I fully concur.

While the ten-area approach I have provided gives you a road map for thorough analysis of the risks and rewards of an offering, it is not realistic to expect an investor to go into full detail on each offering considered. However, even in a cursory review, you should have its basic structure and those three basic considerations in mind as a guide.

To whatever degree you probe for information, then weigh and balance the indicators, the "three P's" will really be the core of your decision. Who are the people? Does the project have potential? Are the proceeds of the partnership sufficient to carry out the partnership objectives? If all of these three considerations give you an overwhelmingly affirmative feeling, you have a more than reasonable chance of success in your venture.

Part Six

THE OUTLOOK FOR THE EIGHTIES

Real Estate Investment Enters the "Growth Stock" Era

IF you are one of the countless millions who could have invested in real estate in the 1970s but let the opportunity pass by, you are probably convinced that by now you missed another good thing. While reading to this point, you have likely been dredging up a lot of old clichés. You may be thinking, "Real estate would have been good, but now it is too high priced." Or you may have decided, "High interest rates will take all the profit out of real estate." Depending on the success of the Reagan administration since the writing of this book, you may even think, "Inflation is necessary for real estate success, and now it looks like our inflation is over."

I can only say, "You are wrong." The timing to get into real estate will never be better than now in the early 1980s. It is difficult to predict with accuracy what the long-term changes in our political, economic, and tax structures will accomplish. But for the decade of the eighties, I see continued, and actually increased, opportunity in real estate investment.

THE "TOO LATE" TRAP

If your thinking does indeed match any of the examples above, you have fallen into the trap that keeps most people forever on the financial defensive. There is a general feeling among investors that by the time they become aware of some important new development, it is time for the market to turn, and they are in fact too late.

Certainly timing should be a critical consideration in any investment strategy. However, to assume the ball game is over simply because you missed the early action is a form of financial paranoia, especially if it is used as an excuse to avoid a decision.

The best approach to an intelligent analysis of the future is to learn from the past, anticipate and apply the effect of all probable changes, and only then make an unemotional forecast.

REAL ESTATE COMES OF AGE AS A "GROWTH STOCK" INVESTMENT

Traditionally, prior to the 1970s, real estate was priced as a multiple of earnings based on current cash flow. A reasonable allowance might be made for increased equity to be earned out of operations, and for potential increases in rents, but these were relatively small considerations. By and large, real estate value came from current cash-flow production.

Today, that value measurement of a decade ago has largely disappeared. Prices of real estate investments now tend to be based on the inflationary expectation of the future, and current return is found in tax benefits rather than in big cash flow. This mystifies potential investors who continue to think of real estate as a typical income-producing investment.

Clearly there has been a most important change in the nature of real estate investment, and to date it has escaped the attention of many sophisticated investors. Real estate has become a "growth stock" type of investment. As a matter of fact, it may be the outstanding "growth stock" of the eighties. Of course real estate is not literally a stock, but I believe the analogy is very appropriate. After all, the stock market with its almost instant quotations is perhaps the most obvious example of how free markets work. Real estate as a market, while not having a formalized quotation system, does share many similarities in its pricing action with stocks.

For those who have never invested in actual growth stocks, let me add a few words of clarification. Suppose you were going to invest in a quiet little company based on its stable operations and the regular production of a cash dividend. Let's suppose the market would require a price per share 10 or 15 times the annual earnings per share. Now, if a large number of people decided that the same company had great potential for the future, perhaps because earnings were expected to increase with inflation, or because an increased demand for their product was developing, or for any other good reason, they would start to buy the stock, and that would push up the price. These buyers would be paying higher prices in anticipation of future growth and future value. As a result, they would have to accept a far lower current return on their investment. Instead of paying 10 times earnings, they might be willing to pay 20 or 30 or even 50 times earnings, depending on the value they put on the anticipated future growth. Over the years, this kind of investment pricing in the stock market has become an accepted phenomenon, and with proper selection many investors have become wealthy through such growth stocks.

I have no doubt that the general price increases in real estate over the last decade have to some extent been the result of more and more professionals viewing it as a growth investment and being willing to pay now for future value. While this concept is not yet broadly held, more and more investors are starting to understand it. As its acceptance spreads, one effect will be to make way for even higher prices, and certainly higher multiples of current earnings.

It is particularly interesting to talk with foreign investors—from Europe, South America, and the Orient. Two things attract them to real estate investment in the United States. First, they feel that despite our economic and political problems, we are still the most stable democracy left in the world. Second, they universally point out how cheap our real estate is compared to that in their home countries. Thus, millions of dollars of foreign money are pouring into U.S. real estate as an inflation hedge and a "growth stock" type of investment. Not only is real estate going to be priced as a "growth stock," but for a short time, under the recessionary and inflationary conditions of the early eighties, real estate is being bought and sold for less than its replacement cost. This makes real estate a bargain.

Because real estate has had such outstanding success in the last decade, there are those who think the party is over. There have been several recent pseudo-economic books predicting deflation and a crash of real estate values. To these doomsayers, I can only reply, "You haven't seen anything yet. The increases in value in the past are nothing compared to what you will see in the eighties." The reasons behind my conviction fill this chapter.

As you know from previous chapters, one of the bedrock reasons for real estate investment profit at this time is inflation. Obviously, you must be concerned with the future course of inflation in the United States as you consider the wisdom of real estate investment.

Our economy may well have some near term improvement, and the rate of inflation may take some encouraging dips. By comparison to the 1980 figure, a reduction to 7 or 8 percent inflation would seem like a miracle. But, in fact, that is still a high rate of inflation, and it would likely be setting the stage for the next round of higher percentages.

As the inflationary battle is being fought, there are other powerful influences that will slowly but surely reduce the availability of real estate investment opportunities, particularly in the residential area. Thus, with each new turn of the inflationary ratchet, as more buyers want real estate as an inflation hedge, the underlying prices will be adjusted upward. While personally I do not desire it, I believe real estate may well become an inflationary fear commodity similar to gold in the late seventies.

RENT-LAG THEORY

The generally accepted situation during inflationary periods is that costs rise, and people who own productive assets at fixed prices benefit. That is true, but it is not quite so simple, because all prices and all values do not rise equally.

Considering the housing industry specifically, I believe there is a definite pattern of price adjustment within the various kinds of housing, and that apartment rents are the last part of the spectrum to rise. This is not a broadly recognized part of real estate economics, but it is important to timing. Right now, I believe it has a major bearing on future profit potential.

To understand this theory you must start with the premise that all types of housing are interrelated in that they offer alternatives. You may own or rent. You may select a single-family detached house, a duplex, a rental apartment, a condominium apartment or villa, a co-op apartment, and so on. Housing represents a broad spectrum of options, but economically these options are interrelated, and what happens to one will eventually have an effect on the others.

In any particular inflationary cycle, the single-family home is generally the first part of the spectrum to increase in price. Builders and developers tend to build only when they can get enough out of each house to cover increases in materials and labor, plus a small profit. In most situations of this kind, buyers tend to pay the increased price because they want the product.

There are occasions when speculative builders may temporarily find themselves with an inventory and no demand, though this does not happen often. The industry is quick to stop production when necessary, and it can react faster than the builders of large multi-family housing projects.

As a result, prices of single-family houses are extremely sensitive to increases in their underlying cost components, and thus to inflation in general. The price of new single-family homes quickly reflects increases in costs of lumber, new union contracts with higher wages, higher land development costs (including such items as sewers and road construction), and even higher construction interest rates (which the new owner must absorb, along with the interest cost he must pay for a mortgage).

The next level of housing inflation is quite logically the used single-family house, since it is directly comparable to the new house. Assume you had a house built for $50,000 three years ago. Last month, a new house was built on the vacant lot next door. It is similar in design, size, appearance, and construction. The only real difference is that it cost $100,000. If you decide to sell, will you accept $55,000, or even $60,000? Not likely. You will carefully consider the minor differences involved, and in all likelihood you will decide to ask $98,500. That is, if you do not decide your fireplace is large enough that you can try for $101,000.

The price you actually sell for will, of course, be determined by demand in the marketplace. Other than during recessionary soft spots, demand continues strong year after year in desirable locations. Chances are you will sell your house for something reasonably close to your asking price, and another example of why used housing is so expensive will have been established.

As used detached single-family homes move to higher and higher levels, larger and larger numbers of would-be buyers are priced out of the market in terms of the space and location they want. This generally creates an increase in popularity for condominiums, both new and used, and their prices start to move up with the strength in that market.

At this point, it starts to make excellent economic sense to convert suitable apartments to condominiums. Real estate owners are always looking for opportunities to create a higher and better use for their property, and condominium conversion does this for existing multifamily dwelling units. As you know, this has been going on at a fast pace in recent years. It has been slowed by high interest rates and the recession, but it is a trend likely to continue for existing apartments.

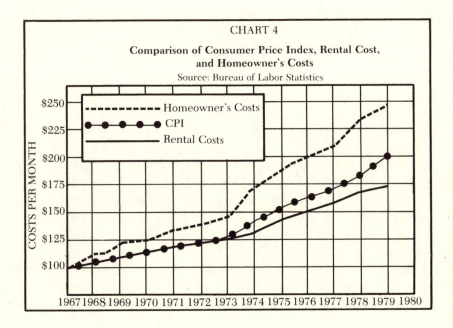

CHART 4

Comparison of Consumer Price Index, Rental Cost, and Homeowner's Costs

Source: Bureau of Labor Statistics

Chart 4 clearly portrays the Rent-Lag Theory. Prior to 1969, increases in cost of living, costs of owning a home, and rentals moved up slowly and proportionately. Then, as inflation became rampant, homeowner's costs soared dramatically higher than the Consumer Price Index, while rental costs inflated at a significantly lower rate than the general cost of living. The result was that by 1980, rental housing became one of the greatest bargains in the U.S. economy, and today rents are poised for a massive upturn.

THE RENT REVOLUTION—THE APPROACHING
PERIOD OF MAJOR INCREASES IN APARTMENT RENT

There are a number of reasons that rental apartments are the last item in the housing spectrum to feel the full force of inflation. First, the ownership of apartment projects is extremely diverse. Since few individual landlords own enough property to be much of a market force in an area, they tend to live in constant fear of negative results if they increase rents in advance of other nearby property owners. They have tended to hold back waiting for someone else to make the first move.

Secondly, in the past most landlords were working with the benefit of older mortgages at relatively low and fixed interest rates. In many cases, the fixed expense involved in paying off the mortgage was 50 percent or even more of the total operating expense. Since this relationship has not been affected by inflation, it has kept the pressure on the landlord relatively low. He could, in fact, hold the line without going broke for a lot longer than other businesses.

Third, during much of the decade of the seventies, the supply of new apartment construction was relatively large, and more than kept pace with the growth of demand. This created a market situation that encouraged landlords to hold the line even if it hurt.

Fourth, it is my observation that apartment owners on the whole have not been an especially capable or professional group. Most owners have tended to be more oriented toward maintaining a high occupancy—i.e., 97 or 98 percent—than to closely watching the financial bottom line. Because they did not know how to market their product, they simply met competition by holding down their rents.

As variable operating expenses increased faster and faster during the seventies, they accepted less cash flow and were satisfied to concentrate on tax shelter and the steady appreciation of sale values.

The result of these conditions has currently created a situation in which cash flow is virtually nonexistent in apartment projects that once produced sizable cash-flow returns. Almost all current investment return now comes from tax-shelter benefits. Moreover, operating expenses as a percentage of the gross income of typical apartment projects have been increasing rapidly over the last decade. Such expenses include property taxes and insurance but not mortgage payments or depreciation. In the early seventies and late sixties, expense factors generally ranged from 33 percent to a very high figure of 38 percent of gross income. Today, true expense figures range from a very low of 50 percent to a high of 60 percent. Many apartment projects are losing money on a cash-flow basis.

The bright spot at this point is the imminence of the upturn phase of the rent-lag cycle in apartment housing. I believe we will shortly see a "rent revolution," in which rents will increase faster than operating expenses.

More than cyclical timing is involved. Numerous other factors—such as the coming shortage of apartments available for rent, to be discussed later in this chapter—will add to the upward pressure. The stage is set, and as soon as the current recession is worked through and household formation resumes its growth, I believe there will be a dramatic rent increase trend that will strengthen the entire apartment industry, and benefit real estate investors.

HOW DO CURRENT APARTMENT INVESTMENT COSTS COMPARE TO REPLACEMENT CONSTRUCTION COSTS?

People who are concerned about a crash in real estate values frequently point out that ridiculously high prices are being paid by investors, and that property today is selling for far more than it is worth. If those perceptions were true, we would indeed have something to worry about. The fact is, they are not true.

How should we measure innate value? How can we be sure we are not caught up in a speculative fever that is temporarily creating artificial prices? I like to think that the replacement cost of any lasting item gives a fair basis for establishing its true value. In other words, if I buy something in good physical condition for about what it would cost to build it, I cannot be too far off in terms of value.

The key fact in refuting a speculative explosion of real estate prices is that replacement construction costs have gone up faster than both sale prices and income value. To get our housing industry back in reasonable balance, either construction costs will have to be drastically reduced or income and sales prices will have to continue to rise. Since I see almost no chance of construction costs being lowered, I believe the near future will bring a dramatic increase in rents, and a continued increase in sale prices.

In the past, a builder-developer could construct an apartment complex, operate it for a period of time while it was rented up, then sell it for about 105 to 110 percent of construction cost. The 5 to 10 percent was considered sweat equity, or the reward for the builder's risk. Today, inflation has pushed construction costs up so high, and so fast, that rental income has not even come close to keeping up. As a result, if some recent apartment construction must be sold, it usually goes for as much as 30 to 40 percent less than current replacement costs.

To be specific, in 1980, apartments completed in 1979 should have sold for about 120 percent of replacement. This would have included the builder's 5 to 10 percent sweat equity, and a premium for the favorable fixed-rate long-term mortgage, which was no longer available on the 1980 market. Instead, such properties sold for 70 to 80 percent of replacement cost. The reason was simply that their income value was too low to attract investment at a higher price. That can hardly be said to be speculative pricing in the marketplace.

THE CHANGING NATURE OF
HOUSING IN THE UNITED STATES

Everyone is familiar with the complete change in our buying patterns in the automobile industry. The "standard" gas-guzzler of ten years ago is now seen as a dinosaur; indeed, it is virtually extinct. As the cost of gasoline exploded upward, our demands in terms of size, speed, and power moved lower and lower. Consumers do not really want to move to smaller cars, but economics have dictated the change, and in a matter of just a few years a new and much lower standard has come into being.

Few people have yet come to grips with the fact that the same thing is happening in the housing industry. The massive nature of the change is not yet obvious, but it is well under way, and I do not believe there is any possibility of stopping the momentum.

Most assuredly, both government and industry will paint the facts over with pleasant words, and we will convince ourselves somehow that the move is not to a lower standard of living, but rather to a smarter or more efficient or easier way of life. However it is perceived, the fact remains that far fewer people will have the option of living in a detached single-family home with private land surrounding it. We will maintain excellent amenities and quality of life superior to much of the world, but increasingly over the next few years most Americans will have to give up some of the space and much of the privacy expected by past generations. Obviously, this will have a dramatically favorable impact on the value of existing apartment projects.

THE SIGNIFICANCE OF SINGLE-FAMILY AFFORDABILITY

First and foremost among the reasons underlying this change in the nature of housing is the relative cost of detached single-family homes. More than 25 percent of American families have been priced out of the market for a median-priced house over the last ten years!

Chart 5 graphically tells the story. It shows that in 1970, median annual cost of owning a home (mortgage payment, taxes, utilities, and so forth) was $2,750 and the median family income was $9,900. Under the traditional rule that a family can afford to pay one quarter of its income for housing, 43 percent of families could afford the median home. By 1980, the comparable figures were $9,300 and $21,700, and only 16.5 percent could afford the median home. By mid-1981, according to National Association of Home Builder estimates, the numbers were $11,480 and $23,500, and only 11 percent could handle the median home. It isn't just house prices that are involved in this runaway inflation, but mortgage rates (which have al-

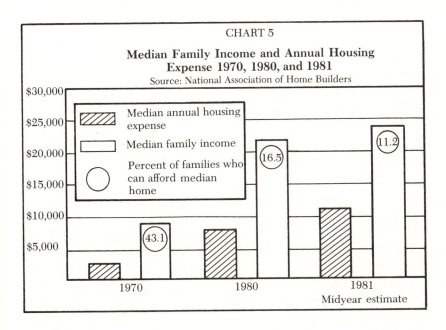

CHART 5

Median Family Income and Annual Housing Expense 1970, 1980, and 1981

Source: National Association of Home Builders

Median annual housing expense

Median family income

Percent of families who can afford median home

most doubled since 1970), utilities, and so on. The result is that most young people cannot even hope to afford a home. Perhaps even worse, fewer and fewer established families can now afford to own one.

WHAT DEMOGRAPHICS TELL US ABOUT APARTMENT DEMAND IN THE EIGHTIES

It has been my practice ever since I became involved with real estate to study demographic projections in an effort to predict the kind of housing demand that will affect my investments three, four, five, and even ten years ahead. In general this has been a good tool. Now, however, an interesting phenomenon is taking shape.

The age group from eighteen to twenty-five years old, traditionally those who are most likely to live in rental apartments, has stopped growing in numbers, and in the 1980s will decline. On the surface, this might indicate a soft apartment rental market in the 1980s. However, there is another demographic development that counters that picture.

The age group from thirty to forty, which is usually associated with first-time home purchases, has been growing rapidly in recent years, and will continue to increase in numbers during the early 1980s. Actually, 32 million Americans reached the age of thirty in the 1970s, and 42 million will become thirty during the 1980s.

As just indicated, very few of those who reached thirty in recent years have been able to buy a first home as they normally would have. Millions of these people have been forced by the new economic circumstances of housing to remain as apartment dwellers. As the ranks of the 30-to-40 age group grows rapidly, millions of additional families will be forced to continue to seek apartments, and the demand is likely to be explosive compared to the supply. Another demographic indicator is the continued high divorce rate, which creates more but smaller household units. Each time a husband and wife opt to live as single parents, or unattached individuals, the demand for another shelter unit is created. There were 1,180,000 divorces between October of 1979 and September of 1980, compared with 708,000 divorces in 1970. The number of divorces per 1,000 of population and per 1,000 married people increased dramatically during this period. These factors must be interpreted as indications of additional growth in the apartment market, especially for those units tuned to the times in terms of size and amenities.

There was a time when successive generations lived together for many years, but I believe the desire for independence is too well established ever to create a desire to return to this bygone tradition. Instead, we can anticipate a steadily increasing demand for more, but smaller shelter units.

WHILE DEMAND IS GROWING, APARTMENT SUPPLY IS SLIPPING

As we discussed the economics of apartment operation through the decade of the 1970s, it probably occurred to you that ultimately these trends and conditions would discourage the building of new apartment projects. It now appears that recent significant increases in interest rates and changes in the terms of mortgages as well as the 1980 recession will make the inevitable a reality. The industry has finally awakened to the fact that without a much higher rent level, it is simply not economical to build new apartments.

Existing buildings are struggling financially despite generally high occupancy. How can developers of new apartments pay the higher costs of construction, and the current skyrocketing interest rates? The answer is simple: they cannot.

Of necessity, construction will be at an extremely low level until rents escalate. The whole key to future supply is whether or not lenders will loan money. There are always builders who will build if loans are available, but without available financial support, builders cannot operate.

Loans were available when perhaps they shouldn't have been during the early seventies, and to some extent even at the end of the decade. They were available because the supply of money was high and the lenders were willing to overlook the reality of the underlying market return. They believed that inflation would bail them out, so they made questionable loans, and eventually many lenders suffered the consequences.

Now, with interest rates at enormously high levels, relatively little construction will be possible. In fact, in 1980 new construction of multifamily rental units was at its lowest level in more than twenty years. Just as important, the net number of rental units available has actually declined as more and more apartments have been converted to condominiums. Michael Sumichrast, chief economist of the National Association of Home Builders, has recently calculated that the supply of nonsubsidized, multifamily rentals is diminishing by 2 percent per year.

Subsidized government housing held fairly steady in terms of new production through the end of the seventies, but even this source of housing will be under great pressure in the next few years as budget-cutting hits Washington. Housing will probably take the limelight as a major political and social problem in 1982 or 1983, but by that time the shortage will be well established.

THE PRESSURE FOR CONDOMINIUM CONVERSION

The demographics of the eighties, plus the inability of many people to buy a single-family detached home, have strong implications for the market for reasonably priced condominiums. Many of the millions who desire to own their own home will inevitably turn to condominium ownership as an attractive alternative. While there is a trade-off in terms of privacy and land, there are usually definite cost advantages, as well as amenities and a desirable lifestyle.

This will create a steady pressure for condominium conversion of existing apartment complexes, and in turn it will increase the opportunity for investors to sell apartments to convertors at high profit. Continued condominium conversions will move the rent levels and values of the remaining rental properties up to a much higher level. The ultimate result will be an economic opportunity to build additional apartment units. Despite this eventual new competition, for much of the eighties the owners of existing apartments should see their investment values grow at a fantastic rate.

FUNDAMENTAL CHANGES IN THE MORTGAGE MARKET

1980 may well be remembered as the beginning of the changes in the mortgage market, which will forever change the real estate business. You will recall that early in this book I explained how the large amount of fixed-interest mortgage debt associated with most real estate investment put inflation to work on the side of the investor. That is how it has been in the past, but it now appears certain that the age of fixed-interest mortgage debt is about to come to an end. Over the next decade this will mean many changes for the real estate investor; right now, I believe it means the opportunities of a lifetime.

In the past, fluctuations of interest rates have been relatively few and far between. Lenders could make long-term loans, secure in the belief that their interest rate would continue to provide a profitable return for many years. Over recent years, as rates moved up at a much faster rate, that confidence became somewhat shaky. Then, in 1980, the violent increases in interest rates created utter devastation in the long-term lending markets. Lenders found themselves borrowing short—that is, paying higher and higher interest for short-term money supplies—while lending long at fixed rates that could not possibly produce a profit. They have found this untenable, and have already started to make fundamental changes in their way of doing business. These changes are a necessity for the lenders. They are also extremely significant in that they mark the beginning of institutionalizing inflation into real estate investment.

Money is merely a commodity, just like gold, silver, corn, or soybeans. Most people don't think of money in this way, but in fact like any other commodity it is available at a price whenever you need it. In the case of money, you buy the use of the commodity, and the price you pay is interest. As with most other commodities, the price of money is determined by the equilibrium between supply and demand. For many years, we have tended to be a capital-surplus country, with ample supplies of money available to satisfy demand, and therefore we had reasonably stable interest rates, although they did tend to move up slowly.

One of the consequences of our excessive inflation in the last decade was that our money became so cheapened we turned from a capital-surplus to a capital-short country. This increased the demand for loans to such an extent that interest rates went through all previous highs.

Lenders have now realized we are living in a very volatile period, and financial planning cannot be made on any assumption of stability. Therefore, they will protect themselves by making long-term loans only with some kind of trigger that will give the lender the right to reevaluate and revise interest rates from time to time. We are currently seeing these developments in both the residential and commercial mortgage markets. The beneficiary of inflation has been the borrower, but with this new development the lender is taking over a great deal of the benefits of inflation.

The basic idea is a "roll-over" mortgage, which has a long-term payoff but which will have to be renewed or rolled over every three to five years as the interest rate is adjusted to whatever the market rate is at the time.

If we continue to be a capital-short country, conditions in the mortgage markets will become even more difficult for the borrower. After all, any supplier with a commodity that is in short supply

and high demand tends to become aggressive. Beyond higher interest rates, we can anticipate creative approaches like joint-venture
positions in return for financing, or a piece of the action in terms of
a percentage of rents to sweeten commercial deals.

Because of the political outcry that will result from these changes,
I have no doubt the government will at some point step in to try to
rectify the matter. I do not expect government action to change the
economic fundamentals at work. In fact, the government is such a
root cause of the problem, due to its own borrowing needs, that it is
helpless to significantly alter the natural forces of the long-term
debt market in real estate.

THE POSSIBILITY OF POLITICAL INTERFERENCE
IN ANTICIPATED FREE-MARKET ACTION

While this chapter has provided a very bullish outlook for real estate
investment in the decade of the eighties, I must also raise a possible
negative development. This would be in the field of politically moti-
vated legislation to control rents and possibly to control condominium conversions.

At this moment, these are merely possibilities, far from certain-
ties, and at worst I believe they will only occur in certain states and
municipalities rather than on the federal level. There are currently
a number of municipalities with various rent- and condominium-
control laws. Should the shortage of rental units become severe, it is
possible that rent control could be federally enacted, but that is
doubtful. It would certainly be contrary to everything the Reagan
administration stands for.

As I have indicated, I do expect a "rent revolution" in which the
general level of residential rents will rise dramatically to catch up
with the cost of construction and other costs involved in providing
desirable housing. It is obvious that such a development will not be
applauded by tenants, although they will have to look no further
than their friendly supermarket to understand that such increases
are justified. Still, tenants are a large voting bloc, and politicians
may well try to help these constituents by passing some form of rent
control legislation.

New York is the only American city that has had a long experience with rent control, and in a form that is completely unrealistic and unfair to landlords. The result has been a total disaster, not only for the investors but, more important politically, to the tenants as well. As a result, if controls do become reality in other areas in the eighties, I believe they will tend to be more realistic, with some form of increases allowed in line with an inflation index. Politicians are probably smart enough not to want to create instant slums for their constituents.

Moderate rent controls would probably cut down somewhat on cash flow for a period of time, but of course this would also have the effect of increasing tax shelter. Given allowable rent increases to match inflation, the cash flow would come back, and might even increase a bit.

Politicians may not want to recognize it, but rent controls virtually assure a severe and continuing shortage of rental housing. While it is virtually impossible to build under current economics, once controls are instituted in an area no developer will even consider building there. This will put existing owners in a unique noncompetitive, permanent monopoly, which in the long run could make values enormous.

My scenario projects that the holding period of investments may well be longer than originally planned. As the housing shortage becomes more and more severe, the politicians will be forced to remove or greatly modify controls to induce new building. This will also vastly improve the income of existing buildings, and the resale value will skyrocket.

Of course, all this is surmise. I would much prefer to see the existing free market continue, and I hope it will. However, we must consider the possibility of controls, and I for one believe that if they come they will create a short-term setback for investors, but a long-term bonanza.

THE BOTTOM LINE IN TERMS OF
REAL ESTATE INVESTMENT TIMING

Over the short term, there are many forces moving real estate investment toward what may prove to be its most golden era. Construction shortfalls in areas such as residential rentals will join with increased demand to create a major upward cycle in rents. During the next few years, this could reverse the decline in cash flow, and add a major dimension to the resale value of existing real estate investments.

Inflation has now been institutionalized into real estate through adjustable interest rates. This will finally force owners to handle their expenses realistically in terms of rent increases. Knowing that debt service is likely to increase in three, four, or five years, owners will be forced to increase rents in anticipation of this increased expense. Thus, for the first time, inflation will be reflected in apartment rents regularly and promptly. From the point of view of tenants, the bargain rates of today will be only a memory. From the point of view of owners, they will be forced to put the business on a proper pay-your-own-way basis. With the recognition that expense increases must be covered by rent increases, there is a strong probability that cash flow will also be reinstituted as a part of the investor's return.

Many existing properties are available now for purchase with large mortgages at fixed rates. While these mortgages have a special value in the face of adjustable interest rates on new construction, the premium investors will have to pay for these properties will eventually be earned back many times over.

Years from now we will look back on the days when interest rates were low and fixed for long periods of time as "the good old days." Investors will say, "I wish I had bought property then." Wishing won't make it happen, but for a little while longer, these kinds of investments are still available to anyone with foresight.

These positive factors increase my anticipation that real estate will be moved by public perception to a highly desirable "growth investment" classification. As values become translated to higher multiples of earnings, those who invest early in the eighties will be richly rewarded.

WHAT DOES IT MEAN TO YOU TODAY AND TOMORROW?

Our entire country is on a debt train that will not stop in the immediate future. The government has created this debt train and now must keep it fueled and running in order to service its own needs.

The unfortunate result is inflation, and that is a hidden tax that burdens those individuals in our society who have worked and produced, but have not been able to get aboard the train. You will either be run over by the effects of inflation and the debt train, or, if you are smart, you will be riding in one of the front cabins, letting inflation work for you.

EPILOGUE

A Better Tomorrow

THIS book was intended as a straightforward guide offering the achievers in our society helpful information about how to benefit from inflation and reduce personal tax burdens. As such, I believe it is complete at this point.

I would, however, like to claim an author's prerogative and include one more element for your consideration. This is a highly personal point of view concerning the long-term desirability of eliminating tax-shelter opportunities along with the political actions and economic conditions that have made them necessary.

The fact is that while my business would not exist in its present form if it were not for inflation and high taxes, I do not view these twin problems as desirable. I deeply fear the consequences of continued inflation and high taxation, and I am committed to encouraging changes in the practices that have created our present situation. Thus, I want to speak here, not in a personal apologia, but rather in an attempt to enlist support for the ultimate and best way for our entire nation to "beat taxes and inflation."

A basic underlying characteristic of the real estate investments described in this book is the preferential tax treatment they receive. While I believe we owe it to ourselves to take advantage of all the

legal deductions available in our tax system, I believe these tax incentives create unrealistic market distortions that lead to uneco-
nomic and less effective real estate markets. They also lead to social
inequities. Why should a person who produces well in society have
to learn about tax shelters in order not to suffer from taxes? Indeed,
the complex games in our tax system create distortions of reality by
which we all lose. This situation isn't likely to change soon. If it
should, the changes would have to occur gradually, given how many
markets have their economics affected by tax considerations. Dras-
tic overnight changes would result in chaos. But in the long run,
wouldn't a system of lower but more equitably distributed taxes for
all make sense?

As a citizen, I am deeply concerned by the human suffering
caused by our inflation and high taxation, and their underlying
causes. Our trend toward the transfer of wealth from those who produce to those who do not I find personally disturbing, but even
more important, I fear what it portends for the future of our country's once great productivity and leadership.

The producers in our society, including the large middle class, are
generally not receiving proper compensation for their labor and
achievement. One of the most vicious effects of inflation is to tax
"successful" people at progressively higher and higher levels as they
earn more, but in fact keep falling behind in terms of buying power.
As a result, instead of achievers receiving the rewards they deserve,
they experience stress and frustration.

Perhaps the most obvious damage created by inflation is to our retired citizens trapped in the nightmare of living on a steadily erod-
ing fixed income. These people include many who worked
diligently throughout their lives, and they deserve better, much
better, from a society that accepted their efforts, encouraged their
thrift, and then created the devastation of inflation. The producers
of today should keep in mind that they will be the retirees of the
future. Can they expect better "golden years" than their parents
are living today?

Those at the lower economic levels of our society are doubly dam-
aged by inflation. They suffer greatly from the erosion of their limited purchasing power. On top of that, the side effects of inflation
greatly decrease their opportunities to move up into more secure

and more meaningful employment. As inflation creates the economic turbulence of boom and bust, those at the bottom seem shackled to their untrained status in a fast-moving, technically oriented world. As cycle follows cycle, the last to be hired and the first to be fired are the young, the minorities, and the so called hard-core unemployable. They rarely have the opportunity to work long enough to get a secure toehold in the system.

It is sad to realize this is the same system that gave hundreds of thousands of immigrant families boundless opportunity and, many of them, undreamed-of success not so many years ago. You may well wonder, how did it change? Where did we go wrong?

Perhaps there is a clue in the fact that for the first 150 years of our history as a country, people generally accepted the idea of taking care of their own welfare. During all those years of growth, our national government involved itself only in truly national and international matters. The government's agenda was small and welfare was not on the list. Individuals, churches, fraternal organizations and, most of all, just plain people helped those who needed help. And we grew and prospered.

Since 1930, welfare has increasingly been an activity of our government. What now is viewed as an established tradition and by many as an absolute imperative has, in fact, been a reality during only 25 percent of our history as a nation!

Inherently, the idea of the government coordinating, financing, and operating welfare programs doesn't seem too bad. After all, most Americans are extremely compassionate; they are perfectly willing to share with others who are less fortunate. As citizens we have always been actively concerned about the welfare of others in our society. Most of us are comfortable with the idea of an economic safety-net spread to help those who cannot help themselves. The problem is that in the last fifty years the safety-net has gotten so large and so institutionalized it has become a snare that threatens our total economy. I believe the move from personal responsibility for our fellow man to government responsibility is, to a considerable extent, at the root of our present economic mess.

Unfortunately, the appetite for government to grow and become more powerful has been operative during these welfare years. The zeal with which politicians and bureaucrats approach the task of

helping the masses has been overwhelming. It has become politically expedient to help everyone in sight with little or no regard for
real need. Necessary assistance has given way to the broader idea of
redistribution of wealth. Many of the recipients of governmental
largesse are fully able to work, produce, and make their own way.
Instead, they have traded incentive and independence for a variety
of government handouts and services.

Over the years, the welfare focus of our government has shifted
from helping those who cannot help themselves to attempting to
solve all social or political issues by spending more and more money.
In the process, many of the ideas and ideals that made this country
the envy of every other in the world have been shoved aside. I
don't, for a moment, believe these ideas have been forgotten, I
think they have been temporarily lost in the confusion.

Politics aside, more and more hard-working citizens are coming
to realize that just because "Washington is paying for it" doesn't
mean it is free. We are all paying for everything the government is
doing for us, and to us. There is a lot of truth in the saying "There is
no such thing as a free lunch."

What's worse is not only have we been redistributing wealth, with
Washington being the Great Redistributor, but we have been waste-
ful in the process. The inefficiency and ineffectiveness of bureaucracy is extremely counterproductive, and the proliferation of
bureaucracy in recent decades has given us the least effectiveness at
the greatest cost. It alone has been a stranglehold on the individual
businessman. Entrepreneurs have become an endangered species.

With increasing intensity, our system of politically based economics has caused us to mortgage the future of our nation. Administration after administration has tried to buy happiness for the voters by
spending more money on social services and middle-class welfare,
and as a result inflation has become permanently rooted in the system. The "Great American Give-Away" has been paid for by simply
printing more money, itself worth less and less. This can be seen as
an indirect but very efficient method of taxation, in that it devalues
the spending power of every dollar in our pockets or our bank accounts. It results in each of us earning more dollars, moving into
higher and higher tax brackets, and ending up with less and less real
buying power.

The absolute irony is that this inefficient and clumsy attempt at middle-class welfare is in fact leading to a greater and greater division in our country between the haves and the have-nots. Inflation and taxes are ravaging the middle class of America, yet the very problem is brought about by the politically based economic excesses aimed at buying votes from this same middle class. Our country is rapidly coming to the point where we can no longer have current gratification at the expense of tomorrow. Our price for decades of give-aways is inflation and counterproductive high taxation. Soon only those who already have assets will be able to accumulate more. The upward mobility that made our country great and produced the world's largest, most affluent middle class is disappearing. Even the American dream of owning one's own home has become out of the reach of many who used to be able to afford starter homes. I believe America is now at a major crossroads.

As an active entrepreneur engaged in organizing investments that take advantage of inflation and taxation, I am frequently asked when I think these problems will be brought under control. By implication, I am being asked if the opportunities in real estate investment will disappear soon. My answer is that for the good of the country, I hope inflation will be controlled in the very near future and that taxation will truly be lowered to reasonable levels. As a practical matter, I believe that this is wishful thinking.

Decades of excess and overspending are behind our current economic situation. It will not be resolved without a great deal of sacrifice over a considerable span of time, a process that will require new thinking and a higher national resolve than I see at this moment. If America is ready to bite the bullet and make the necessary sacrifices, then at best we are ten years away from a stabilized economy based on high productivity, individual responsibility, and fiscal restraint.

Until I see real change in the making, I will continue to concentrate on real estate investment as the best answer to both inflation and taxation. However, I will also spend a part of my energy to try to encourage the changes in economic and governmental action needed for a stable future. The fact that when this change is achieved there may be no need for limited-partnership investment as it exists today does not disturb me at all. I see no inconsistency in taking the best possible advantage of current conditions while trying to improve those conditions for the future.

As an investor, I know there will always be outstanding opportunities. Today, conditions dictate real estate limited partnerships, because of tax advantages and the value of leverage in fighting inflation. If we regain stability and real growth at some point in the future, I suspect real estate will still have great value, but it will become intrinsic instead of being tied to inflation and tax shelter.

I am very proud to be an American. I am proud to be part of a country that offers freedom of opportunity, and thus the constant hope of improvement. I want my children and their children to enjoy at least as much freedom as I do, and I believe the best way to assure this is to leave them an unmortgaged economy built on pride, hard work, and self-reliance. I believe our current economic chaos is a threat to our freedom, and I pray we still have the chance to turn it around and make it strong once again. Currently there are signs that we may take the necessary hard road to preserve and enhance our freedom, but it will be a long process.

Meanwhile, I sincerely hope the information and ideas presented in this book prove valuable in helping the producers in our society to help themselves. If I have contributed in any way to your financial well-being, I will have accomplished my primary goal. My further hope is that as your financial security becomes stronger, you will focus some of your attention on the security and well-being of our country. I hope you will broaden your political and economic knowledge and thinking to seek out new ways to contribute to the future of our country. As a personal achiever, the greatest thing you can do to safeguard your future is to become an active participant in the restoration and preservation of the greatness of America.

APPENDIXES

APPENDIX

1

Sources of Additional Information

THE following list of sources has been compiled to help the interested reader pursue additional information on real estate and tax-advantaged investments in general. For your convenience, each source has provided a brief description of the information and services it provides.

BRENNAN REPORTS
William G. Brennan, Inc.
Valley Forge Office Colony
P.O. Box 882
Valley Forge, Pa. 19482

Brennan Reports, a monthly publication, is devoted exclusively to tax-shelter investments and sophisticated tax planning. At least three available investments in such diverse areas as real estate, oil and gas drilling, and equipment leasing are reviewed in each issue, with emphasis on economic potential, tax aspects, and prior performance. Samples can be obtained from the above address.

HALL REAL ESTATE GROUP
18311 West Ten Mile Rd.
Southfield, Mich. 48075

The Hall Real Estate Group is a coordinated group of affiliated companies that discover and develop capital-gain and tax-shelter opportunities for limited partners in real estate and related businesses. It acquires, manages, markets, and syndicates rental real estate. A turnaround specialist, the Hall Real Estate Group brings underachieving properties to successful operation, as well as acquiring and operating currently successful properties with good future potential.

NATIONAL REAL ESTATE INVESTOR
6285 Barfield Rd.
Atlanta, Ga. 30328

National Real Estate Investor is a monthly newsmagazine that serves the fields of development, investment, financing, and management of income-producing property. Each issue contains regular features such as city-area reviews, theme stories dealing with industry trends, news departments, and columns by industry experts.

NATIONAL TAX SHELTER DIGEST
9550 Forest Lane, Suite 604
Dallas, Tex. 75243

National Tax Shelter Digest is the only monthly magazine devoted exclusively to tax-advantaged investing for the average taxpayer. The publication is not an advisory service, and the content is generic. Members of its Tax Incentive Advisory Council are among the top experts in the country on oil and gas, real estate, equipment leasing, financial planning, agriculture, business, and other forms of tax-advantaged investing.

QUESTOR ASSOCIATES
115 Sansome St.
San Francisco, Calif. 94104

Questor Associates is a financial and economic consulting firm with particular emphasis on real estate. Headquartered in San Francisco, Questor serves individual, corporate, institutional, and public-sector clients on a noncontingency basis. The firm's central service is applied economic analysis. Specific areas of specialization include development strategy and coordination, valuation, legal economics, feasibility studies, investment analysis and policy, and a comprehensive range of real estate consulting services.

THE REAL ESTATE SECURITIES AND
SYNDICATION INSTITUTE (RESSI®)
430 North Michigan Ave.
Chicago, Ill. 60611
(312) 670-6760

RESSI® is an organization of over 3,000 members who are specialists in the creation, issuance, analysis, promotion, marketing, and management of real estate securities.

Established in 1972 as an affiliate of the National Association of Realtors, RESSI® works to protect its members' right to syndicate with a minimum of state and federal regulation. RESSI® is dedicated to promoting ethical conduct among those in the real estate securities field and to providing real estate professionals with highly competent instruction on how to properly work within the field.

RESSI® serves its members as a vital information link between securities regulators and the real estate industry. Through its two national publications, *The RESSI Review®* and *The Real Estate Securities Journal* (see following descriptions), and frequent legislative and regulatory bulletins, RESSI® gives its members updated information on constantly changing real estate regulations and legislation.

The RESSI Review® is the official monthly newsletter of the Real Estate Securities and Syndication Institute. Published monthly, the *Review* is available only to RESSI® members, offering them an up-to-date source for the latest in legislative and taxation developments affecting the real estate securities industry, as well as information on state and national institute activities. A subscription to the *Review* is included in the membership dues for all RESSI® members.

The Real Estate Securities Journal, published quarterly, contains in-depth, original articles on all aspects of the real estate securities industry. Articles are authored by recognized experts including real estate practitioners, attorneys, and accountants. Emphasis is on providing state-of-the-art coverage on critical industry issues. All RESSI® members receive the *Journal* as part of their dues. Nonmembers may subscribe for $60 for four issues, $100 for eight issues.

THE STANGER REPORT
20 Bigham Ave.
Rumson, N. J. 07760

The Stanger Report, a monthly newsletter, features expert advice involving oil and gas partnerships, real estate partnerships, general tax-shelter strategy, regulatory issues, and important tax-shelter investment news and recommendations. Each issue provides in-depth analysis of potential and actual economic benefits of recommended tax shelters and researches the inherent problems and risks in these investments. The newsletter demonstrates which transactions make sense and tells why, and analyzes each tax-shelter recommendation for its investment merit.

Public Limited-Partnership Sponsors and Their Offerings

Sponsors	Name of Fund Series	Objectives	Types of Properties	Location of Properties
Angeles Realty Corporation	Angeles Partners		Primarily existing apartment, garden apartments	Twelve states, primarily Sunbelt
Angeles Realty Corporation	Angeles Park Communities, Ltd.		Existing mobile-home park communities	Primarily Sunbelt states
The Balcor Company	Balcor Pension Investors Debt Vehicle	1. Current cash distributions 2. Capital preservation 3. Maximizing cash through equity participations	Primarily residential and commercial properties	Throughout United States
The Balcor Company	Balcor Realty Investors	1. Tax shelter (primary) 2. Capital appreciation 3. Tax-sheltered cash distributions	Primarily residential and commercial properties under construction or planned for construction, some mobile homes	Throughout United States

Minimum Investment	Year of Inception	General Partner	Sold Through	Contact for Additional Information
$1,000 per unit, minimum 5 units	1971	Angeles Realty Corp.	NASD brokers, primarily through regional member firms	Angeles Realty Corp., 1888 Century Park E., Los Angeles, Calif. 90067
$1,000	1980	Angeles Realty Corp.	NASD brokers, primarily through regional member firms	Angeles Realty Corp., 1888 Century Park E., Los Angeles, Calif. 90067
$5,000	1979	Partnership of Balcor corporate officers	Registered NYSE and NASD listed major brokerage houses and other NASD registered brokers	Local stockbroker
$5,000	1973	Partnership of Balcor corporate officers	Registered NYSE and NASD listed major brokerage houses and other NASD registered brokers	Local stockbroker

Sponsors	Name of Fund Series	Objectives	Types of Properties	Location of Properties
The Balcor Company	Balcor Income Properties	1. Tax-sheltered cash distributions 2. Capital preservation 3. Capital appreciation	Existing income-producing residential and commercial properties	Throughout United States
The Balcor Company	Balcor Equity Properties	1. Capital appreciation 2. Tax-sheltered cash distributions 3. Tax shelter	Primarily existing residential and commercial properties	Throughout United States
W.P. Carey & Co., Inc.	Corporate Property Associates (CPA)	1. Cash distributions from operations 2. Generation of depreciation to be offset against a portion of rental income 3. Preservation and protection of limited partners' capital 4. Appreciation in value 5. Equity build-up from mortgage amortization	Net leased industrial and commercial property	Throughout United States
Consolidated Capital Equities Corp.	Consolidated Capital Properties	1. Preservation of capital 2. Capital appreciation 3. Quarterly tax-sheltered distributions 4. Equity build-up 5. Generate tax losses	Existing income-producing residential and commercial properties	Throughout United States

Minimum Investment	Year of Inception	General Partner	Sold Through	Contact for Additional Information
$3,000	1976	Partnership of Balcor corporate officers	Registered NYSE and NASD listed major brokerage houses and other NASD registered brokers	Local stockbroker
$3,000	1980	Partnership of Balcor corporate officers	Registered NYSE and NASD listed major brokerage houses and other NASD registered brokers	Local stockbroker
$2,500, $1,500 (for an IRA account)	1978	1. Individual, William P. Carey 2. Corporate General Partner, Carey Corporate Property, Inc., Subsidiary of W.P. Carey & Co., Inc.	Exclusively through E.F. Hutton	Mr. James L. Umluaf, Executive Vice-Pres. W.P. Carey & Co., Inc. 600 Montgomery St. San Francisco, Calif. 94111 Mr. David Driscoll 2nd Vice-President W.P. Carey & Co., Inc. 689 Fifth Avenue New York, N.Y. 10022
$3,000 in most states	1978	Consolidated Capital Equities Corporation and Consolidated Capital Management Company	NASD brokers	Local broker

Sponsors	Name of Fund Series	Objectives	Types of Properties	Location of Properties
DeAnza Corporation	DeAnza Properties XI—Ltd.	1. Capital appreciation 2. Cash flow 3. Income-tax benefits	Five existing residential properties including two apartment projects and three mobile-home communities	Throughout United States
Equitec Financial Group	Equitec 81 Real Estate Investors	1. Capital appreciation 2. Cash flow	Commercial and industrial properties	Primary Sunbelt states
First Capital Investment Corporation	First Capital Income Properties, Ltd.	1. Preservation of capital 2. Cash distribution (tax-sheltered) 3. Capital appreciation—debt reduction 4. Capital appreciation in value of assets	Existing income-producing commercial real estate—shopping centers, warehouses, and office buildings	Florida and southeastern United States
Fox & Carskadon	Century Properties Funds	1. Capital appreciation 2. Preservation of capital 3. Provide cash distributions (tax-deferred) 4. Equity build-up	Existing or to be built garden apartments and conventional inflation-sensitive, income-producing real estate with conservative leverage in growth areas	Sunbelt western states
Fox & Carskadon	Preferred Properties Funds	1. Capital appreciation 2. Cash flow (tax-deferred) 3. Preservation of capital 4. Equity build-up	Primarily existing hotels that are business and travel oriented in major metropolitan areas, plus additional inflation-sensitive	Western and Sunbelt states plus business-oriented hotels in other areas in major metropolitan areas

Minimum Investment	Year of Inception	General Partner	Sold Through	Contact for Additional Information
$5,000	1980	Herbert M. Gelfand	NASD brokers	Local Merrill Lynch broker
$3,000	1981	Equitec Financial Group, Inc.	Equitec Securities Corp.	Mr. Jan Hoeffel, Corp. Vice-Pres. of Marketing, Equitec Financial Group, P.O. Box 1109 Lafayette, Calif. 94549
$5,000	1975	First Capital Properties Corporation Managing General Partner, Seth Werner, Preston Haskell	A selling group of 50 to 60 NYSE and NASD-registered firms	Marketing Department First Capital Companies 1-800-327-0378
$5,000	1970	1. Fox & Carskadon Financial Corp. 2. Century Partners (officers of the partners)	Most major NYSE firms and smaller regional NASD firms	Local stockbroker
$5,000	1980	Montgomery Realty Company, an affiliate of Fox & Carskadon	Most major NYSE firms and smaller regional NASD firms	Local stockbroker

Sponsors	Name of Fund Series	Objectives	Types of Properties	Location of Properties
Fox & Carskadon (cont'd)			commercial properties in growth areas	
Integrated Resources, Inc.	National Property Investors	1. Capital growth through appreciation 2. Cash distribution 3. Some tax shelter 4. Equity build-up	Primarily garden apartments	Throughout United States
Integrated Resources, Inc.	American Property Investors	1. Partially tax-sheltered cash distributions 2. Appreciation and equity buildup	Long-term net leased industrial and commercial properties	Throughout United States
JMB Realty Corporation	JMB Income Properties, Ltd.	1. Cash distributions (fully sheltered) 2. Capital appreciation	Existing commercial, office buildings and shopping centers	Throughout United States
JMB Realty Corporation	Carlyle Real Estate Limited Partnership	1. Cash distributions (tax-sheltered) 2. Sheltering of other income 3. Capital appreciation	New or yet to be completed multiple residential and commercial properties	Throughout United States
LRH Income Properties, Ltd.	LRH Income Property	1. Cash flow (tax-sheltered) 2. Capital appreciation 3. Equity build-up	Existing commercial, office and retail	Primarily Eastern United States

Minimum Investment	Year of Inception	General Partner	Sold Through	Contact for Additional Information
$2,500 in most states	1977	Subsidiary of Integrated Resources, Inc.	NASD registered brokers	Broker
$2,500 in most states	1972	Subsidiary of Integrated Resources, Inc.	NASD registered brokerage house	Broker
$5,000	1973	Affiliate of JMB Realty Corp.	Major NYSE listed brokerage firms	JMB Realty Corp., 875 N. Michigan Ave. Chicago, Ill. 60611
$5,000	1971	Affiliate of JMB Realty Corp.	Through NYSE brokerage firms, regional and local brokers	JMB Realty Corp., 875 N. Michigan Ave. Chicago, Ill. 60611 or local stock brokerage or regional broker
$5,000	1979	A corporate affiliate of Loeb Partners Realty	Shearson Loeb Rhoades brokerage houses and regional broker/dealers	Alan L. Gordon, Vice-President & Treas. Loeb Partners Realty 521 Fifth Ave. New York, N.Y. 10175 or their local Shearson Loeb Rhoades

Sponsors	Name of Fund Series	Objectives	Types of Properties	Location of Properties
The Robert A. McNeil Corporation	McNeil Real Estate Public Funds	1. Preserve and protect the partnership's original invested capital 2. Provide capital gains through potential appreciation of partnership property 3. Provide quarterly distributions of distributable cash from operations that do not constitute taxable income 4. Build up equity through the reduction of mortgage loans on partnership properties 5. Generate tax losses (which are not expected to be significant) during the initial years of the partnership that may be used by holders to offset other taxable income	Primarily existing apartment complexes, office buildings, shopping centers and/or other income-producing properties	Secondary cities throughout the United States with exception of the Northeast
Paine Webber Properties, Inc.	Paine Webber Income Properties Limited Partnership	1. Current cash distribution (fully sheltered in early years) 2. Equity build-up	Existing apartment complexes, offices, and shopping centers	Throughout United States

Minimum Investment	Year of Inception	General Partner	Sold Through	Contact for Additional Information
$5,000 3 units for IRA is available, except as stated in prospectus	1965	1. Robert A. McNeil 2. Pacific Investors Corporation—a wholly owned subsidiary of R. A. McNeil Corporation 3. Allen Cymrot	NASD member firms NYSE firms and regional firms	Local securities brokers
$5,000	1979	1. A wholly owned subsidiary of Paine Webber, Inc. 2. Seller retains 10-50% gen-	Paine Webber, Jackson & Curtis system	Local Paine Webber broker or Paine Webber Properties, Inc., 100 Federal St., Boston, Mass. 02101

Sponsors	Name of Fund Series	Objectives	Types of Properties	Location of Properties
Paine Webber Properties Inc. *(cont'd)*		3. Capital appreciation		
Public Storage, Inc.	Public Storage Properties	1. Cash flow (80% taxable) 2. Appreciation 3. Safety	Build mini-warehouses, owned free and clear	Major cities throughout the United States
University Group, Inc.	Varies according to the program	Varies according to the program	Apartments, shopping centers, office buildings, industrial parks	Throughout United States

Minimum Investment	Year of Inception	General Partner	Sold Through	Contact for Additional Information
		eral partner interest and management of the property		(617) 423-8150
$2,500	1976	1. Public Storage, Inc. 2. B. Wayne Hughes	NASD member firms; NYSE firms	Mr. William Savage, President, Capital Market Group Public Storage, Inc., 94 South Los Robles Ave., Pasadena, Calif. 91101
Varies	1971	Dr. Martin L. Rosenzweig, Raymond T. Burns, Donald H. McClelland, Jack Cohen, Stuart S. Greenberg	Major NYSE brokerage firms and NASD firms nationally	Mr. Randall P. Sanders, Vice-President University Group, Inc. 666 East Ocean Blvd. Long Beach, Calif. 90301

National and Regional Brokerage Houses and the Sponsors They Carry

NOTE: Each of the brokerage houses listed was provided the opportunity to respond to a request for information to be included in this appendix. Inclusion or exclusion is in no way a reflection of the quality of product or services of the brokerage houses included below.

Brokerage House	Public Partnership Investment Sponsors	Private Sponsors
Dean Witter Reynolds, Inc. 3000 Town Center Suite 95 Southfield, Mich. 48075 (313) 355-1620	American Properties Investment Balcor Pension Investors Balcor Equity Properties Balcor Realty Investors Carlyle Century Properties Fund First Capital JMB Preferred Properties Public Storage REAL Winthrop Partners	Balcor Continental Wingate Conventional Real Estate CRI Government Subsidized Housing Highly Leveraged Leasebacks JMB NHP Winthrop Financial

Brokerage House	Public Partnership Investment Sponsors	Private Sponsors
Manley Bennett McDonald & Co. 100 Renaissance Center 25th Floor Detroit, Mich. 48243 (313) 353–0630	The Balcor Company Carlyle Consolidated Capital Income Trust Consolidated Capital Special Trust Consolidated Capital Properties Integrated Resources American Properties Investment Integrated Resources National Properties Investment Integrated Resources American Leasing Investment The Robert A. McNeil Corporation Shurgard	Amurcon Low Income Section 8 Housing Continental Wingate Low Income Section 8 Housing
McDonald & Company 2100 Central National Bank Bldg. Cleveland, Ohio 44114 (216) 623-2000	First Capital Properties Corporation The Robert A. McNeil Corporation Omni Oil & Gas Drilling Texland Petroleum, Inc.	
Merrill Lynch & Co., Inc. One Liberty Plaza 165 Broadway New York, N.Y. 10080 (212) 637-7455	DeAnza Properties JMB Income Properties MLH Properties	

Brokerage House	Public Partnership Investment Sponsors	Private Sponsors
Mutual Service Corporation 100 Renaissance Center Suite 2780 Detroit, Mich. 48243 (313) 259–4000	Angeles Realty Corporation The Balcor Company Carlyle Securities Corporation Consolidated Capital Securities Corporation Integrated Marketing, Inc. JMB Realty Corporation Landsing Securities Corporation Public Storage, Inc. The Robert A. McNeil Corporation Second Western Income Realty Trust	American Development Corporation Continental Wingate Epic Associates Hall Real Estate Group
Smith Hague & Company 539 City National Bldg. Detroit, Mich. 48226 (313) 963–5535	The Balcor Company	Amurcon Continental Wingate Capital Corporation Hall Real Estate Group Northern Equities
Shearson Loeb Rhoades & Co. 2 World Trade Center New York, N.Y. 10004	The Balcor Company Colonial Self-Storage The Robert A. McNeil Corporation Shearson Property Investors Shearson Murray Properties	Calmark Properties Continental Wingate Corporation Epoch Properties Lincoln Properties Robert A. McNeil Corporation

APPENDIX 4

Largest Public-Partnership Sponsors Ranked By Total Dollars Raised*

NOTE: In no way does the inclusion or exclusion of any organization reflect on the merits of their offering or operation.

Rank	Sponsor	Total Dollars Raised
1	JMB Realty Corp.	$318,070,000
2	Integrated Resources, Inc.	$294,858,000
3	Consolidated Capital Corp.	$245,859,000
4	Fox & Carskadon Financial Corp.	$232,744,000
5	The Robert A. McNeil Corp.	$215,271,000
6	The Balcor Company	$ 91,245,000
7	Public Storage, Inc.	$ 60,246,000
8	University Group, Inc.	$ 52,313,000
9	DeAnza Corp.	$ 37,794,000
10	First Capital Properties Corp.	$ 37,182,000
11	Smith Barney Real Estate Corp.	$ 37,036,000
12	Angeles Corp.	$ 36,796,000
13	Foster & Marshall, Inc.	$ 25,457,000
14	Equitec Financial Group	$ 22,882,000
15	W. P. Carey & Company, Inc.	$ 20,587,000
16	Merrill Lynch, Hubbard, Inc.	$ 15,000,000
17	Paine Webber Properties, Inc.	$ 10,255,000
18	Loeb Rhoades Hornblower Income Properties, Inc.	$ 7,332,000

*As of December 31, 1979, provided courtesy of Questor Associates.

Guide to Property Inspection

THE following outline covers all aspects of property inspection that I believe should be carried out by a General Partner prior to offering a property for syndication as a limited partnership. The depth of proper inspection is indicated by my inclusion of a detailed list of specific items to be checked in some areas. These are simply examples; in fact, a similar detailed list is used in each of the general areas listed below.

This material is included as a guide to individual investors with the thought that it may be helpful if you desire to inspect a property yourself before investing. It is extremely doubtful that an investor would have either the opportunity or desire to cover all of the elements listed below. Nevertheless, this list may suggest some areas for personal inspection, and others for discussion with the General Partner or representative.

PHYSICAL INSPECTION

· Unit description—Includes description, condition report, and cost to correct on such items as balcony, carpet, central air, dishwasher, disposal, drapes, dryer, fireplace, hood vent, locks, patio, refrigerator, stove, thru-wall air conditioners, washer, and windows.

- Grounds description—Includes compactor, drainage, fencing, flowers, lawn, number of carports, number of parking spaces, outside lighting, pavement, playground, sidewalks, sprinklers, swimming pool, tennis courts, trees, and shrubs.
- Building description
- Clubhouse description
- Construction history
- Construction materials and condition
- Maintenance work order procedures
- Preventative maintenance programs
- Maintenance contracts
- Deferred maintenance
- Equipment
- Parts inventory
- Mechanical systems
- Vacant unit condition

RENTAL ADMINISTRATION EXAMINATION

- Rental rules and procedures
- Rental accounting procedures
- Occupancy and turnover by month and year
- Vacancy summary by unit type
- Vacancy summary by building
- Delinquency analysis
- Notices-to-vacate analysis
- Lease expirations summary
- Rent rate history
- Analysis of rent rate potential
- Other income
- Competing projects analysis

OPERATIONS EXAMINATION

- Amenities—This includes description and rating of such things as boat and camper storage area, clubhouse, dog run, laundry, nursery, pet policies, picnic area, children's play area, pool, saunas, security, social program, tennis courts, whirlpool, etc.
- Purchasing procedures
- Accounts payable procedures
- Move-in and move-out procedures

- Office equipment and furniture
- Labor
- Tenant interviews

COMPETITION

- Identification and location of all competitive projects
- Shopper inspection of each competitive project
- Evaluation of competitive amenities
- Competitive rent schedules
- Competitive floor plans and sales literature
- Analysis of comparable values

MARKET AREA ANALYSIS

- Description and demographics—This includes work with the local chamber of commerce, libraries, and other sources to determine such things as the general nature of the area, work and traffic patterns relative to the property, school availability and reputation, character of the neighborhood, economic outlook for the area, public transit availability, employment outlook, etc.
- Zoning

APPENDIX 6

Glossary

Accounting rate of return Commonly used in real estate, this method of measuring investment returns compares all after-tax cash benefits (cash flow, tax savings, and sale or refinance proceeds) to the amount of the investment for the period of time the funds were invested. Its weakness is that it treats all returns as equal without regard to their timing. A refined and more comprehensive method that adjusts for timing can be found in Chapter 11 (see also discounted rate of return).

Appreciation The growth in value of any possession or investment. Appreciation is frequently a result of inflation, but in the case of real estate it may also be due to such other factors as improvement in operations, neighborhood changes, and shortage of available similar properties. Potential appreciation is an important consideration in selecting investment properties.

At risk Dollars "at risk" are any money or property contributed as investment, or any notes to which one is personally liable. In all investments other than real estate, individuals can deduct losses only up to the amount they have at risk. In real estate, the government provides for additional tax basis that allows for greater deductions.

Blind pool   A real estate investment for which specific properties have not been selected or purchased at the time the investment is made. This is most often a condition of public limited-partnership offerings. The general type of property to be purchased is described, and the investor relies on the ability and judgment of the General Partner to make favorable purchases.

Brokerage houses   Companies engaged in the purchase or sale of financial securities as the (usually commissioned) representatives of individual investors. Many brokerage firms (or houses) currently offer real estate limited-partnership investments and other tax shelters as well as the more traditional stocks and bonds.

Capital expenditure   ·The outlay to purchase any asset with a useful life of over one year. The tax treatment for such an expenditure allows the asset to be "capitalized": its cost is deducted over its useful life according to the applicable depreciation method rather than as an expense in the current period. In a real estate limited partnership, such capitalization may be a disadvantage. Items that are capital expenditures as opposed to currently deductible expenses serve to lower the current tax benefits to the partners.

Claim of exemption   Limited-partnership interests may be sold without official registration with the state securities bureau if the issuers meet certain state standards for a "claim of exemption." They may claim an exemption based on the securities laws of the federal government and/or the states in which the partnership·is offered. The exemption itself may require a filing of certain materials, which may in fact be very similar to the registration filing, or it may require no filing at all. The conditions of a claim of exemption vary by state and according to the type of offering.

Conflict of interest   A situation in which there is or may be a divergence of opinion or actions regarding the functions, capabilities, or constitution of a General Partner. For example, a General Partner who owns a management company that he wants to employ in a limited partnership may have a conflict of interest with regard to rental scales, rates to be charged, results to be expected, etc. Investors should be made aware of all such potential conflicts and be satisfied that any and all decisions will be made in their best interest.

Conversion The opportunity to pay tax at favorable capital-gains rates after deducting any losses as computed at higher ordinary-income rates. This is a primary benefit of real estate investment under the Internal Revenue code.

Debt, fixed vs. variable rate The concepts are the same for mortgage debt as for any other type of debt. As long as inflation remains a condition of the national economy, fixed-rate debt will be a valuable asset. See Mortgages, fixed vs. floating rate.

Deferral The opportunity to pay later what you otherwise would have owed now. See also Recapture.

Democratic rights This term refers to the actual or nominal voting rights of limited partners as recommended for national application by the North American Securities Administration (formerly Midwest Securities Commissioners). Past guidelines by this body have been adopted by a number of states as part of their state securities laws. The concept of "democratic rights" suggests that partnerships allow for votes by the limited partners on such decisions as sale of the partnership assets, refinancing, and dissolution or termination of the partnership. There is considerable controversy as to whether or not these rights give too much management control to the limited partners and thereby cause limited partners to lose the advantage of a limited-liability position.

Depreciation There are two basic methods of computing property depreciation, *straight-line* and *accelerated.*

Straight-line depreciation is computed by dividing the life of the project over its costs. For most real estate a fifteen-year life is used, resulting in a depreciation deduction of 6.66 percent of the total cost each year. For example, a $900,000 building with a fifteen-year life is depreciated $60,000 per year.

Accelerated depreciation on real estate allows for declining balances ranging from 175 to 200 percent, depending on provisions of the tax code regarding the type of property under consideration. *Double-declining-balance depreciation* is the 200 percent maximum. For example, a $120,000 asset with a fifteen-year life—which under straight-line would depreciate at $8,000 a year—would have a double-declining-balance depreciation of $16,000 in its first year.

In the second year, however, the doubled depreciation factor of 13.33 percent would be applied to a declined balance of $104,000 ($120,000 less the first year's depreciation) to produce a second-year depreciation of $13,863.

Dilution   A common term for the percentage of interest in a partnership, or share of a partnership's profits, that is taken by the General Partner, thereby "diluting" the limited partners' interest.

Discounted (or internal) rate of return   A method of measuring investment return that discounts all future returns of an investment to a present value, according to cash flow of monies invested and received. Although more complex than the accounting rate of return, this method is usually more advantageous because it takes into account the time value of money. The consideration is especially important in real estate partnerships with heavy tax losses in early years. For more detail on this method, see Chapter 11.

Due diligence   A term that signifies willing spirit; it can be applied in either of two ways. Most commonly it refers to the investigation work that is done by a securities firm into the nature of an investment and of the sponsor of that investment; it describes how assiduously the firm checks out the details of and facts behind the investment and the sponsor. A second use of the term relates to the checking out of the property by the sponsors themselves. Adequately investigating and appraising the project's physical state, finances, and significant background data is what is commonly referred to as "due diligence."

Exotic shelters   Tax-sheltered investments of an unusual and high-risk nature. Exotic shelters as of this writing would include movie deals, highly speculative art investments, cattle, and other tax shelters that have originated largely as loophole or write-off schemes. In terms of security of investment and IRS allowance, such exotic tax shelters are far more risky than such legislatively intended shelters as real estate, oil and gas, and venture capital.

"Fair, just, and equitable" doctrine   An accepted securities-industry doctrine that allows many state bureaus to determine and look beyond the question of whether or not an offering discloses all of the information that would allow an investor to make a fair, just, and equitable decision. In effect, it implies that the securities administrator has the power to decide whether or not an offering as presented for registration or exemption meets the administrator's standards for fairness to the public. In states that apply this doctrine, an administrator can actually renegotiate the terms of an offering and/or refuse a sponsor's request to offer a syndication, if the administrator feels that the syndication is not fair, just, and equitable.

Fees, front-end The common term used to describe what is paid to the sponsor or his affiliates out of the syndication proceeds. These may be paid in the first year of a syndication or over the period of the syndication, spread over a number of installments.

Fiduciary A relationship founded in trust and legally requiring loyalty, full disclosure, full accounting, and the application of skill, care, and diligence. A General Partner has a "fiduciary duty" to investors.

Foreclosure A termination of all rights of the mortgagor (property owner) and liquidation of the property covered by the mortgage. Upon foreclosure an investor may owe taxes without the benefit of cash from the investment.

Full disclosure A securities term referring to a requirement in securities law that an investor be told all the pertinent data about a particular investment. In certain types of securities transactions, it may refer to a predetermined set of information. In general, however, it refers to the concept of disclosing all of the appropriate and pertinent data, particularly that which might be necessary for an investor to make an informed decision.

Issuer The actual legal entity offering a particular investment. In most cases the issuer is the partnership itself.

K-1 Schedule The Internal Revenue Service form that must be supplied by partnerships annually to give each partner the information necessary to reflect the partnership interest and financial operation in the partner's tax return.

Leverage The financial advantage of an investment that controls productive property of greater value than the cash invested. Leverage is usually achieved through the use of borrowed money. It is particularly powerful in real estate investing because of the high percentage of property value that can be financed by long-term mortgages.

Liquidity The amount or range of immediately available cash or cash equivalents. Cash equivalents would be investments that could be turned into cash at once, principally stocks.

Long-term capital gain The profit on an investment that qualifies to receive favorable income tax treatment due to the period of time it has been held. At present, 60 percent of any long-term capital gain is exempt from ordinary federal income tax, no matter the individual's tax bracket.

Mortgages, fixed vs. floating rate Until 1980 most mortgage loans were made at a fixed interest rate, which was then applied to the unpaid balance of the loan throughout the life of the mortgage, usually twenty to thirty years. While inflation caused interest rates on new mortgages to rise, this did not affect preexisting fixed-rate mortgages. Today, because of the rapid climb in interest rates, many lending institutions prefer floating rates. These are frequently referred to as VRM (Variable Rate Mortgages) or RM (Renegotiable Mortgages). Specifics vary, but in a typical case the mortgage will have a fixed term of thirty years, with an interest rate fixed for only three years. Every three years that rate will be adjusted up or down a maximum of 1.5 percent, depending on the movement of certain economic indices. During inflationary times, a fixed-rate mortgage is usually advantageous to the buyer.

Nonrecourse loans Loans, usually long-term mortgages, for which no partner, limited or general, assumes personal liability. In most cases, the debt is secured by the property itself. Nonrecourse loans are important because under current tax law, a real estate investor can only take losses greater than his investment if the loans against the property are nonrecourse. Other investors cannot use nonrecourse loans in their tax basis.

Offeree representative Under federal guidelines, an attorney or CPA or Registered Investment Advisor may act as offeree representative and receive a fee from one party or another for referring potential investors to a registered representative. That fee must always be fully disclosed in writing to the investor.

Partitioning   A legal term referring to the right of an investor in a joint venture to ask for a proportionate share of an asset to be divided out from the whole of the ownership of the venture. In most limited partnerships there is a prohibition against partitioning—that is to say, a partner may not request the court to divide a jointly owned property, giving a certain portion of it to each partner, but rather must acknowledge maintenance of the partnership interest as an indivisible and entire asset.

Partnerships and partners   A *partnership* is a legal entity established under the ownership of two or more interests jointly engaging in a business enterprise. This form of organization differs from a corporation in several ways. Advantageously, corporate tax is eliminated as the profits of the enterprise are passed through to the partners before taxation, and each individual owner pays personal income tax only on his share. Disadvantageously, each partner is personally responsible for any liabilities of the partnership.

A *general partnership* is one in which all the partners are fully liable for the debts and acts of the partnership. Investors who expect or desire to participate on a passive basis should not, in most circumstances, invest in a general partnership, as their liability will extend to items that are beyond their control. Instead they should invest in a limited partnership, which will limit their liability.

A *limited partnership* is a unique form of partnership that provides limited liability to the investors, the limited partners. The taxation of the limited partnership is favorable to the limited partners in that taxes are passed through directly to the partners, unlike the case of a corporation, which is taxed at the corporate level and then again on dividends. Nevertheless, a corporation liability can be limited, and in many ways it can be said that the investors get the best of both worlds.

Limited partnerships may be either *public* or *private*. The terms refer to the type of security registration involved in offering partnership interests for sale to investors. *Public limited partnerships* usually are registered with the Securities and Exchange Commission as well as various state bureaus, and interests are sold to a large number of investors in those states. *Private limited partnerships* meet regulations for exemption from the time-consuming and costly registration process and therefore can be sold to only a limited number of investors; they are usually available just to residents of a particular state.

A *General Partner* is the individual or entity that is responsible for the operation of a partnership. The designation usually refers to a member of a class of partners or a partner in a limited partnership that makes the decisions and has the liability for the acts of the partnership.

A *limited partner* is an investor in a limited partnership. A limited partner's liability is limited to the amount of money that partner invests or agrees to be liable for. In many respects, limited partners are similar to shareholders in a corporation, although they can receive tax advantages not available to corporate shareholders.

Payback   A method of measuring investment return that determines the length of time required for an investor to recover his investment. As a greatly simplified example, an investor with a $10,000 investment in a real estate partnership with combined tax savings and cash flow of $2,500 per year would achieve a four-year payback. In some private limited partnerships with tax-loss ratios greater than 1.7 to 1, a taxpayer in a 50 percent or higher tax bracket receives almost complete payback immediately, thus having to invest little or none of his own funds.

Preopening costs   New construction costs in the building of a project. Primarily these would include interest on the loan prior to opening, salaries and personnel, marketing, and other administrative costs prior to opening. These costs are generally not deductible and must be capitalized over a period of time in a syndication. They do not include the actual construction costs of the property.

Private placement   The sale of a private limited-partnership interest under securities regulations that preclude advertising and limit solicitation only to prospects of certain qualifications of residence, income and net worth, and/or investment expertise.

Rates of return   See *Accounting rate of return* and *Discounted rate of return.*

Real Estate Investment Trust (REIT)   A special type of fund with inherent benefits for real estate investment not present in normal stock corporations. REIT shares are broadly traded, as is any other stock, but the trust is allowed to distribute profits without previous corporate taxation. Tax losses cannot be passed through to shareholders, but must be used against profits of the trust.

Real Estate Securities and Syndication Institute (RESSI®) An institute of the National Association of Realtors dedicated to the improvement of professionalism within the real estate syndication industry. It was first formed in 1972 and has state chapters as well as a national organization.

Real estate stock corporations Companies, usually listed on major stock exchanges, that are particularly involved in real estate development, management, or investment. Ownership of their stock offers an indirect method of investing in real estate.

Recapture That part of a gain on sale equal to the amount of depreciation taken in excess of the allowable straight-line depreciation, which must then be treated as ordinary income.

Registered investment advisor An individual who is registered both in Washington (under the Registered Investment Advisors Act of 1940) and with his or her local state securities bureau as an investment advisor. In some states, a registered investment advisor is allowed to refer the sale of securities and receive offeree representative fees, but only under full disclosure to the client. Alternatively, registered investment advisors may charge for reviewing deals for clients, either on a time and services basis or on a retainer basis.

Registration A term that refers to the securities filing for a public partnership. Not all securities require a public filing, and for people who seek a private-placement exemption, the process is very similar to registration filing.

Registered representative An individual such as a stockbroker who has passed a securities exam and is licensed to sell securities with any of the major brokerage firms, and also some of the smaller local firms that are members of the National Association of Securities Dealers. In addition, some states allow SECO (Securities and Exchange Commission Only) broker-dealer firms that specialize in a limited line of product. Their salesmen are also required to be Registered Representatives.

Rent control   Legislation that establishes an artificial method of determining rental ceilings.

Rent lag   A current phenomenon of the realty market: the fact that rents have moved up much more slowly than have current property costs. In all likelihood, rents are due for an explosive "catch-up" increase in the near future. Rental property purchased during a rent-lag phase should experience a substantial increase of income with inevitable improvement in the housing market.

Revenue Act of 1980   The main provision of this federal act was to allow that, upon death, a limited partner's tax basis increases to the market value at the time of death, thus relieving heirs of an inheritance tax for the investment as was required under prior law.

Risk factors   A section of the offering memorandum that describes the various risks of making the investment. Some of these factors apply to the specific characteristics of the actual project, while others are more general risks that apply to all offerings.

Roll-over mortgage   A loan that matures periodically every three to five years—at which point the interest rate is changed (See Mortgages, fixed vs. floating rate). Such a mortgage may come due in its entirety but still have a clause allowing for the interest rate to go up based on a specified formula, or it may be established that the loan "rolls over" a different interest rate at periodic intervals.

Section 1231 assets   Trade or business property subject to an allowance of depreciation when held for more than one year. Such assets qualify for long-term capital-gain treatment only if profitable; if unprofitable, they are treated as ordinary loss for tax purposes.

State securities bureau   The department of a state government charged with protecting investors and regulating the offering of securities within that state. Such agencies may be a good source of information concerning the reputation of General Partners, and they can advise a prospective investor if a particular security has met the requirements for legal sale.

Stepped-up basis The provision of the Revenue Act of 1980 increasing the tax basis of a limited partner's interest at the time of death to the value listed in the estate-tax return. This allows the possibility of increasing the tax basis without any income tax being paid.

Syndicators A common term for the people or entity that actually put together an investment opportunity and raise the money. Primarily the syndicator is a person or organization involved in the money-raising function of the investment.

Tax basis An investor's basis in the property, which includes initial cash investment plus income previously taxed, minus losses, cash received, and any share of the liabilities.

Tax deferment In a tax shelter, tax dollars are either put off until a later time or converted to a lower tax rate. In the case of tax-deferred dollars, or in the event of a tax deferment, losses are taken in a current period, and an equal gain is taken at a later time. In other words, a $10,000 loss today becomes equal to a $10,000 gain some years later; the taxes have thereby been deferred.

Tax-loss-to-investment ratio The tax shelter anticipated for an investment compared to the dollars invested. A 1.2-to-1 ratio anticipates $1,200 of tax loss for each $1,000 of investment. For an investor sheltering income in the 50 percent bracket, this would mean that tax savings would pay for 60 percent of the investment. High ratios (2 to 1 or more) may (but do not necessarily) indicate higher risks or questionable deductions, and should be considered only by those who can afford a high-risk investment.

Tax preference A claimed item that is allowed special deductions or special treatment in the tax code and is thereby subject to a preference tax. There are many such items, but for purposes of this book the only significant ones are the accelerated depreciation over straight-line method and intangible drilling costs in oil operations.

Tax Reform Act of 1976 Established the new "at risk" rules, under which an investor in a limited partnership can receive tax losses only for the period during which he has money "at risk." Under prior law, an investor could receive losses for the entire tax year (or that portion of the tax year during which the partnership existed) even if he or she invested late in the year.

Tax Reform Act of 1978 Further curtailed benefits of most tax-shelter investments, with the notable exception of real estate.

Tax shelter An investment with paper losses that can be used to lower one's otherwise taxable income. In other words, the tax loss from the tax-shelter investment is a write-off against regular salary or other income, and therefore "shelters" that income.

Turnaround The art of dramatically improving the performance and value of distressed and/or underproductive real estate. Turnaround property investments frequently provide exceptional profit opportunities, but to mature successfully they require special turnaround knowledge and experience on the part of the managers or General Partners.

INDEX

Index

Accountant, 18, 55, 66, 110, 144
  compensation of, 111
  role of, 113, 155, 168, 187, 194, 227
  as source of investment informa-
    tion, 134
Accounting, 196
Accounting rate of return, 168–69,
  172, 289
After-tax dollars, 10, 14, 27
  and rate of return, 144, 167, 168,
    172
Apartment houses, 37–38, 163–64,
  245–47, 248, 252
  effect of recession on, 184–85
  as tax shelter, 70
Apartments
  supply/demand, 246, 249–51,
    255–56
Appreciation, 289
Assumptions, 194–95
  in prospectus, 232
  review of, 174–75
At risk, 105
  defined, 289–90
At risk regulations, 80, 81, 98, 299

Attorney(s), 18, 66, 110, 149
  compensation of, 111
  role of, 112–13, 155, 187, 195, 198
  as source of investment informa-
    tion, 134
Audit(s), 69, 106, 155–56, 233
  limited partnerships and, 94–97

Bankruptcy, 20, 162, 185
Banks. *See* Financial institutions
Blind pool, 45, 130, 137, 174, 194
  defined, 290
  description of, in prospectus, 190
Blind pool syndication, 55
Blue-sky laws, 44, 193
Borrowing, 18–19, 223
  See also Leverage
Brennan Reports, 267
Broker(s), 114, 129, 130, 131, 136
  commissions of, 133, 178
Brokerage houses, 59, 130, 131
  defined, 290
  sale of private limited partner-
    ships by, 45, 46, 132, 133
  sponsors carried by, 282–84

Builders, 243, 251
Buildings, special-purpose, 165
Business, 16
Business continuity, 147, 231
  plans for, 124–25
Buying power, 10, 11, 13–14, 15, 19,
  259, 261

Call provisions, 198, 234
Capital, 154, 196, 198
  liability for, 197
  See also Liability
Capital expenditure
  defined, 290
  projected, 174–75
Capital gain(s), 88, 173, 195, 209,
  227
  long-term, 294
  taxation of, 68–69, 72–73, 74,
    87–88, 90, 91, 291
Carnegie, Andrew, 25
Cash flow, 29, 39, 68, 72, 173, 191,
  196
  in apartment building invest-
    ment, 246, 255, 256
  tax loss and, 83–84
  and taxable income schedule, 113
  vs. property maintenance, 84
Cash-flow planning, 222, 223, 224–
  25
Claim of exemption, 192
  defined, 292
Commercial properties, 158–61
  effect of recession on, 184, 185
Communication, reporting, 122–24,
  147
Competition, 155, 233, 288
Condominium conversion, 164, 244,
  251–52, 254
  prohibition of, 156, 158
Conflict of interest
  defined, 290
Conflict of interest, potential, 111–
  12, 114, 121
  evaluation of, 234

information on, in prospectus,
  190–91, 192
Construction, 30, 66
  of apartment buildings, 245,
    246–47, 250–51, 252, 255
  and cost of acquisition, 181–82
  costs of, 98, 246–47, 251, 296
Conversion, 71–73, 83–84, 87–88, 291
Corporation(s), 295
  double taxation of, 34
  real-estate-oriented, 33–34
  real-estate stock, 297
Costs
  of construction, 98, 246–47, 251,
    296
  of housing, 248–49
  preopening, 296
Crestwood Commons (property),
  48–52, 180

Debt, 9, 18, 256
  fixed vs. variable rate (defined),
    291
  fixed-rate, 21, 32, 252
  liability for, 22
  national, 31
  and tax basis, 75
  variable rate, 21–22
  See also Mortgage(s)
Debt service, 83, 256
Dedication, 120
Deferral, 70, 71, 83–84, 86, 87–88
  defined, 291
  See also Tax deferment
Democratic rights, 119, 149
  concept defined, 291
Depository Institutions Deregula-
    tion and Monetary Control
    Act (1980), 20
Depreciation, 16, 29, 67–71, 77–78,
    90, 298
  accelerated, 223, 291, 299
  defined, 291–92
  double-declining-balance, 291–92
  straight-line, 291

Depression(s), 31, 233
  deflationary/inflationary, 156
Developer(s), 132, 243
  as General Partners, 125
DIF System, 94
Dilution, 179
  defined, 292
Disclosure, 144, 200, 229–30
  of fees, 177
  full, 121, 293
  re potential conflict of interest,
    111–12, 234
  in prospectus, 190, 233
Discounted (internal) rate of return,
    170–71, 172
  defined, 292
Diversification, 227–28
  limited partnerships and, 38–39
Documentation
  evaluation of, 137, 187–202
Dollar, value of, 11
Due diligence, 41
  defined, 292
  See also Property(ies), inspection
    of

Economic conditions (U.S.), 4, 9–24,
    30–32, 258–63
  local, 154, 233
Economic Recovery Act of 1981,
    90–91
Economic Recovery Tax Law, 1981,
    69
Economic security, personal
  rules for, 17–24
  See also Financial security
Economies of scale, 37–39
Estate planning, 110
Estate tax, 298
  stepped-up basis for, 88–89
Exemption. See Claim of exemption;
    Registration/exemption
Exemption orders, 200
Expenses (projected), 174
Experience, competence, 120

Fair, just, and equitable doctrine,
    200
  defined, 292–93
Federal Deposit Insurance Corpora-
    tion, 20
Federal Reserve System, 31
Fees
  front-end, 19, 176–77, 183, 293
  of General Partner, 153, 176–83,
    233–34
  of offeree representative, 294–95
  of underwriter, 191
  See also General Partner, cost for
    services of
Fiduciary
  defined, 293
  General Partner as, 118, 293
Field, Marshall, 25–26
Financial advisors, 107–14, 134, 144
  compensation of, 111–12
  role of, 110–12, 188
Financial institutions, 19–20
  See also Interest; Savings
Financial management rate of re-
    turn, 171
Financial planning (personal), 24,
    78, 113
  professional advice re, 110
  for real estate investment, 205–28
  See also Step Investing Plan
Financial projections
  in prospectus, 191, 194–95, 231–32
Financial security, 205–28
  See also Economic security
Financial statements, 123, 191
Financing (projected), 174
  See also Leverage
Foreclosure, 223, 226
  tax effect of, 77–78
Full disclosure, 121, 293

General Partner(s), 35, 39, 74, 76,
    86, 112, 234, 290
  affiliated companies of, 121, 177,
    192, 234

General Partner(s) *(cont'd)*
and audits, 95–96
corporate, 127
cost for services of, 38, 98–105, 153, 176–83, 233–34
decision-making powers of, 84, 117, 118–19, 120
defined, 296
desirability rating for, 139–47
disclosure of investment results by, 144
essential qualities of, 119–25
evaluation of, 135–39
fiduciary duty of, 118, 293
financial strength of, 182, 230
information re, in prospectus, 189–90, 192, 230–31
inspection of property by, 286–88
key to investment success, 117–28, 166, 230
legal position of, 118
liability of, 201 *(See also* Liability)
as manager, 42, 118–19, 122, 123
ownership interest of, 176, 177–78, 182–83
plans for continuity, 124–25, 147, 231
problems handled by, 144–47, 231
problems with, 148–49
removal of, 197
reputation of, 130–31, 139, 140–44, 146, 153, 174, 177, 182, 188, 199, 230, 231, 234, 298
responsibilities of, 40, 41, 43, 72, 129, 149
and reviewing assumptions, 175
and sale of limited partnership interest, 54
selection of, 37, 43, 117–28, 129–49, 183, 199
selection of limited partners by, 132
services of, 178, 179–80
variety among, 125–27

See also Conflict of interest, potential
General partnership
defined, 295
Government (the), 26, 28–32
intervention in real estate market, 156–57, 233, 254–55
role of, in inflation, 10–11, 30–32, 254, 256
tax policy of, 64–66
and welfare, 260–62
Growth stock
real estate as, 239–57

Hall, Craig
The Real Estate Turnaround, 3
Hall Real Estate, 1, 39, 41, 48, 84, 94, 124, 171, 180, 181, 183, 185–86, 195, 201, 217, 267
Hall Securities Corporation, 114
Hall Sun-Key Associates, 52–53
Hand, Learned, 65
Home ownership. *See* Housing
Honesty, integrity, 119–20, 139
Housing, 90, 157, 163, 250, 255, 262
changing nature of, 247–49
costs of, 248–49
rental, 66
subsidized, 251
See also Apartments
Housing industry, 242–45, 247
See also Construction

Incentives, 29–30, 90, 106
tax shelters as, 64–66
Income, 17–18, 26
projected, 174
See also Cash flow; Tax shelter(s)
Income tax. *See* Taxes
Income tax returns
Form *4625*, 103–4, 106
Form W4E, 78
reporting limited partnerships on, 105–6
Schedule E, 101–2, 105–6

Industrial properties, 162–63
Inflation, 9–13, 16–17, 18, 21, 63, 170, 205, 239, 257
    benefiting from, 32, 215, 216
    and debt, 18, 19
    effects of, 16, 242–45, 247, 258–63
    institutionalized into real estate, 253, 256
    and leverage, 82
    rate of, 11, 14, 32
    real estate investment and, 25–36, 80, 156, 242, 252–53
    and rental rate, commercial property, 159, 160
    role of government in, 10–11, 30–32, 254, 256
Inflation hedge, 10
    real estate as, 26, 32, 242
Installment credit, 45–46, 49, 51, 59, 196, 197
Installment sale, 86–87
Installment Sales Revision Act of 1980, 86
Interest
    costs, 18, 22
    on savings, 9, 19, 20
Interest rates, 18–19, 22, 205, 252–53, 256
    adjustable, 19, 253, 256
    fixed, 252
    and housing industry, 250, 251
    See also Debt
Internal rate of return. See Discounted rate of return
Internal Revenue Code, 64, 291
Internal Revenue Service, 29, 64, 66, 68, 69, 81, 92–106, 155–56, 194
    on tax shelter, 92–94
International Financial Planners, 110
Investment(s)
    borrowing for, 223
    diversification in, 20–21, 38–39, 227–28
    economic and tax elements in, 155–57
    evaluation of, 153–86
    exotic, speculative, 21, 156 (See also Tax shelter[s], exotic)
    safe, 205
    tax-advantaged, 267–69
    turnaround, 145, 158, 180
    See also Limited partnerships; Real estate investments; Return on investment
Investment advisor, registered defined, 297
    See also Financial advisors
Investment decisions, 17, 39
Investment funds (personal), 20–21, 53–54, 58, 206, 207, 212–15
    pooling of, 37–38
Investment letter, 199–200
Investment objectives
    balance between tax shelter and profit, 51–52, 56, 66, 77, 79–80
Investment opportunity, 26, 39
Investment plan, long-range, 206
    See also Financial planning (personal)
Investment portfolio, 38–39, 110, 165
Investment units, 59, 130
    resale of, 53–54, 192–93, 296
Investor(s), 58–59, 212
    foreign, 241
    high-income, 45, 56, 215–22 (See also Tax bracket)
    as professional client, 108–10, 113
    reviewing assumptions re offering, 174–75
    small, 18, 45, 127, 163
    as source of investment information, 137–38
    suitability standards for, 54, 58, 59, 132, 193, 199, 200, 234–35
    vigilance by, 148–49

Investor questionnaire, 199
Issuer, 129
    defined, 293

K-1 Schedule, 97, 99, 100, 105, 106,
        123, 147
    defined, 293
Kurtz, Jerome, 93

Land, 164–65
Landlords, 245–46, 255
Leases
    commercial property, 159–60
    industrial, 162, 163
Leverage, 27, 32, 46, 161, 177, 178
    defined, 81, 293–94
    and depreciation, 67–68
    value of, 81–83
Liability, 68, 75, 80, 294
    described in Partnership agree-
        ment, 197–98
    legal advice re, 112
    of limited partners, 22, 35–36, 81,
        118, 201–2, 234, 296
    in partnerships, 295
Limited partner, 35
    defined, 296
    delegation of responsibility to
        General Partner, 117–18
    selection of, 70–71, 77–78 (See
        also Suitability standards)
    voting rights of, 119 (See also
        Democratic rights)
Limited partnership(s), 27, 35–36
    balance sheet in prospectus, 191
    control in, 117–18
    defined, 295
    liability in, 22 (See also Liability)
    prohibition against partitioning
        in, 295
    relation with tax audit, 94–97
    reporting of, on income-tax re-
        turns, 105–6
    restrictions on resale of interests
        in, 53–54, 192–93, 296

reward and cost factors in, 47–59
sale of, 46, 129, 130
selection of limited partners in,
        70–71, 77–78
tax basis in, 75
tax benefits of, 65–66 (See also
        Tax law; Tax shelter[s])
term and dissolution of, 196–97
value of, 37–46
See also Partnership agreement;
        Private limited partnerships;
        Public limited partnerships
Limited-partnership certificate, 234
    amended, 201–2
Liquidity, 21, 34, 39
    defined, 294
Litigation, 155, 233
Location, 155, 232, 233
    of commercial property, 160, 161
Loopholes, 17, 29, 64
    See also Tax law
Losses, 28, 30, 196
    excessive, 93
    See also Paper loss

Management, 196
    of apartment houses, 163, 164
    of commercial property, 159
    of industrial properties, 162, 163
    of office space, 161
    of real estate, 34, 37–38, 41–42
Management company, 42
Market area analysis, 288
Market statistics (projected), 175, 288
Middle class, 10, 261, 262
Money
    price of, 253
    time value of, 170, 171, 173
Money-market funds, 15, 18, 21
Mortgage(s), 9, 18–19, 205, 245, 294
    fixed-rate, 256
    fixed vs. floating rate, 256, 294
    roll-over, 253, 298
    See also Debt; Interest rates
Mortgage market, 252–54

National Association of Realtors, 297
National Association of Securities Dealers, 297
National Real Estate Investor, 268
National Tax Shelter Digest, 268
Negative capital account, 76–77
Negotiation, 40–41
New York City, 254–55
Nonrecourse loans, 80, 105
defined, 294
North American Securities Administration, 291
North American Securities Administrators Association, 119

Offeree representative
defined, 294–95
Offering
description of, in prospectus, 192–93
evaluation of, 229–36
specified asset, 137
Offering document
Risk Factors section, 154
See also Prospectus
Offering memorandum. *See* Prospectus
Office properties, 161–62
effect of recession on, 184, 185
Oil and gas exploration, 21, 81

Paper loss, 29, 33–34, 49, 50, 82, 300
depreciation as, 67–71
Partitioning, 196
defined, 295
Partnership(s)
defined, 295–96
See also Limited partnership(s)
Partnership agreement, 35, 149, 187, 195–99
summary of, in prospectus, 193
Partnership form
Schedule K-1, 99, 100, 105, 106, 123, 147, 293
Partnership meetings, 123–24

Payback, 173, 183
defined, 296
Personalized Tax Analysis, 216–22
Planning
value of, 228
See also Financial planning; Tax planning
Politics, 90
inflation and, 10–11, 31
and tax shelters, 65
Private limited partnerships, 44–46, 83, 84, 153
advantages and disadvantages compared with public, 172–73
annual meetings, 123–24
defined, 295–96
disclosure of investment results by, 144
economic projections in, 174
exempt from SEC registration, 44, 131–32, 200
financial advice re, 109–10
limit on number of investors in, 44, 59
locating local sources of, 132–35
sale of, 130, 131–32
See also General Partner(s); Leverage; Limited Partner
Private placement, 44, 45
defined, 296
Professional consultants, 18, 94, 96, 97–98, 105, 187–88, 194
selection of, 110–11
See also Accountant; Attorney; Financial advisors
Profitability, 27, 32
Profits, 16, 26, 66, 73, 79–80, 88, 196
of General Partner, 181, 182, 193, 294
leverage and, 82–83
timing and, 42–43
See also Capital gain(s)
Promoter, 129

Property(ies), 39, 153
acquisition of, 180–82, 185–86, 191
description of, in prospectus, 190
economics of scale in, 37–38
evaluation of 232–33
financial assumptions re, 194–95
inspection of, 138, 157–58, 286–88, 292
location of, 155, 232, 233
maintenance of, 84
physical problems of, 154, 233
sale of, 42–43, 46, 86–87, 168, 195, 223, 225
selection of, 165–66
See also Apartment houses
Prospectus, 97, 155, 177, 187, 188–95, 200, 219
analysis of, 229–36
evaluation of, 137
financial information statement in, 191
for public limited partnerships,131
Public-housing programs, 156–57
Public limited partnerships, 44–46, 53, 59, 109, 123, 127, 153, 167, 174
defined, 295
General Partner fees in, 177–78
leverage in, 83
locating, 130–31
rate of return in, 172
registered with SEC, 200–1
sale of, 130
sponsors (largest), 285
sponsors and offerings, 270–81
suitability requirements for, 58
Purchasing power. *See* Buying power

Questor Associates, 268

Rate of return. *See* Return on investment
Reagan, Ronald, 10, 13, 16, 69, 90

administration, 14, 31–32, 157, 239, 254
Real estate, 21, 28, 29–30, 297
price of, 242
purchase of, 39, 40–41
reflects inflationary increases, 27, 253, 256
as tax shelter, 79–91
types of, 158–65
value of, 28, 67, 80, 82, 156, 240–42, 246–47
Real Estate Investment Trusts (REITs), 34–35
defined, 296–97
Real estate investments
acquisition stage of, 41
and capital gains profits, 88
economic value of, 79–80
evaluation of offering, 229–36
financial objectives of, 166–67
financial planning for, 205–28
importance of professionals in, 27, 28
indirect, 297
and inflation and taxes, 25–36
information sources re, 267–69
opportunity in, 239–40, 262–63
passive, 2, 26, 32, 33–36, 117
profitability in, 27, 32
prospects for, 239–57
risk in, 75–76, 97–105 (*See also* Risk[s])
role of government in, 28–32
size of first, 206–15
special deduction problems in, 98
tax treatment in, 45–46, 258–59 (*See also* Taxes; Tax shelter[s])
timing of, 183–86, 255–56
See also Limited partnership(s); Private limited partnerships
Real estate market, 240
government policy and, 156–57, 233, 254–55
Real-estate-oriented corporations, 33–34

Real Estate Securities and Syndication Institute (RESSI), 135, 268–69
defined, 299
Real Estate Securities Journal, The, 269
Real estate stock corporations, 299
Real Estate Turnaround, The (Hall), 3
Recapture, 56, 70–71, 72–73, 209, 223, 224, 227
defined, 297
on negative capital account, 76–77
Recession(s), 19, 31
and real estate investment, 183, 184–85, 186
Refinancing (projected), 174
Registered Investment Advisors Act, *1940,* 297
Registered representative
defined, 297–99
Registration/exemption, 44, 45, 131, 137, 192, 200, 295–96
defined, 297
Rule 146, 44
Rule 147, 44
See also Claim of exemption
Rent(s), 185
apartment, 242, 245–46, 251, 252, 256
commercial property, 159–60
industrial properties, 162
inspection of administration of, 287
office space, 161–62
Rent controls, 156, 158, 254–55
defined, 298
Rent lag
defined, 298
Rent lag theory, 242–45
Reputation (General Partner), 130–31, 139, 140–44, 146, 153, 174, 177, 182, 188, 199, 230, 231, 234, 298

Reserves, 154, 207, 232, 233
RESSI Review, The, 269
Return on investment, 27, 47–53, 153, 166–73, 183, 232
of commercial property, 161
methods of calculating, 51, 168–71
See also Accounting rate of return; Discounted rate of return; Payback
Revenue Act of *1980,* 299
defined, 298
Ringling, John, 25
Risk(s), 22, 23, 26–28, 58, 153, 163, 165, 173
evaluation of, 154–57, 233
in financial institutions, 19–20
limiting, 27
set out in prospectus, 188, 189–90, 298
tax-law, 97–105, 194, 226
in tax-shelter investment, 75–78
See also Tax shelter(s), exotic
River View (property), 56–57
River View Apartments, 84–86
River View Associates, 84–86

Safe harbor rules, 127
Sale of property, 42–43, 46, 86–87, 90, 168, 195, 223, 226
Savings, 9–10, 14–15, 19
SECO broker-dealer firms, 297–99
Section 1231 assets
defined, 298
Securities, 44
Securities and Exchange Commission, 44, 148, 201, 295
Guide *60,* 144, 188
private limited partnerships exempt from registration with, 44, 131–32, 200
Securities bureaus, 200–1
See also State securities bureaus
Securities law(s), 131–32, 188, 189, 192, 293

Securities salesmen, 129, 136
    See also Broker(s)
Selection
    of financial advisors, 108
    of General Partner, 37, 43,
        117–28, 129–49, 183, 199
    of investment property, 165–66
    of limited partnerships, 70–71,
        77–78
Shelter(s). *See* Tax shelter(s)
Specified asset offering, 137
Speculation, 21, 23, 156, 157, 176
    See also Tax shelter(s), exotic
Sponsor(s), 129, 131, 166
    carried by brokerage houses,
        282–84
    of public limited partnerships,
        270–81, 285
Stanger Report, The, 269
State securities bureaus, 44, 58, 137,
        148, 295
    defined, 298
    and documentation, 200
    registration of investment advi-
        sors by, 297
    as source of investment informa-
        tion, 134–35, 139
State securities laws, 44, 54, 188,
        189, 193
Staying power, 53–55, 84, 182, 233
    of General Partner, 28, 154
Step Investing Plan, 39, 215–22, 227
Stepped-up basis
    defined, 299
Stock market, 16, 26–27, 33
Stocks, 9–10, 26, 294
Subscription documents, 187, 199–
        200
Suitability standards
    for investors, 54, 58, 59, 132, 193,
        199, 200, 234–35
    in prospectus, 193
    in public limited partnerships, 58
Sumichrast, Michael, 251
Sunset Manor (property), 145–46

Syndication, 134, 135
Syndication costs, 98–105
Syndication fee. *See* Fees, front-end
Syndicators, 129, 132
    acquisition of property by,
        180–82
    defined, 299

Tax adjustment, 95–96
Tax advisor, 55
Tax analysis. *See* Personalized Tax
        Analysis
Tax basis, 73–75, 77, 298
    defined, 299
    and estate tax, 88–89
    stepped-up, 299
Tax brackets, 13–14, 52, 78, 110,
        167, 205
    and amount of shelter, 208–9
    and benefits of limited-partner-
        ship investment, 55–58
    See also Suitability standards
Tax code, 67
Tax court, 95, 98
Tax deferment, 26, 70–71, 72
    defined, 299
    See also Deferral
Tax law, 29, 64–65, 80–81, 86,
        90–91, 98, 193, 194, 216, 223,
        233
    changes in, 90, 155–56
    and risks in real estate invest-
        ment, 97–105
Tax planning, 215–22
Tax policy, 64–66
Tax preference, 56, 70, 223–24
    defined, 299
    set-aside concept, 226–27
Tax reform, 90
Tax Reform Act, of *1976,* 80, 209
    defined, 299–300
Tax Reform Act of *1978*
    defined, 300
Tax shelter(s), 17–18, 26, 29–30, 39,
        50, 167, 173, 258

Tax Shelter(s) *(cont'd)*
abuses of, 93
amount of, 206, 208–15
as cornerstone of economic survival, 63–78
defined, 66, 294, 300
examples of, 48–52
exotic, excessive, 65, 81, 96, 194, 223
General Partner fees and, 178–79
inflation-oriented, 21
information sources re, 267–69
Internal Revenue Service position on, 92–94
need for professional advice·re, 110
offsetting cash investment through, 50, 51
in public limited partnerships, 45
ratios of, 55
real estate as, 79–91
and suitability, 58
tax-loss-to-investment ratio, defined, 299
Tax risks in, 75–78, 97–105
See also Tax preference
Tax Shelter Digest, 131
Taxation, double, 34
Taxes and tax system, 10, 13–14, 28–29, 51, 258–63
consequences for, described in prospectus, 193–94, 195
and foreclosure, 77–78
of high-income people, 215–16
investment information re, 123
as investment power, 50, 51, 63–64
real estate investment and, 25–36
withholding, reduction of, 78
See also Capital gain(s)
Taxpayers, 28–29, 92
Tenants, 185
apartment, 254, 256

commercial, 159, 160
industrial, 162, 163
of special-purpose buildings, 165
Time value of money, 170, 171, 173
Timing, 42–43, 53, 71, 239–40
of acquisition of properties, 185–86
of duration of investment, 54–55
and investment opportunity, 39
of real estate investment, 183–86, 255–56
and return on investment, 173
of turnover, 42–43
Track record. *See* Reputation (General Partner)
Turnaround
defined, 300
Turnaround investments, 145, 159, 180
Turnover
timing of, 42–43

Underwriter, 129, 191–92
Unemployment, 31
United States
economic conditions, 4, 9–24, 30–32, 258–63
U.S. Congress, 17, 20
tax laws by, 29, 64–65, 90–91
U.S. Treasury bills, 21

Value, investment, 28
Venture-capital investment, 81

Wall Street brokerage firms, 45, 46, 127
Wealth
redistribution of, 259, 261–62
Welfare
government and, 260–62
Work ethic, 10

About the Author

At the age of thirty-one, Craig Hall is a phenomenon in the real estate field: he entered it at the age of eighteen with $4,000 saved from summer jobs, and today his firm's affiliated assets are well over $350 million, with operations centered in very large Michigan and Texas realty companies, all part of the Hall Real Estate Group. In addition to his business operations, Mr. Hall has been president of the Michigan chapter of the Real Estate Securities and Syndication Institute, a member of the Board of Governors, Legislative and Taxation Committee of the National Real Estate Securities and Syndication Institute, a member of the National Association of Realtors, Michigan Real Estate Association, National Apartment Association, and Builders Association. Mr. Hall is a member of the State Securities Advisory Committee to the Corporation and Securities Bureau of the State of Michigan. He is also the author of *The Real Estate Turnaround*.